Creating Multimedia on Your PC

Creating Multimedia on Your PC

TOM BADGETT
COREY SANDLER

John Wiley & Sons, Inc.

New York • Chichester • Brisbane • Toronto • Singapore

Copyright © 1994 by John Wiley & Sons, Inc.

Library of Congress Cataloging-in-Publication Data

Badgett, Tom
    Creating multimedia on your PC / by Tom Badgett and Corey Sandler.
      p. cm.
    Includes index.
    ISBN 0-471-58928-4 (alk. paper)
    1. Multimedia systems. 2. Microcomputers. I. Sandler, Corey,
1950-   , II. Title.
    QA76.575.833 1993
    006.6--dc20   93-5422
                                                CIP

Printed in the United States of America

10 9 8 7 6 5 4 3 2 1

To our families with thanks for their support and understanding of the writer's crazy lifestyle.

T.B. & C.S.

Acknowledgments

Two authors' names appear on the front of this book, but a book is the work of countless numbers of people. We'd like to thank John Wiley & Sons for publishing this book, with special thanks to Tim Ryan for his capable (and patient) editing and guidance. Tim spent hours working at home, on his own time, checking our procedures and redoing our drawings.

Special thanks, also, to IBM and the many professionals there who conceived and produced the Ultimedia Tools Series CD-ROM that is included with this book. We haven't seen a better sampling anywhere of what's available in the multimedia world today. We especially appreciate the time spent by Michael Minard at IBM for getting us together with the right people inside and outside of IBM to answer questions and gather resources.

To the many companies who loaned us additional multimedia software or supplied screen captures and slides to help illustrate concepts, we extend our thanks. This list is just too long to attempt in this section. You'll see their products mentioned throughout this book.

Finally, thanks to Multimedia Solutions in Alcoa, TN, for spending time showing us real-life client applications as well as the latest in presentation technology.

Contents

Introduction

You found it! This book has all the software and instructions you need to start building multimedia presentations now. With the expert advice, multimedia design tips, and the software on the enclosed IBM Ultimedia Tools Series CD-ROM, you can set up your own "multimedia studio" and start creating multimedia today!

This book/CD set gives you:

- Advice on buying multimedia equipment
- Design tips and strategies for creating multimedia presentations
- Software you need to start building multimedia now
- An overview of the software on the market today
- Great examples of multimedia presentations

What's on the CD?

IBM has taken a lot of time to assemble the best software in the industry and put it all on one CD-ROM. Not only will you find a number of fully working programs, but you'll find demos, multimedia tutorials, cool animation samples, motion video clips, a glossary of multimedia terms, and more. A whole orchestra of information is waiting for you to play it! The entire CD itself is a multimedia event—one of the finest examples of a multimedia presentation you'll ever see.

Figure I.1 gives you a quick peek.

Figure I.1
CD-ROM
Ultimedia Tools
Opening Screen

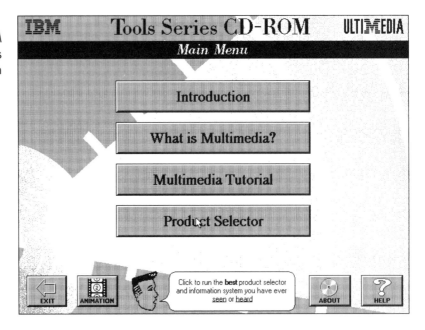

Table I.1 is a partial list of the fully functioning software on this CD.

Table I.1 Ultimedia Tools Software	
StoryBoard Live! 2.0	Fractal Design Painter
Multimedia Toolbook	Wave for Windows
IconAuthor	Action!
Animation Works Interactive	LinkWay Live!
Mannequin Designer	Master Tracks Pro
Media Master	Trax
PhotoFinish	Quest 4.0

In all you'll find at least 58 programs and demos on this CD. You won't find a better collection of software to take for a test spin. By using this book and the IBM Ultimedia Tools Series CD, you'll not only learn how to create multimedia presentations, you'll experience the most popular software on the market today and discover what's right for you.

Great, but What Is Multimedia?

What is multimedia? You can find a lot of different answers to this question, but the clearest, most direct answer comes from IBM: "Multimedia is the merging of video, audio, graphics, and text in a multi-level, computer-based production that can be experienced interactively." With this simple statement, IBM has recognized the key to multimedia: graphical images, sound, and animation combined to produce a learning tool that people use *interactively*. Multimedia does not mean "sit on the couch and stare at the screen." Multimedia means "get up and do it!"

Every day there are more examples of multimedia creations all around us. You may have seen one of these examples, shown in Figures I.2 through I.5.

Figure I.2
Department Store Kiosk

A customer approaches a kiosk near the entrance of a department store. By touching the screen a few times, she displays a picture of several refrigerators. A price and a few lines of information appear beneath each one. She touches a picture and the screen fills with a full-motion video of a salesperson describing the major features of the selected model. During the presentation, she wants to know more about the freezer section, so she touches the freezer area.

The video jumps directly to the discussion of the freezer. Satisfied, the customer touches an icon at the bottom of the screen to present an order screen. The product information is already filled out; she merely touches an alphabetic display to spell her last name and select her full name and address from the offered list. A printer inside the kiosk spits out an order confirmation, which she retrieves and carries to the rear of the store where she can confirm account number and delivery information.

Figure I.3
Executive in
Conference
Room

An executive enters a conference room where several department directors await her report. She inserts a videotape into a player attached to a projection television system, and her entire report—complete with computer-generated spreadsheet graphs, motion video, bar charts, text, and narration in her own voice—is played for the group.

Figure I.4
Training PC
Showing
Multimedia
Screen

An inventory clerk clicks on a program group, opening a window to a network-based multimedia training system that shows him the next in a series of interactive lessons he's pursuing. Today he's learning how to use the network to post complex transactions up the network to a mainframe host. The instruction is through motion video, sound, and interactive questions and exercises.

Figure I.5
Elementary
Classroom
with Students
and PCs

A second-grader is sitting in front of a multimedia system in his school library. The screen shows a multi-color map of North America. A computer voice asks the student to touch his home state, which he does. The voice, calling him by name, next encourages the student to find the state capital, his home town, and other information. The instruction continues with motion video sections showing native industries and scenes, color pictures, and sounds of the student's state geography.

You get the idea—multimedia can be about as broad as your imagination and it can fit into just about any business or personal endeavor. It's a great way to present information because it's quick and intuitive; it's a great way to teach because people are more likely to remember things they see and interact with, and it's fun!

We'll explore many uses for multimedia in this book, showing you how it can solve business, training, and education problems. We'll also show you how to use many specific software products to build your own multimedia applications. And we'll discuss the major multimedia hardware and software components you'll need to pursue this fascinating technology path and apply it to your own needs.

Conventions Used in This Book

We've tried to keep this book as easy to access and use as the technology it talks about. Therefore, we won't set up a lot of special codes or conventions that you (or we!) have to remember. However, there are a few things you can keep in mind as you work with this material that might make getting started with this book—and multimedia—a little easier.

Most of the applications you'll be using work best with a mouse, so we use the regular mouse lingo you're probably already familiar with:

- "Click" on a menu choice or on-screen icon means simply to move the mouse pointer to the specified object and press the left mouse button once quickly.

- "Double click" on an object means press and release the left mouse button twice in quick succession.

When we talk about program names, we usually present them in this book in the same way as the software vendor. IBM's StoryBoard Live! is a good example. The name of the program includes an exclamation point at the end. Other programs may have an unusual combination of upper- and lowercase characters, and so on.

However, when it comes to executable files, such as AUTOEXEC.BAT, we'll present those in all uppercase letters.

Where Do I Go from Here?

We've designed this book/CD set so you can jump in about anywhere to get the information you need. The three major parts are:

Section I: An introduction and discussion of multimedia concepts and the tools required to use multimedia.

Section II: A section of instructions and tips for creating your own multimedia presentations with the software tools found on the CD-ROM.

Section III: The IBM CD-ROM. This disk includes at least 58 demonstration applications and presentations from IBM's Ultimedia Tools series along with some text to show you how to use them. A number of these demonstration programs provide functioning, interactive screens where you can explore software features, and even design some practical presentations of your own.

If you would like more information about the hardware you need to run multimedia, turn to page 9 in Chapter 1. If you feel relatively comfortable with the multimedia concept and you already have the hardware you need to run multimedia applications, jump to page 33 in Chapter 2 and get started putting your ideas into sound and motion.

Whatever your procedure in using the information provided in this book, you should approach multimedia with an open mind, ready to learn some new computer techniques and prepared to change the way you receive and present information.

 In case you can't wait another second to play with the CD (we don't blame you!), insert the CD into your CD-ROM drive; at the DOS prompt, switch to that drive and type **UTSDOS** if you are using DOS, or enter UTSOS2 at the OS/2 prompt. Have fun!

Multimedia Hardware and Software

AN OVERVIEW

You've probably heard the terms *multimedia* and *multimedia presentation* for a long time, but maybe you weren't completely sure what they meant. In the past, multimedia has meant little more than combining slides, maybe tape-recorder sound, and perhaps overhead projection into a presentation. Although some presentations got fairly complex, a lot of equipment was required, and making changes to a finished production could turn into a major operation.

Today, a properly equipped PC and a little experience will let you produce on-screen, projected, or video presentations that rival those of professional producers. Today's multimedia tools include computer graphics, motion video, CD-ROM, audio tape, and more, all on your desktop PC.

From its simple beginnings, multimedia personal computing is maturing as hardware and software vendors refine their products

1

and work together to set common software and hardware standards. IBM, for example, is working not only to develop industry-wide standards, but by bringing together the products of many vendors under its "Ultimedia" umbrella, it's making multimedia technology accessible to a broader range of PC users. And many other companies are cooperating to move multimedia from technical theory to hands-on reality.

If you already have your multimedia PC up and running and you just can't wait to get your hands on some of the software supplied with this book, turn now to Chapter 2. We'll show you how to build a real multimedia presentation step by step with IBM's Storyboard Live!

Multimedia Technology

One factor responsible for the seemingly sudden growth of multimedia systems in 1992 was an overall lowering of cost for the hardware needed to drive multimedia utilities. CD-ROM readers, for example, that had previously cost around $1,000 could be purchased for around $300, though these were relatively slow machines. Figure 1.1 shows a typical CD-ROM reader and disks from IBM.

Figure 1.1
IBM CD-ROM II
Drive

Furthermore, by the end of 1992, PCs with high speed, 32-bit processors configured for multimedia applications were available for around $2,000. That's about half what a similar system would have cost just two or three years before—*if* it had even been available. And mainstream vendors such as IBM are now pre-packaging multimedia systems with all the memory, CD-ROM readers, sound cards, and disk storage required to let you jump immediately into producing your own multimedia applications. Figure 1.2 shows an IBM Multimedia PC.

Figure 1.2
IBM
Multimedia
Computer
System

If you have a CD-ROM player, you can work with the disk we included in this book to learn more about Multimedia right now. Insert the CD-ROM disk into the player, select the proper drive (Type **F:** then press **Enter** if your CD-ROM reader is on drive F:, for example), then type **UTSDOS** at the DOS prompt. If your are using OS/2, type UTSOS2 at the OS/2 prompt in a full-screen OS/2 session. From the main menu, click on Introduction and follow the instructions that appear.

For example, the Tandy Sensation!, shown in Figure 1.3, is displayed prominently in the consumer electronic sections of most Radio Shack stores, where it plays a continuous demonstration program of pictures, motion video, stereo sound, and high-resolution color.

Figure 1.3
Tandy
Sensation!
Multimedia
System

This kind of "hardware horsepower" at such affordable prices has made it possible to design software systems that would have been impractical or too expensive just a few years ago. These software systems from IBM and other vendors are interactive, user friendly, and incorporate more than just color text and pulldown menus. Today's software uses graphics images, photographs, sound, and motion video. Some multimedia presentations even place several of these image types on the screen at once, as you can see in Figure 1.4.

Moreover, multimedia systems—once specialty computers suitable for a limited number of users—are becoming consumer items.

Figure 1.4
Sample
Multimedia
Screen with
Multiple Image
Types

Right: Through Lutheran Brotherhood's fraternal programs and member volunteers, Lutheran Brotherhood and its branches provided more than $1 million for victims of Huricanes Andrew and Iniki in 1992.

◄ In 1992, Lutheran Brotherhood provided more than $7 million in Congregational Matching Funds throughout the nation.

Meanwhile, Radio Shack and other vendors are beginning to market *information systems* that are really computer-driven CD players designed to connect to your television set. The Tandy Information System is shown in Figure 1.5.

Looking more like video games than computers, these systems access informational and entertainment CDs from encyclopedias and atlases to databases, music, videos, and games, as shown in Figures 1.6, 1.7, and 1.8.

Use the CD-ROM supplied with this book to see a sample multimedia presentation. Here's how:

Select the drive letter for your CD-ROM reader (type **F**, then press **Enter** if it's on your F: drive, for example), type **UTSDOS**, then press **Enter**.

At the main menu, click on the Animation button to see a sample presentation.

If you have a sound card, you'll hear sound as well as view graphic images on the screen.

Figure 1.5
Tandy Video
Information
System Player

Figure 1.6
Multimedia
Encyclopedia
Screen

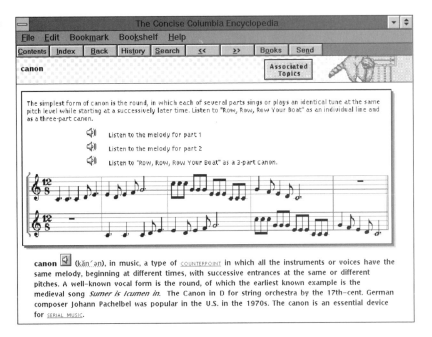

Figure 1.7
Multimedia
Atlas Screen

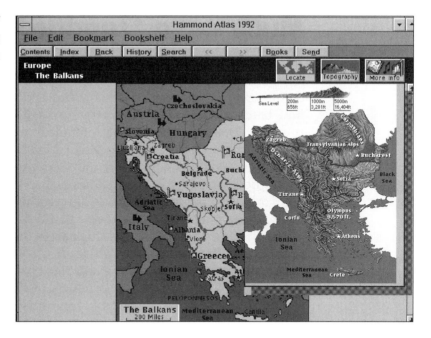

Figure 1.8
Battle Chess
Game Screen

Multimedia Standards

As mentioned earlier, one major development that's helping to make multimedia more easily accepted is industry-wide standards, definitions that industry designers agree to and that specify how hardware and software operate. As with any mainstream computer application, a successful multimedia application depends on common standards being applied to it industry-wide. As computer technology evolves, there are bound to be some incompatible developments, but companies such as IBM and Microsoft are working to get industry-wide agreement on hardware and software capabilities for multimedia platforms. IBM's multimedia hardware and software tools are part of the Ultimedia series of products. IBM has also brought leading software vendors on board and made their products available as part of the Ultimedia Tools Series. You can identify products in this series by their logo, shown in Figure 1.9. For more information, you can contact IBM at 1055 Joaquin Road, Mountain View, CA 94043.

Figure 1.9
The IBM
Ultimedia Tools
Series Logo

Another group, called the Multimedia Marketing Council (1730 M Street NW, Suite 707, Washington, DC 20036, 202-331-0494), tests and certifies hardware and software products as Multimedia PC Specification compliant. Companies whose products have been certified by the council are authorized to display the Multimedia PC Logo.

In addition, the Interactive Multimedia Association (IMA) is working to establish cross-platform multimedia software standards. IBM is among the companies working directly with IMA to achieve software and data compatibility across a variety of MPC hardware. This type of compatibility is particularly important as different multimedia hardware shows up together on networks.

In general, the council (and the widely accepted industry guide-lines) call for manufacturers to include at least the following hardware for multimedia systems:

- An IBM or IBM-compatible personal computer (see the information below on minimum PC configurations)
- A CD-ROM drive
- An audio board
- Microsoft Windows 3.1 or later
- Amplified speakers (or headphones)

Presently, the minimum configuration for the PC portion of a multimedia platform is as follows:

- 80386SX CPU
- 2Mb of RAM
- VGA or VGA+ adapter and display
- CD-ROM drive with CD-DA outputs (CD-ROM XA audio is an option)
- Hard drive
- One floppy drive
- Two-button mouse
- 101-key keyboard
- Audio board
- 1 serial port
- 1 parallel port
- 1 MIDI I/O port (probably included with your sound card)
- 1 joystick port (included with your sound or graphics card)

Again, these specifications are the minimum configuration recommended by the council and generally accepted by hardware and software vendors. Some multimedia applications may require more memory or more disk storage. And, whenever you're working with an OS/2 or Windows-based application, more memory is generally better. Many experienced Windows users, for example, say that 8Mb of RAM is the minimum configuration. And, a 486-based machine (available at very reasonable prices today) will naturally give you better results than the minimum 386-based units.

In addition, newer systems that include VESA-standard (Video Electronics Standards Association) direct bus video and hard-disk controllers offer significantly better performance than conventional machines.

There are standards recommendations for the CD-ROM reader component of multimedia systems, as well. The minimum recommendation under the MPC2 specification is for a drive with a maximum seek time of 300 milliseconds and a sustained transfer rate of 300Kb per second. These are sometimes called "double speed" drives. Older drives with 1000 ms seek time and 150Kb transfer rate are too slow for most multimedia applications. (For more information on multimedia CD-ROM drives, see the discussion on CD-ROM hardware later in this chapter.)

Much of the multimedia-oriented software and support data is supplied on CD-ROM. So, you should consider adding a CD-ROM reader to that basic system. (You'll find additional information on how to select and install CD-ROM and other multimedia hardware in the next part of this chapter.) This hardware addition will cost you an extra $300 to $800, depending on the features you select, options you choose, and other products that may be bundled with your CD-ROM package.

A sound card is also part of the "not-required-but-fairly-necessary" hardware components of a true multimedia system. Several multimedia software packages can use the built-in computer speaker for sound output, but the level will be low and the overall quality of your multimedia sound will be much lower than if you install a full-featured sound card.

Sound hardware such as the Creative Labs Sound Blaster and the IBM M-Audio capture and playback adapter, for example, lets you connect stereo cables directly from your CD-ROM drive, providing high-quality, high-level sound from CD-ROM-based applications. You can even load a software package that lets you play conventional CD music disks.

You'll want some basic software to round out your multimedia platform, as well. First, consider Microsoft Windows 3.1, Microsoft Windows for Workgroups (based on Windows 3.1), or

IBM's OS/2 as the minimum operating environment. Of course, if you're using Windows (instead of OS/2) you'll need DOS, too. If you have a version of DOS earlier than 6.0, consider upgrading. The cost of upgrading is minimal, the number of additional features compared to DOS 5.0 is significant, and the process painless (as long as you stay away from disk compression). Besides, DOS 6.0 offers significant advantages over earlier versions, even the popular DOS 5.0. Among the pluses you get with DOS 6.0 is improved memory management, including an excellent auto configuration program that helps you optimize memory usage with a variety of applications. DOS 6.0 also includes such desirable features as an anti-virus program, real-time disk compression, a backup and restore utility set that actually works and is easy to use, a disk defragmenter, and a whole lot more. In addition, our experience has shown that the latest versions of DOS are highly compatible with applications designed for early releases. You should have very little if any difficulty in making the transition.

Likewise with Windows. If your computer experience to this point is based on DOS and its applications, you'll have to learn a different way of interacting with the system and with your applications. You may even have to spend some time fine-tuning some older applications to work reliably with Windows. But the process is relatively easy and well worth the effort as you begin to work with multimedia. Remember, too, that Windows operates in conjunction with DOS, so you can elect to run some applications in DOS alone rather than through Windows when required, but Windows will be there for your multimedia applications when you need it.

You can avoid the entire DOS/Windows dilemma by using OS/2 2.1, which not only runs DOS and OS/2 applications, but will run Windows 3.1 applications as well. OS/2 has many advantages over Windows, including better memory management and crash protection. However, OS/2 requires more system resources and the number of software packages designed to run with OS/2 is fewer than for DOS.

As you work with multimedia applications, you'll also accumulate a variety of utility software packages to support individual needs.

These might include drawing and screen capture software to help you prepare images to include in multimedia presentations.

Most sound hardware includes some software tools for audio capture and editing, but third-party products also are available to help you capture sound, music, or narration, edit it, and incorporate it into your presentations.

Multimedia Sound Hardware

Today, when you load a multimedia application you'll hear narration, synched sound with motion video, music, and sound effects. Most sound cards include a microphone input and stereo audio output. Some of these cards supply speaker-level audio at up to four watts, others supply line-level sound for you to attach your own amplifier and speaker combination.

Current multimedia standards require that sound cards convert sound at a sampling rate of 22.05KHz or higher. That means the converter hardware and software capture 22,050 samples of sound every second. (*Hertz*—Hz—is a term for cycles per second.) That is the minimum for MPC compliance. Microsoft Windows, for example, supports sampling rates at half (11.025KHz) and twice (44.1KHz) the minimum.

The higher the sampling rate the better audio quality you can achieve, but large sampling rates also require more storage space. You may find that for some applications the lower sampling rate is sufficient to produce the quality required. Many voice-only applications, such as narration, may not suffer with the lower sampling rates. On the other hand, if you mix audio with different sampling rates, the user of the program will notice a difference in the sound quality of the different segments.

When a software application generates sound to be played through external speakers, the sound is in digital form (an electronic *representation* of the sound), like any other computer data. Digital sound information can be stored on hard disk or CD-ROM, and it can be converted to analog sound for output to your speakers "on the fly" through instructions from the software. For more information about multimedia PC audio, refer to Appendix C.

Digital audio—represented like any other computer data in the form of positive and negative (1's and 0's)—can be sent through the computer's integral I/O bus to a plug-in sound card. However, audio amplifiers and speakers handle information in an analog format, a direct representation of the physical sound waves that all sound produces. That means some conversion must take place inside the card.

The analog to digital and digital to analog conversion takes place in dedicated hardware that is part of the sound board. A DAC (digital to analog converter) transforms sound from the computer format to standard format, while an ADC (analog to digital converter) converts sound from the outside world into digital format recognized by the computer.

In addition to sampling rate, digitized sound quality is affected by the number of bits used to store the samples. Older sound cards—and some of the currently available devices—were 8-bit products. Each sample in an 8-bit card is only eight bits wide. That means that all of the components of the digitized sound wave must be represented by a maximum of 256 values ($2^8 = 256$). Newer sound cards, on the other hand, capture and digitize sounds with 16 bits of resolution, giving up to 65,536 possible values to describe the digitized sound ($2^{16}=65,536$). Obviously, a 16-bit-wide sample can produce truer, better-quality sound than an 8-bit-wide sample.

High-end sound cards used for multimedia applications frequently support 44.1KHz sampling rates, using 16-bit resolution and stereo. This produces sound quality comparable to audio CD sound. And, since you can use CD-based audio as a source of music or sound effects for your multimedia presentations, this level of sound quality is a sensible minimum for you to try to achieve. Not all sound cards support 16-bit samples, and some of those that do won't capture stereo sound. However, with today's technology, it costs very little more to have 16-bit stereo sound, so when deciding on the type of card you'll install, look for this higher level of capability, included in such products as IBM's M-Audio capture and playback adapter.

There is a down side to this high quality with multimedia presentations, however. One minute of 16-bit, 44.1KHz-sound requires about 10.5Mb of hard disk space. At the low end, 8-bit samples at an 11.025KHz rate, one minute of digitized sound requires about 6.355 Mb of storage.

MPC-compliant sound hardware has a way around the high storage requirements of quality, digitized sound: *MIDI* (musical instrument digital interface). MIDI is a form of synthesized sound that can be produced by a multimedia application program on the fly, instead of storing it on a hard disk.

Digitized sound is "recorded" in computer format to a hard disk. Synthesized sound is composed by software and played on external, MIDI-compliant hardware, or through sound boards that include MIDI features. In general, with today's technology, the external MIDI hardware produces better quality than PC-board MIDI hardware, though the internal hardware is getting better all the time.

MIDI hardware synthesizes audio by electronically generating the sound wave combinations required for a specific sound. The computer MIDI sound port captures the instructions for re-creating the sound on the synthesizer rather than recording the actual sound in digital format. By the same token, computer software can generate MIDI sounds by sending instructions for producing specific frequency combinations to a MIDI device.

By using a separate synthesizer for sound input and output, storage requirements are reduced drastically from digitized audio. An hour of stereo MIDI sound can be represented in the computer with about 500Kb of storage.

Sound boards intended for multimedia applications include on board FM MIDI synthesis chips. This relatively low-end approach to reproducing MIDI can still produce reasonably high-quality sound output.

High-end devices—to this point usually external products, but a technology that is moving inside the PC case—use "wave table" synthesis for the highest quality sound. Wave table synthesizers use ROM-based digitized sounds of the actual instruments they're emulating. A violin, piano, trumpet, and so on are recorded, then the individual sounds are digitized and stored in ROM. This is how electronic organs and synthesizer keyboards achieve such realistic sound. The perceived quality of wave table MIDI devices is noticeably higher than FM sound synthesis.

As with other areas of multimedia, MIDI sound needs the proper direction to produce products that are consistent and provide a high level of sound quality. The MIDI Manufacturer's Association is one group that is pushing MIDI research and the setting of standards.

The present MPC-standard for MIDI includes the following guidelines:

- A minimum of 128 sounds, including instruments such as harp, bassoon, and marimba, as well as effects such as applause and gun shots
- Standardization of instrument (sound) assignments so that MIDI calls to any playback device will always produce the same sound result

The future of computer-based audio may be with a technology different from what is in common use today, however. *Digital signal processors* (DSPs), programmable chips that can handle all of the digital and synthesis audio requirements of the MPC standard, offer much broader functions than simple DACs and ADCs.

In addition to handling standard audio functions, DSPs are compact and can be programmed for such additional functions as:

- Audio compression and decompression
- Video compression and decompression
- Speech recognition
- Voice mail
- Data and fax modem
- Telephone or answering machine
- Speakerphone

The compact design and broad features made possible by DSPs will spawn a line of computers with sound technology designed into the motherboard as well as compact sound cards that offer more features than today's offerings.

But already sound-processing capability is extremely important in the PC market. In late 1992, for example, there were about half a dozen sound boards on the market. When this book was published in late 1993, there were over 50. Many of these boards also have a *SCSI* (Small Computer System Interface, pronounced "scuzzy") port that you can use to plug into a CD-ROM player. We'll discuss SCSI interfaces in detail later in this chapter.

These boards offered a wide range of features, to be sure, and the most popular card with an estimated 60 percent of the market remained the Sound Blaster. Still, the fact that the number of sound cards on the market quadrupled in just a few months shows the massive changes under way in the PC market, changes that should cause you, the user, to weigh carefully how you configure any new desktop machine you purchase. One key to success is to purchase multimedia-ready machines from a single vendor. IBM's "Ultimedia" series, for example, comes configured with compatible sound and other hardware.

CD-ROM Players

Three types of optical storage are commonly used with personal computers today: CD-ROM, write once, read many (*WORM*) drives, and magneto-optical (*MO*) drives. CD-ROM is read-only technology, WORM lets you write data once and read it many times, while MO technology is read/write. Each of these has its own application niche, and all of them may be used with multimedia applications. The most common of these, however, is CD-ROM.

General Technology

The laser technology used with computer optical storage disks is similar to that used with popular CD audio disks. In fact, many computer optical drives can be used to "play" computer data or regular music CDs, depending on the software you use with your drive.

All three optical types share a common technology: lasers. A laser is a highly focused, highly controlled beam of light that can be used to record data on special media, or to read pre-recorded data.

To record information on optical media, a laser beam burns out any location that will store a logical 1 and leaves blank any location that will store a logical 0. This laser is controlled by electronics that translate the computer data into the appropriate "burn/no burn" instructions and tell the laser mechanism where to place the data on the disk. Except for WORM drives, such laser activity is reserved for the software company or data provider that generates the master disk. When you use a laser disk , the laser device inside your drive only produces enough light to define the burned locations to internal electronics, or to precisely position a read/write head for conventional magnetic recording in the case of MO drives.

The result is a rigid platter similar to a CD audio disk that contains 600Mb or more of read-only data, in most cases. You can place this disk in an optical reader that uses a laser beam to scan the disk and translate that information into usable computer data.

A CD-ROM disk is a rigid plastic platter with a center hole to accept the drive spindle. On top of the rigid plastic disk is a reflective coating that forms the signal recording surface. On top of that is a protective layer designed to preserve the data.

To improve data integrity at the user end, original data is enhanced with error correction information before it's written to the optical platter. Coupled with intelligent electronics in the ROM reader, this error-correction code can help rebuild correct data even if the disk surface is damaged.

WORM drives are used more for archival applications or where you need to store large amounts of data in one location and then transfer that information to another site. WORM drives work sort of like CD-ROM drives, except that the more powerful writing laser is built into the drive.

MO drives are actually magnetic storage devices that use laser technology for precise head positioning, allowing data to be placed much closer together than would be possible with conventional head positioning technologies. MO drives can store up to 600Mb of data on a single 5.25-inch disk, but you must turn the cartridge over to access all of the data because present standards don't provide for dual-head designs.

Optical Advantages

Optical technology offers some obvious advantages, including:

- Storage density (600Mb or more on a 5-inch disk)

- Easy sharing of data with other users

- High data integrity (short of a serious scratch or dent on the surface of the disk itself, there isn't much that can make optical data inaccessible)

There are advantages from the producer or distributor viewpoint as well. A master laser platter is made with an electronically controlled laser that physically burns or pits the surface of the disk as data is written. Once this master disk is produced, however, distribution disks that contain graphics, maps, reference text, or computer software can be "pressed" in much the same way as old-fashioned photograph records. Such pressings can be made quicker, easier, and cheaper than copying magnetic data.

How reliable is this error-correction and detection scheme? That depends on whose figures you believe, and how you interpret the data, but CD-ROMs are *very* reliable. For example, it's unlikely that your CD-ROM reader will find errors at a rate any higher than one bit in each quadrillion (10^{15}) bits. That's actual wrong data read *and detected*. That means the CD-ROM reader might get a wrong bit once in each 10^{15} bits read, but the system is extremely good at finding the errors it gets, missing only one wrong bit in two quadrillion disks read—disks, not bits. All this doesn't mean that your reader can interpret every bit on every disk you have, of course, but it does mean that the reader won't blindly feed your computer wrong data.

Based on the same technology that makes CD audio such a pleasure to listen to, CD-ROM drives bring high capacity, practically indestructible, read-only data storage to the desktop at an increasingly reasonable price.

Optical Disadvantages

As long as you consider the inherent limitations to optical technology—chiefly, the relatively slow access and transfer speeds—there are few disadvantages to optical storage. Until recently, cost was a factor, but even high-speed drives that offer performance well beyond the basic multimedia standards requirements today are reasonably priced.

And, the traditional disadvantage that optical is for read-only applications is lessened on two fronts: WORM and MO drives are available at constantly falling prices, and applications such as reference programs, graphics libraries, and more have been developed that don't require read/write capability.

Cost is a factor for MO technology. The drive mechanisms can cost as much as $6,000, and each data cartridge is $300 or more. However, access times are excellent and for multimedia applications that require a lot of storage on a medium that can be transferred among various computers, MO technology fills the bill well. And as the technology becomes more widely distributed, the prices are likely to fall.

Another important consideration is access and transfer speed. While a SCSI interface—the most common interface for optical devices today—is capable of transferring data at 5Mb per second, optical drives achieve less than 300K per second (typically 250K or so). In addition, except for MO technology, optical products offer extremely slow data access time when compared to most hard disks.

A typical internal hard drive can access data in 18- to 22-milliseconds, for example, while a CD-ROM drive takes up to 450 milliseconds (that's nearly half a second!) for the same task. Drives such as IBM's CD-Rom II offer 280-millisecond access time, but still, if you need high-speed online storage, a high-capacity hard disk is a better choice than a CD-ROM.

Although we'll see increasing use of MO and WORM technologies for multimedia applications as prices come down, in the near future the majority of optical drives for multimedia will remain CD-ROMs.

CD-ROM Standards

There are several working standards used by a variety of CD-ROM manufacturers, and some CD-ROM drives are capable of reading two or more of them.

Formats

The earliest, and for a time the most popular, CD-ROM data format was the High Sierra Group's High Sierra format. This was a popular disk structure definition until the ISO (International Standards Organization) began looking at CD-ROM technology. The HSG wanted their format to be accepted as an international standard, and when they approached ISO with it, the acceptance was good. The committees did, however, make some minor changes to form a superset of HSG called ISO9660. The majority of drives in use today conform to this format standard.

This is an interesting standard, in that the directory structure for a given disk is actually written twice: once in PC format and once in 68000-based format. By placing it on the platter both ways, a single disk and player can be used with a variety of computer systems.

This format works fine for conventional text or graphics data where the read head is positioned at the start of the data and reads data until the end of the requested data is reached. In multimedia applications, including motion video and animation, however, this is not always good enough. One reason is the increasing need for sound to be included as part of the visual data.

With the ISO standard, text and other visual information is placed at one location on the disk while the sound that accompanies it is somewhere else. If you're displaying information that requires some background music, say, or voice-over narration, this is probably okay. If the application is motion video or an animated game, on the other hand, it's difficult to maintain synchronization between voice and lip movement when the read head has to travel back and forth across the disk looking for display and sound data.

A newer standard, CD-ROM XA (for *eXtended Architecture*) stores sound and picture data in an interleaved format (data, sound, data, sound, and so on) so that during an animated or motion video read, the head stays in the same place, reading display and sound data alternately. It's up to the application using the data to sort out the information and route it properly within the PC, as it always has been, but keeping sound and picture data together on the disk offers a considerable speed advantage.

Incidentally, the idea for this technique actually came from the existing audio disk process. Left and right stereo information is stored like this so the read head simply moves across the disk picking up first a little data for the left channel, then a little data for the right channel and the electronics route it sequentially to the proper amplifier and speaker. The speed of the CD data access makes it seem that stereo sound data is actually being read simultaneously.

Obviously, XA capability is an important feature to look for as you shop for a CD-ROM reader for your multimedia system. Notice, however, that many vendors advertise their products as "XA ready," which may mean that you can convert to XA capability, perhaps by adding a new ROM or by performing some other upgrade. Question sales personnel to find out whether the unit you're purchasing is, indeed, capable of XA support as sold.

Notice that Apple Computer uses its own format, *hierarchical file system* (HFS), which is the same format used on Apple magnetic hard disks.

CD-ROM Speed

Standards for PCs that support multimedia hardware and software have been established by Microsoft and others. These standards require a little better performance from CD-ROM hardware than many existing devices are able to provide, but even the Microsoft standards will probably have to be updated as multimedia applications mature.

The basic standards for multimedia CD-ROM drives, for example, specify access times of 300 milliseconds and sustainable transfer rates of 300K or better. Older drives may require up to 1.5 seconds to find specific data, and these often have transfer rates that simply slow multimedia products down to the point that they become impractical or so frustrating that they obviate the benefits of the technology.

In fact, the older MPC specification of one-second access and 150Kb transfer standard fast became outdated. Newer drives from companies such as IBM, NEC, Texcel, and others use *double-spin* (or double speed) technology that achieves access times of 280 milliseconds and transfer rates of 300Kb per second.

So, don't be misled by discount drive advertisements that claim "MPC standards compliant," or other words that indicate these drives support the latest technology. Although some companies still aren't supplying double-speed drives, if you're serious about your multimedia applications, don't settle for a drive that just meets the standards. Shop for double-speed units with access times under 300 milliseconds and sustained transfer rates of 300K per second or better.

In addition to the XA and speed requirements, CD-ROM drives you intend to use for multimedia applications should also be Kodak Photo CD compatible. Photo CD is a technology that places conventional 35mm photographs on a CD-ROM disk for playback on special readers through your television set. However, because the basic CD-ROM technology is the same whether it's designed for music, television playback, or computer data, it's a relatively easy task to load Photo CD images into your computer from a CD-ROM reader. Many of the drives available today support *single-session* Photo CD. That means you can write one set of images to the disk and read the images, but if you have a second set of pictures burned into the disk, your computer won't be able to find them.

If photographic images are likely to be an important part of what you do with your multimedia computer platform, specify *multi-session* Photo CD compatibility. Within a reasonable time this multi-session compatibility likely will be standard. However, ask questions before you buy a CD-ROM reader and don't settle for the vendor's claim that a specific drive is Photo CD compatible. It doesn't cost anything extra (usually) to get multi-session compatibility, so demand it as part of your CD-ROM reader specifications.

The SCSI Interface

Whether you already use a SCSI device or not, if you add a CD-ROM or other optical device to your computer, you certainly will. SCSI is a relatively fast, parallel interface that got its start with early desktop machines, moved into the minicomputer world, and now is regaining popularity with small machines. CD-ROMs are SCSI devices that need a SCSI card inserted into your computer so that the CD can communicate with your PC.

Two forms of SCSI are common today: SCSI-1 and SCSI-2. An emerging standard, SCSI-3, promises better standard definitions, improved performance and "maps" to other high speed I/O protocols.

The SCSI-2 definition is being changed to address the needs of today's changing computer marketplace, particularly CD-ROM, WORM, MO, printers, and scanners. These devices are showing up on multimedia workstations and PCs, and SCSI generally is the interface of choice for them.

And work goes on toward proposed specifications for the next generation, SCSI-3, which will offer significant enhancements over SCSI-2. For one thing, SCSI-3 likely will support mapping to a fiber-optic serial channel compliant with the newly implemented 100Mb per second FDDI serial channel. Other expected features for SCSI-3 include a greater number of individual components, longer cable runs, and a smaller, 68-pin connector. In addition, SCSI-3 is being implemented in modules, an approach that makes for shorter documentation, faster approval of individual components, and ease of updating in the future. And, by "tightening" the standards in SCSI-3, it will be easier for developers to design compliant products, reducing implementation problems that plague some SCSI installations today.

SCSI is an important part of your CD-ROM purchase decision because of the latitude in today's standards. For example, many of today's sound interface cards, discussed earlier, include a SCSI interface designed to support a CD-ROM drive. The idea is that you can install a sound board and attach a CD-ROM drive without the need for another SCSI interface board. The reality of the situation is, however, that the sound card you choose may not support a wide range of SCSI-interfaced CD-ROM readers.

The Creative Labs' Sound Blaster board, for example, is probably the most popular of all sound cards today, with virtually any multimedia application compatible with it. However, the Sound Blaster's included SCSI interface is far from standard and is compatible with only the Matsushita CR-521 CD-ROM (or the Panasonic equivalent) reader supplied by Creative Labs. This is not an industry standard interface; it is a proprietary SCSI-like interface.

On the other hand, you can install a Pro Audio Spectrum sound card from Media Vision and achieve broad-based SCSI compatibility that supports just about any vendor's standard CD-ROM drive. Unfortunately, this SCSI compatibility is achieved at the sacrifice of industry standard sound. Although the company promotes the Pro Audio Spectrum series as Sound Blaster compatible, our experience (and the experience of many users) is that you probably won't get satisfactory results with the Pro Audio boards if your applications support only Sound Blaster. However, if the applications you want to use with this board include a specific installation configuration for the Pro Audio boards, everything should be all right.

Most CD-ROM vendors are aware of these problems, so consult your salesperson carefully before purchasing CD-ROM, SCSI interface, and sound cards. Fortunately, there generally is no problem installing multiple SCSI interfaces on the same computer bus. So, if you already have a sound card installed and find that its integral SCSI interface won't work with your CD-ROM drive, for example, you likely can add a SCSI card dedicated to the CD-ROM drive without any problem.

Obviously, if you can combine a sound card and SCSI interface, that's the better choice because it frees up additional bus space and saves the cost of the extra card. If, however, that course won't work for you, simply purchase a SCSI interface recommended by your supplier and install it in addition to your sound card.

CD-ROM System Software

Because the basic PC architecture wasn't designed with CD-ROM in mind, it's a pretty sure bet you'll have to use some additional software to make it play. For example, you'll probably need a disk driver installed in CONFIG.SYS to inform DOS about your optical drive, how it works, what interface it uses, and so on. These drivers make the optical device appear like a conventional hard disk drive. Sometimes you'll need an additional driver to help DOS use the SCSI interface (these software drivers will be packaged with your CD-ROM drive).

In addition, you may use one or more programs in your AUTOEXEC.BAT file to install CD-ROM extensions to Windows so Windows knows about your CD drive and how it works.

Don't worry. With all of these you'll be told during installation about the software your systems needs and how to install it.

In addition to such utility software, you may opt for other optical software, particularly a caching program to improve I/O performance. One such package—CD Speedway from Tiger Software—buffers data from CD-ROM onto a conventional hard disk or RAM disk, improving access time drastically—up to 1000 percent, according to the company. As with any caching software, how well it works depends on your application and how you use it, but if you're frustrated by the speed of CD-ROM data access, such a utility may be the answer.

High-Resolution Display

Although IBM-compatible PCs have used a variety of display formats over the years, PCs purchased within the past few years almost certainly are equipped with some form of VGA (*Video Graphics Array*) display adapter and a compatible monitor. Standard VGA provides for 16 colors with a screen resolution of 640 pixels by 480 pixels. This standard has been around since 1987, however, and there have been a number of improvements to basic VGA. If you are configuring an existing system for multimedia, or you are purchasing a new one for multimedia applications, you should specify a VGA display capable of 1024×768 resolution. Also, a graphics co-processor or accelerator may be desirable and you should consider a local bus system for best display performance. With high end VGA hardware you can display 256 colors or more.

Video and Screen Capture

Among the sources for images to use in your multimedia presentations are motion video and computer screen captures. Motion video and captured still images from video sources will take on increasing importance in multimedia computing. Until fairly recently, the hardware required for capturing video from external sources such as VCRs or video cameras was too expensive for casual applications. Now, however, hardware capture boards from a variety of sources are becoming inexpensive enough for about any multimedia application. For details on video capture and editing technology, see Appendix D.

Capturing computer screen images is an easier and less expensive process. All that's required is a software package compatible with the applications or environments you want to capture.

If you're using Microsoft Windows applications, for example, you'll need a different screen capture utility than you will for DOS-only applications.

Why would you need a screen capture utility? You won't unless you want to use an image from one of your software packages as part of a multimedia presentation. This actually is a common requirement for multimedia projects for such applications as training computer users how to use specific software, for including graphs, spreadsheet, or database information within a presentation, and for sales and promotion of computer software.

Depending on the screen capture utility you use (some multimedia software, such as IBM's Storyboard Live!, for example, include a screen capture utility) you may capture computer screens directly to a disk file or use the Windows Clipboard to store the image temporarily before loading it into an editor or formatting utility.

In addition, the list of file extensions in Appendix E shows some common graphics formats and the filename extensions associated with them. Some screen capture utilities support only a few formats, while others let you save a captured image in about any format you like to make it easy to incorporate it into a multimedia presentation.

Scanners

Another of the "useful but not required" additions to a multimedia system is a scanner. Scanners work a little like a copy machine to convert photographs or other printed images into digital form. Once the paper image has been digitized, you can load it into your computer, edit it, merge it with other data, and save it on disk.

There are several basic scanner configurations you can use to fill a variety of image digitizing requirements:

- Hand-held scanners that can capture one-half page or less with a single pass

- Page scanners that capture one side of a single sheet with each pass; these scanners process pages like single-sheet copiers; the pages have to be removed from any book or other binding
- Flat-bed scanners that can capture pages from books or other bound sources; these come in a variety of sizes

Scanners attach to your computer through the serial port, the parallel (printer) port, a SCSI port, or a proprietary interface (one used only by one vendor). In addition, you must install software to capture images as they're transmitted through the port into your computer. Two levels of software generally are required:

- A port driver to enable the interface hardware to communicate with DOS and/or Windows
- Applications software to capture, display, and store images digitized by the scanner

In addition, you may need software to edit the captured images (this may be part of the scanner software package or you may purchase a separate editing application) or to convert the graphics image format into text readable by another application. Such OCR (*optical character recognition*) conversion software is necessary because scanned images are imported into the computer in a graphics format—TIFF, PCX, or another image format—and not a text format.

Obviously, you don't need a scanner to create a successful multimedia configuration, but it can be a useful addition, particularly when you want to incorporate existing graphics (including photographs) into a presentation.

Input Devices

Part of the multimedia hardware standard calls for several input devices, including a mouse, a sound card, MIDI port, and a joystick port. We've provided information on MIDI and sound cards earlier in this chapter. Here we'll consider other input devices.

Mice

There's no substitute for the keyboard when you're manipulating text, whether in a word processor, a database, or a spreadsheet program. However, when the majority of your work consists of selecting items from a menu, pointing to or moving an object, and selecting from a menu, a mouse is much more convenient. All MPC-compliant computers are equipped with some form of mouse. If your PC doesn't have one, get one.

Joysticks

Joysticks used to be only for games. Now, with multimedia applications, the joystick and other input devices may take on more importance. You won't need one for all MPC applications, but you might want one for some things. Consult your software documentation for guidelines.

Trackballs

Think of a trackball as an upside-down mouse. Like the mouse, the ball rests loosely in a cavity where the moving ball is tracked by sensors as it turns horizontally and vertically. The advantage of a trackball is that it can be incorporated into a keyboard platform, eliminating the need for extra desk space. Instead of moving the hardware across the desk, you move your hand to spin the ball. This can be attractive when desk space is at a premium, or when you want to make interactive multimedia presentations on laptop or notebook computers.

With mouse, trackball, or joystick, the resolution of the device may be a concern with drawing, editing graphics images, and creating other multimedia operations. Resolution is the ability of an input device to interpret small distances. Newer mice designs generally support 400 points per inch (ppi) resolution, double that of earlier models. Some products even support resolutions of 700, 1000, or more ppi, but beyond about 700 ppi the device becomes almost too sensitive to use.

Higher resolution with a mechanical or opto-mechanical mouse is based on more holes in the light wheel or more physical segments for the mechanical brush to pass over. Resolution with an optical mouse is determined by the spacing between the horizontal and vertical grid lines and the ability of the mouse electronics to read the grid.

Resolution is more important in some applications than others. Using a mouse for word processing or a spreadsheet requires only the ability to move the cursor to a letter or a cell, both relatively coarse selections. If you're manipulating graphics, however, higher resolution could be important.

One difference you'll notice quickly between a low resolution and a high resolution mouse, assuming everything else stays the same, is the speed of on-screen movement. The high resolution mouse seems much more sensitive and quicker.

Many input devices let you vary the *sensitivity*—the relationship between the distance moved on the desktop and the distance moved on the screen. A higher sensitivity means that a smaller movement is required to move the pointer farther on the screen.

Similarly, acceleration usually can be varied through software settings. *Acceleration* is the relationship between the speed and distance of mouse movement and the speed and distance of cursor movement. As you move the mouse faster, the on-screen pointer or cursor moves farther with each pulse received; cursor distance is reduced as the mouse slows down.

Light Pens

Another input device, though less common, is the *light pen*. Shaped like a pen, but with a trailing cord, a light pen lets your computer register positions on the screen when you point. The pen does this through internal electronics that can detect changes in brightness that occur as the electron gun in the picture tube scans the screen. Like the joystick, the light pen may be a nice addition for some applications, but it is not required.

You can use the light pen for anything that requires pointing. For example, with a painting program, you can draw on your monitor screen with a light pen as if it were filled with ink and the screen were paper. The light pen is used in graphics editing so artists need only point to the screen or circle design elements they want to change or move.

Although the light pen can be well applied in some multimedia interactive applications, it's a low resolution device, limited to the sharpness of your monitor.

Tablets

If your applications require a lot of custom drawings and designs, then you'll probably need a digital tablet. These devices hook up to a serial or dedicated port and support high-resolution drawing, custom templates, and more. A tablet isn't something every user needs, but for some applications they are quite useful. Contact your local multimedia hardware dealer for details.

Touch Screens

The touch screen gives the computer a way of detecting what part of the screen you're pointing to with your finger. This technology can detect the presence and location of your finger on or near the display screen of the computer. Touch screens have been effectively used to interface computers with a general public not versed in the intricacies of computing, enabling them to point at the function they wish to carry out. It's in this area that multimedia producers should look to touch screen technology. A sales or promotional presentation, for example, could well be controlled through a touch-screen interface. No keyboard would be required and very little training would be needed for anyone to use the presentation. A simple on-screen prompt or a printed sign usually is all that is required.

Pen Computing

For many users, the best computer is one without cursor keys, mice, or keyboard. That's the theory of *pen computing*, soft-screen technology that lets you turn your handwritten notes into information the computer can digest.

Although pen computers currently have limited use in multimedia applications, as the technology evolves they may take on a stronger role.

Multimedia: Your Next Step

If you already have a CD-ROM player installed and you have a sound card working, then you're well on your way to placing multimedia power at your fingertips. (If you have a CD-ROM player and you haven't already experimented with the Ultimedia Tools software included with this book, refer to the box on page 3 of this chapter to get a taste of what's on this disk.)

If you have a working CD-ROM, go on to Chapter 2, where we introduce you to designing and building multimedia presentations with IBM's Storyboard Live!, using the demonstration software included with this book. Notice that Storyboard Live! is designed to work with a wide variety of hardware configurations, so as long as you can load the demo, you don't need a lot of memory, nor do you need a sound card to step through the tutorial in the next chapter.

If you don't have a CD-ROM reader and you'd like to know more about configuring your existing PC for multimedia, or you want to consider purchasing a dedicated multimedia machine, then use the information in this chapter to help you decide what features you want to add to your existing machines or to guide you in purchasing a multimedia PC.

Using IBM's Storyboard Live!

AN INTRODUCTION TO MULTIMEDIA AUTHORING

Multimedia applications probably aren't like any other software you've ever used. In the conventional computing world, you usually pick one word processor, for example, and you stick with it. With multimedia, however, it's unlikely that you'll settle on a single software program to handle all your needs. The range of possibilities in multimedia is so great that it often takes several different programs to put together the right presentation.

The good news is that you can use the IBM CD-ROM included in this book to evaluate more than 16 multimedia software packages and select the right software for you. The demonstrations and working models of popular multimedia software packages included on this disk will give you a good idea of the applications available, and will give you a great head start to finding the one that best suits your needs.

A popular package that you can use for a variety of applications, and one that demonstrates graphically how to go about designing and producing a multimedia presentation is IBM's *Storyboard Live!*, which is included on the CD-ROM supplied with this book.

33

In this chapter, we introduce you to the world of multimedia presentations with a hands-on discussion of Storyboard Live!, and you'll learn how to produce a practical application with the demonstration version of Storyboard Live! included on the CD-ROM disk.

What Is Storyboard Live!?

Storyboard Live! is an *authoring tool*, which means that it can be used to assemble existing graphics, sound, and video images into a finished presentation. Storyboard Live! then goes further to enable you to draw your own artwork, capture images, and edit graphics, sound, and motion video.

Use the IBM Ultimedia Tools CD included with this book for a quick overview of StoryBoard Live!:

1. Switch to your CD-ROM drive and type **UTSDOS** at the DOS prompt.
2. Choose Product Locator from the main menu.
3. Use the scroll bar to find the StoryBoard Live! icon.
4. Choose it and select "Demonstration" from the StoryBoard Live! information card on the left of the screen.

This DOS-based product has been around longer than most multimedia applications, making it a familiar product to a number of business presentation producers already. And, because of its origin in the pre-Windows, pre-multimedia era of personal computing, Storyboard Live! works with computers that don't have MPC-specific hardware such as sound or video cards. In addition, this program will function well with relatively limited disk and memory resources.

The name for this program comes from the way motion picture or documentary productions are planned. Such productions are often viewed as a "story" and are organized into "pages" or modules and then placed on a timeline to show where each module appears. With Storyboard Live! and many other multimedia products, presentations are designed and built around these storyboards. Figure 2.1 shows how a rough storyboard for a simple film might look.

Figure 2.1
A Simple
Hand-Drawn
Storyboard

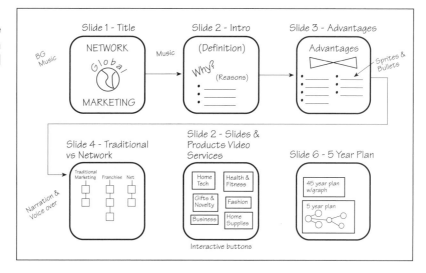

Storyboard Live! consists of five separate modules:

• Electronic Presentation
• Picture Taker
• Picture Maker
• Story Editor
• Story Teller

Here's how to load Storyboard Live! to display the opening screen shown in Figure 2.2:

1. Choose Product Locator from the main Ultimedia Tools screen.
2. Click on the Down Arrow at the bottom of the scroll bar at the right of the display until StoryBoard Live! is listed.
3. Select Storyboard Live! then click on Working Model in the Storyboard Live! window.

This arrangement is typical of a number of multimedia products that contain all of the utilities you need to produce text and graphics images; arrange them in a desired order; add music, sound, or narration; and present the images in a slide show or presentation format.

Figure 2.2
Storyboard Live!
Opening Screen

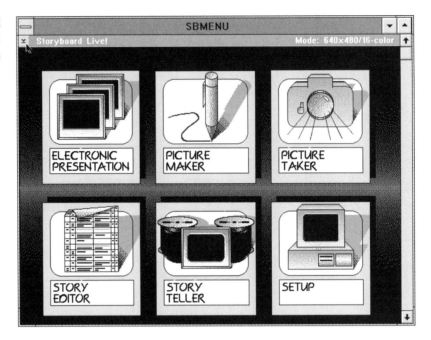

We'll use these modules and more to produce a simple multimedia presentation with the Storyboard Live! sampler included with this book.

Basic Operation

Although Storyboard Live! is a DOS-based application, it has a sophisticated graphical interface and supports a mouse pointing device.

To enter one of the program modules, simply click anywhere within the graphics image that represents the module you want to run. Note that you don't have to click on the name at the bottom of each graphics image; you can click anywhere within the image to launch the chosen module.

When you've finished with a given module, you can return to the main Storyboard Live! menu by clicking on the Exit icon at the upper-left corner of the current module screen. Also, with some modules, such as Electronic Presentation, you can choose File Exit to return to the menu. In addition, if you have called a module from inside another module, the File menu will show the calling module name instead of Exit as the last entry on the pulldown menu.

If you have worked with Macintoshes, you'll find some features of Storyboard Live! very familiar. For example, to open a menu, you point to the main menu choice, then hold down the mouse button to display the secondary menu. As you move the mouse, each menu item is highlighted in turn. You make a selection by highlighting it and then releasing the mouse button.

You can use Storyboard Live! modules in any order. (With the production version of the software you can even load individual modules from the DOS prompt, bypassing the main menu.) The order you choose depends a little on the type of presentation you're building. Also, note that some modules can be called from within other modules, so you don't necessarily have to go through the main menu to jump from module to module.

For example, the Electronic Presentation screen includes a selection for Story Editor to let you enhance a frame or add information to the presentation. In addition, you can click on Edit Frame from the Electronic Presentation screen to launch a frame builder module that in turn may run the Picture Maker module for frame editing.

Getting to Work on a Presentation

Let's get right to work. After all, you want to use Storyboard Live!, not just read about it, right?

In this section you'll learn hands on how to produce a short but practical presentation with Storyboard Live!. Later, in Chapter 3, you can learn how to start from a basic idea or concept and work through a finished presentation in Storyboard Live! or any other presentation product. Don't worry too much about the intricacies of the design, just concentrate on becoming familiar with the procedures for building this presentation. While other presentation programs may do more than Storyboard Live!, they may also be more difficult to use. However, the *general* process you'll use to build the sample presentation with Storyboard Live! is the same *general* process you'll use with other packages.

The Message behind the Presentation

For this example, assume you want to produce a short presentation detailing a network marketing plan. This presentation is designed to teach people who want to start their own businesses the basic concepts of *network marketing*, a concept that is gaining popularity.

In general, network marketing works like this: A large corporation offers a range of products for sale through a "network" of other businesses or individuals. The small businesses and individuals often pool their time and money to market the corporation's products. They purchase the products from a single corporation, which in turn purchases merchandise from dozens or even thousands of other companies.

For example, suppose individual *A* decides to begin a network marketing group. He contacts the main supplier, establishes an account, perhaps sets up a territory, and decides on a product line or lines. Products flow from the company to the individual. He, in turn, contacts other people—individuals *B*, *C*, *D*, and so on—to work within the same network. Each of these persons can establish his or her own network so that eventually dozens or hundreds of individuals are working together. Their line of supply is through the originator of the network. Total sales volume, and therefore profit, for the network is the sum of everything moved by all persons in the network. In this way, individual businesses benefit from the sales volume of others in the network.

And, because network marketing can make available virtually any goods and services most of us are likely to need, and because merchandise typically is purchased through catalogs or computerized online services, network marketing is becoming increasingly popular.

The message in this presentation is that networking is an innovative concept whose time has come, a marketing method that offers many benefits over conventional designs. Moreover, we want to show the audience how they can learn more and how to get directly involved. We'll keep this sample presentation very short so that you can learn the basics and move on to your own designs. We'll show you exactly how to do the first three slides in the presentation; after you see how it's done, you can complete the presentation or start your own presentation on a different topic.

The audience for this presentation is diverse, including anyone who may be interested in starting a business of their own using a network design. For this reason, we must keep the design of the presentation fairly simple and avoid jargon. In addition, we need to anticipate the broad range of questions that are likely to arise and try to answer them in the presentation.

The medium for this presentation will be the computer screen itself, but an MPC presentation such as this one could be transferred to video tape relatively easily with the proper VGA-to-NTSC interface board.

When you've finished the design stage of preparing to build a presentation, you should have an outline—similar to the one in Figure 2.3—that shows the general makeup of the presentation you're designing.

Building the Initial Screens

As we mentioned before, Storyboard Live! is an authoring tool. When working with most authoring tools, you first create all the artwork, sounds, and animation for your scenes, or boards. When that is finished, you combine all the pieces and organize

Figure 2.3
Preliminary
Outline for
Networking
MPC
Presentations

Preliminary Outline
Network Marketing Presentation

I. Title
A. Networking Marketing title
B. Single frame graphic—"Global" theme

II. Introduction
A. Definition of Network Marketing
B. Reasons people are attracted to Network Marketing

III. Advantages
A. Animated bulleted list
B. Narration with music

IV. Traditional vs Network Marketing
A. Traditional Marketing flow diagram
B. Franchise Marketing flow diagram
C. Network Marketing flow diagram

V. Products and Services
A. Graphics annd motion video "buttons"
   1. Home Tech
   2. Health & Fitness
   3. Gifts & Novelty
   4. Fashion
   5. Business
   6. Home Supplies
B. Series of slides linked to each button
   1. Picture of typical item
   2. Narration of product examples
   3. Name brand emphasis

VI. Year Plan vs 5 Year Plan
A. Two windows
   1. 45-year "traditional" business plan
      a) Description
      b) Graph
   2. 5-year networking plan
      a) Description
      b) Network drawing
B. Narration
C. Music
D. Voice over

them into a timeline according to your storyboard design. So the first thing you'll do now is design the opening screen for your presentation.

As you can see from the story outline in Figure 2.3, the first slide in this sample presentation is a title slide. Begin presentations with a descriptive title slide, something that establishes the topic and sets up the presentation.

To create images in Storyboard Live! you can:

- Use a scanner to input images from company brochures and other promotional material
- Capture photographs from Kodak's Photo CD
- Use professional images or clip art
- Design and draw images with Picture Maker

The title slide shown in Figure 2.4 was produced with the Storyboard Live! Picture Maker module and art included in the SBLive demo.

Figure 2.4
Networking
Opening Slide

The retail version of Storyboard Live! includes about 800 pieces of art you can use for your presentations. The version supplied with this book is more limited—about 75 images—but you can use these samples as a starting place for your own work.

Before you begin using Storyboard Live! to design a presentation, you should create a subdirectory on your hard disk that you'll use to store the individual presentation components and the Storyboard file itself. We suggest that you create two directories:

one called MPC off of the root and another called SBLIVE off of the MPC subdirectory.

To create this directory structure, type the following:

CD
MD MPC
MD MPC\SBLIVE

Now, if you want, you can create still another directory under the SBLIVE directory to hold the network marketing show:

MD MPC\SBLIVE\NETWORK

Remember, you'll be using some information from the CD-ROM disk and you can't save anything back to this drive. Besides, a dedicated hard drive directory for each presentation makes it easy to back up data, to copy it to a floppy disk or other media so you can take the entire show to another machine, or to delete the presentation and all of its components if you want to.

Since we're going to modify an existing piece of artwork for our initial screen, we must first load that artwork. To do that, you have to load the Ultimedia Tools menu and start Storyboard Live!.

To start Storyboard Live!:

1. Switch to your CD-ROM drive and type **UTSDOS** at the DOS prompt.
2. Click the Product Selector, then scroll down through the list until you see Storyboard Live!.
3. Click on Storyboard Live!, then select Working Model.

Creating the Title Screen

The first thing we're going to do is create all the artwork for the different screens in this presentation. To do that, we'll use the Storyboard Live! Picture Maker to alter some existing artwork that comes with the Ultimedia CD.

To load an existing piece of artwork into the Picture Maker module:

1. Select Picture Maker from the main Storyboard Live! screen. The Picture Maker screen shown in Figure 2.5 is displayed.

Figure 2.5
Picture Maker
Screen with
Labels

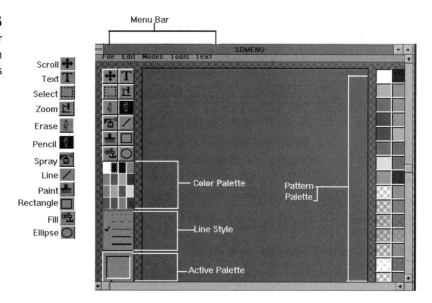

2. Click on File and select Get Picture. The GET Picture file dialog shown in Figure 2.6 is displayed.

Figure 2.6
GET picture
file Dialog

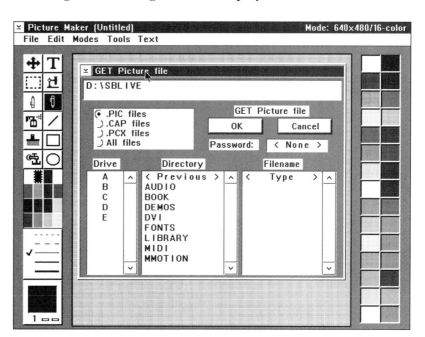

3. Select the drive where your CD-ROM reader is installed from the Drive column. (If the CD is on drive F:, for example, click on F in the Drive column. Storyboard Live! will display a list of directories in the next column.)

4. Use the scroll bar at the right of the Directory column to find the IBM30000 directory, then select that directory.

5. Click on All Files in the file definition box, then choose the WORK directory in the Directory column.

6. Choose TUTORIAL from the list of subdirectories under the WORK directory.

7. Scroll down through the File column until you find DEMO1A.TEM. Select this file, then click on OK. Storyboard Live! loads the template shown in Figure 2.7.

Figure 2.7
DEMO1A.TEM
Displayed in
Picture Maker

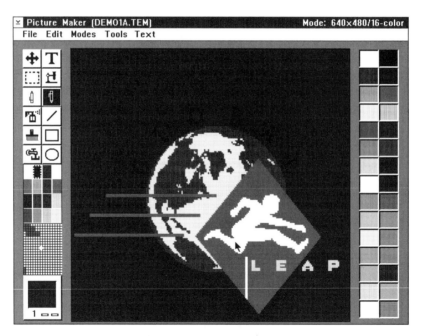

We chose this image because it was already available on the CD, and because it can help carry the "global" networking theme we want for this presentation. Remember, however, that this image is stored on your CD-ROM, so you can't save it back where it came from. Instead, save it to your hard disk:

To save a file from the CD onto your hard drive:

1. Use File Save Picture to display the SAVE Picture file dialog shown in Figure 2.8.

Figure 2.8
SAVE Picture
File Dialog

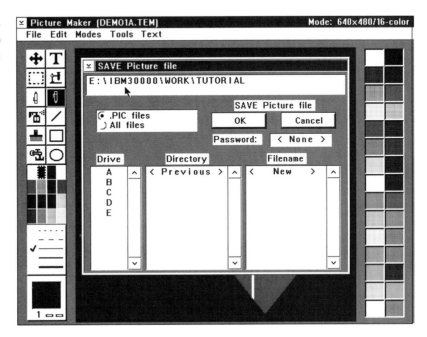

2. Choose the directory you created earlier for this show from the list under the Directory heading.

3. Click on New in the Filename column of this dialog. Enter the filename **NET00001.PIC**. Press **Enter** to set the name and store the image to disk.

Remember that you can only specify the *.PIC format with the Storyboard Live! sampler. Using filenames of this type lets you see quickly what shows the slide files are in and the order in which they're designed to appear. However, this scheme only works when you've planned carefully before you start designing the slides. If you work on images for a show before you're sure of the order in which they'll appear, you may wish to establish a more descriptive file-naming system to help you track images as you arrange them into a show.

Now that you have the original image stored in a safe place, you can edit it to develop the opening slide for the networking slide show. First, you'll remove the word LEAP from the display.

To edit the existing figure, do the following:

1. Click on the Paint icon and select the red color from the color bars at the right of the Picture Maker screen.

2. Select Tools from the main Picture Maker menu and choose Full Screen from the pulldown list. This lets you see the entire Picture Maker image without the tool bars on either side, making it easier for you to edit the image.

3. Move the pointer over the L inside the red diamond and click the left mouse button. Picture Maker removes the tools and menu and displays a magnified image of that area of the frame within a small menu box. If this box doesn't appear, press the Spacebar to display the Menus box and select Zoom.

4. Position the Brush icon over the yellow L in this image.

5. Press and hold the left mouse button, then move the Paint icon across the yellow L and the yellow E to paint out these unwanted letters. Use the magnified viewer inside the menu box to make sure you cover all of the yellow pixels in these letters.

6. Click on Menu at the bottom of the magnify box and select the blue color from the color bars at the right of the screen.

7. Move the pointer into the image again and click the left mouse button to switch to full screen display.

8. Position the Paint icon over the blue A. Press and hold the left mouse button.

9. Move the Paint icon across the letter A to paint over it. Use the magnified image inside the Menus box to help you cover all of the yellow pixels. Use the same procedure to paint out the letter P.

10. Use File Save Picture to store the modified version of the global picture to the same directory and filename where you stored the original. Save your work after each successful step. if you make a mistake, you can retrieve the last version of the image and start again from that point.

Next, we'll construct the text title for this slide. You'll use the text tool to enter the word *NETWORK* at the top of the slide and *MARKETING* at the bottom of the slide. In addition, you'll use the Select tool to move the Globe image slightly upward on the screen to make room for the text at the bottom.

If at any time during construction of this slide you make a mistake, simply return to the menu, select the background color from the bars on the right of the screen, and paint over the letters. Then select the color you're using for letters again, and start over. When you have the word "NETWORK" looking the way you want, save the image again before starting on "MARKETING."

To add text that completes Slide 1:

1. Select Modes from the menu and choose Crosshair. This will display a large crosshair on the slide, making it easier for you to position the text and globe.

2. Select Text from the menu and choose Set Attributes to display the Set Attributes dialog shown in Figure 2.9.

Figure 2.9
Set Attributes
Dialog

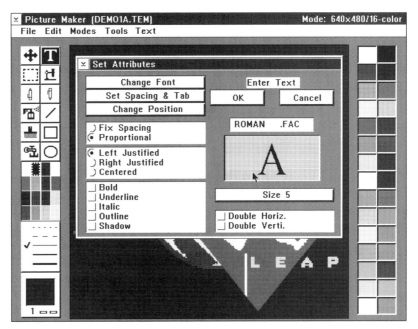

3. Click on the red color bar in the box to the left of the dialog to set the text color to the same red as the diamond that overlays the globe on this slide.

4. Click on the size bar until Size 5 is displayed, then click on OK.

5. Click the right mouse button twice to display the crosshair cursor.

6. Position the insertion point (the intersection of the crosshair lines) about one inch from the top of the screen and about half an inch from the left of the screen.

7. Press the left mouse button to remove the crosshairs and set the position for the first text character. A large blinking underline cursor will appear.

8. Press the **Caps Lock** key, then type **N E T W O R K**, placing a space between each character.

9. Press the right mouse button to end text input.

If you make a mistake, simply press **Backspace** to erase the previous character. After you've pressed the right button to set the text, you can remove the entire word by returning to the menu, selecting the background color from the bars on the right of the screen, and painting over the letters with the paint tool. Then select the color you're using for letters again, select the text tool, and start over. When you have the word NETWORK looking the way you want, save the image again.

To make room for the word MARKETING at the bottom of the slide, you need to move the globe image up slightly.

To move the globe image, do the following:

1. Click on "Menus" at the bottom of the Menus box to display the Picture Maker tool bar and menu.

2. Select the Selector tool from the menu bar, then position the cursor anywhere on the slide image and click the left mouse button. This will remove the menu and tool bar and display the crosshair cursor again.

3. Move the intersection of the crosshair to the upper left of the screen so that the horizontal line just clears the wrap-around

"Global" characters at the top of the globe image. The vertical line should just clear the horizontal red bars at the left of the display.

4. Press and hold the left mouse button and draw a box around the entire graphics image. Release the mouse button after you've positioned the box correctly. A moving dotted line should surround the globe image, as shown in Figure 2.9A.

Figure 2.9A
Selected Globe
Image in Title
Screen

5. Position the insertion point anywhere inside the dotted lines. Press and hold the left mouse button to move the globe image up on the screen. Position the image so that the upper line that surrounds the globe rests just under the letters in the word **N E T W O R K**, as shown in Figure 2.9B. Release the mouse button to set the position. Depending on how you moved the image, a portion of the old image may remain on the screen.

6. Click on the Menus button. Select the Paint icon and click on the dark blue color in the tool bar. Click in the active pattern box (which looks like a small TV screen at the bottom of the tool bar) to set that color.

Figure 2.9B
Edited Globe
Image in
Storyboard Live!

7. Click anywhere inside the graphics image and use the Paint icon to remove any unwanted portions of the image that remained after you moved it.

8. Click on Menus and use File Save Picture to store the modified image.

Now you're ready to type the word MARKETING at the bottom of the slide.

To place the word MARKETING at the bottom of the slide:

1. Select the text tool from the tool bar.

2. Click anywhere on the slide image to remove the menu and tool bar. Use the crosshairs to position the insertion point about one inch from the bottom of the screen and about one inch from the left margin.

3. Type the word **M A R K E T I N G** in all caps, placing a space between each letter. The finished slide should look similar to the one in Figure 2.10.

4.   Use File Save Picture to store the image one final time.

Figure 2.10
Finished
NETWORK
MARKETING
Slide 1

Creating the Introduction Screen

This next slide offers additional information about network marketing. Figure 2.11 shows how this slide will look.

Figure 2.11
Network
Marketing
Slide 2

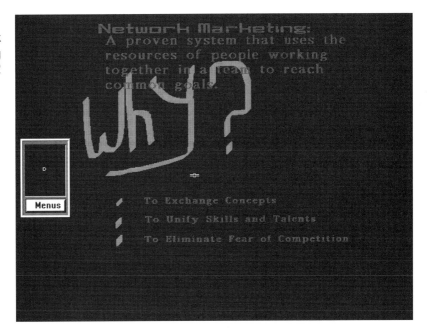

Slide 2 uses a combination of computer-generated text and free-hand letters. We were simply striving for variety in the slides and for a way to focus the viewer's attention on the points made in the bulleted list. You could use other techniques to achieve the same thing, including graphics images, varied size and type of fonts, different colors, and so on. With Storyboard Live!, you can experiment with a variety of designs to achieve one that fits your needs. This slide introduces you to the concept of freehand drawing (but with an *easy* image), just to show you it really isn't difficult to use the Picture Maker drawing tools to produce your own designs.

Now you're ready to work on Slide 2, which we call the Introduction. You'll also use Picture Maker to construct this slide, so the first step is to clear the editing screen.

To clear the screen:

1. Select Edit and choose Clear.
2. Click on OK when Picture Maker asks for confirmation and the screen is cleared.

To begin creating Slide 2 (Introduction):

1. Click on the Text symbol.
2. Select light red text by clicking on the red color bar.
3. Position the mouse pointer at the upper-left corner of the screen and press **F2**. This displays the Set Attributes dialog shown in Figure 2.12.
4. Click on the Change Font button. The GET font file dialog shown in Figure 2.13 is displayed.
5. Select MODERN.FAC to choose the Modern font and click on OK to return to the Set Attributes dialog.
6. Click on the Size button until Size 3 is displayed.
7. Select Bold at the lower-left corner of this dialog and click on OK to return to the Picture Maker main screen.

To type the first line of text for this slide:

1. Position the cursor near the top center of the screen.
2. Type **Network Marketing:**.

3. Press the right mouse button to set the text.

4. Use File Save Picture to store this slide as NET00002 (or use the naming convention you have chosen).

Figure 2.12
Picture Maker
Set Attributes
Screen (F2)

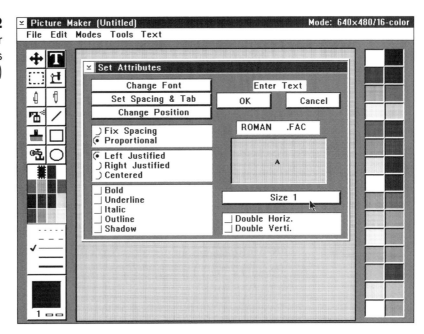

Figure 2.13
GET Font file
Dialog from
Picture Maker

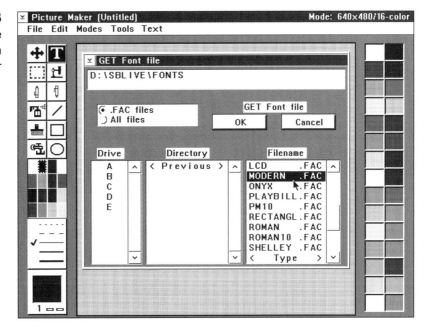

Next you'll freehand the word "Why?", slanting upward from the middle-left area of the screen. You can experiment with positions and "fonts" until you have the effect you want.

To create freehand text:

1. Select the paintbrush symbol from the tool bar and click on the light violet color square from the color group at the right side of the screen.
2. Position the cursor at the lower-left area of the screen, press and hold the left mouse button and freehand-draw the word **Why?**, slanting up the screen.
3. Save the file again when you're satisfied.

Now add the remaining text to the screen by doing the following:

1. Select the Text symbol and position the insertion point beneath the first line of text, then press the left mouse button.
2. Press **F2** to display the Set Attributes screen and choose Change Font.
3. From the GET Font file dialog, select Roman and click on OK to return to the Set Attributes dialog.
4. Click on the Size button until font size 2 is displayed, then click on OK to return to the Picture Maker screen.
5. Type the next four lines of text, as shown in Figure 2.11, pressing **Enter** at the end of each line. Notice that the text overwrites the freehand Why? we drew earlier.
6. Click on File Save Picture to save the file.

Next, create the irregular bullets under the word "Why?", like this:

1. Select the paintbrush again and choose the light violet color from the color group at the right side of the screen.
2. Position the cursor where you want the first bullet to appear, press and hold the left mouse button and move the mouse slightly to produce a small blotch of color.
3. Repeat the previous step for the remaining bullets in this list.
4. Save the file.

To insert the three phrases beside the bullets that you just drew:

1. Select the text symbol and position the insertion point beside the first bullet in the list.
2. Press **F2**, set the text size to 2, then click on OK.
3. Type **To Exchange Concepts**.
4. Press the right mouse button to set the text.
5. Move the insertion point beside the second bullet and type the second line.
6. Repeat the process for the third line in the list.
7. Save the file with the same filename you used earlier.

> Don't worry too much about precise positioning of text and other Picture Maker objects. You can move them. Choose the selector symbol from the tool bar (the dotted rectangle second from the top on the left side of the bar) and mark a block on the screen. Select Mode and choose Move, then position the mouse cursor over the object, hold down the left button, and move the object where you want it. If you change your mind about the location before you release the left button, press the right button and release the left button. The object returns to its original position.

Creating Sprites

For the next slide (an animated slide with music background), we'll use a specialized version of the Picture Maker editor called the Sprite Editor. The completed slide looks like the one in Figure 2.14.

To access the Sprite Editor, select File and choose Exit to return to the main Storyboard Live! menu. Choose Story Editor from the menu.

When the Story Editor is on the screen, select Modes and choose Sprite Editor from the menu. You should see the Sprite Editor screen shown in Figure 2.15.

Figure 2.14
Networking
Slide 3—
Bulleted List

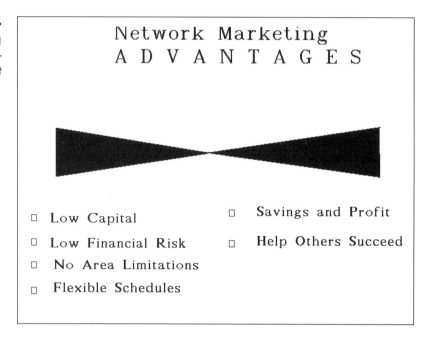

Figure 2.15
Sprite Editor
Main Screen
with Labels

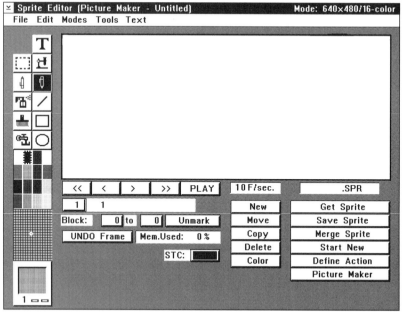

A Storyboard Live! *sprite* is a picture or text that moves according to pre-programmed instructions. For this slide, we'll create a series of text lines that start from a point on the screen and then grow at a rate of 30 frames per second to full size. This is a good technique for emphasizing points or items in a list during a presentation. In addition, we'll start this slide with some background music, then stop the music for narration about each point as it appears.

To generate the slide shown in Figure 2.14, we'll need about 10 individual sprites, which we'll install one at a time on the storyboard when we start building the presentation later in this chapter.

First, lets build the six short phrases for the bottom of this slide:

- Low Capital
- Low Financial Risk
- No Area Limitations
- Flexible Schedules
- Savings and Profit
- Help Others Succeed

Create each of these items as separate sprites for maximum flexibility in designing a presentation.

Here's how to build the first sprite in this series:

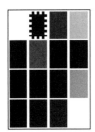

1. Click on a color attribute box at the bottom of the tool bar to specify a color for the text in this sprite. We used the dark red (red/orange) color.
2. Click on Start New from the Sprite Editor screen. The Start New Sprite dialog shown in Figure 2.16 is displayed.
3. Select Text from the Sprite Type list on the left side of the screen. The Animation Effects window shown in Figure 2.17 is displayed.
4. Accept the default animation effect, which is Grow From a Point. That means the text in this sprite will start as a very small dot on the screen and grow to full size.
5. Click on Set Sprite Size to display the Sprite Editor screen with the sprite box surrounded by a dotted line.
6. Use the mouse to shrink the size of the sprite so that the bottom border is about midway in the second icon in the tool bar. Leave the width of the sprite box at the default. You can see how this should look in Figure 2.18.

Figure 2.16
Start New Sprite
Dialog from
Sprite Editor

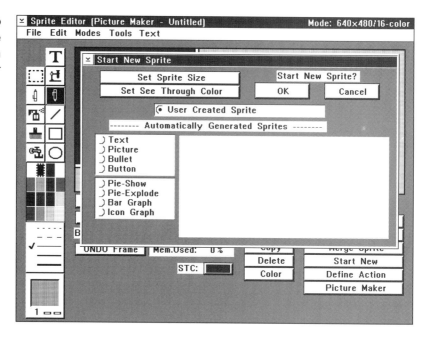

Figure 2.17
Animation
Effects Window
from Sprite
Editor

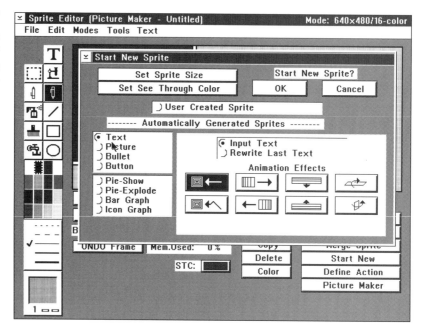

Figure 2.18
Set Sprite Size
Display in
Sprite Editor

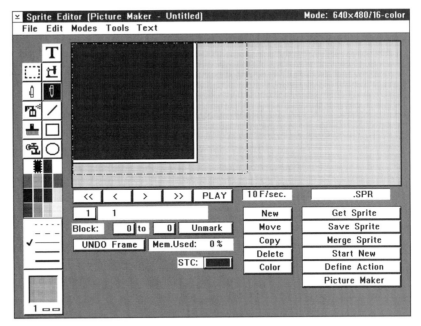

7. Click on Input Text to display the Set Attributes dialog. The Roman font file should be selected.

8. Click on Size until Size 3 is displayed on the size button. Accept the other defaults by clicking on OK.

9. A set of blinking crosshairs is displayed. Use the mouse to move one crosshair to the left side of the sprite box and press the right mouse button to fix it.

10. Type the text for the first sprite: **Small Capital**.

11. Press the right mouse button to fix the text and display the Start New dialog again. Click on OK and the Sprite Editor will ask if it's okay to clear current memory. Click on OK.

12. Watch as the editor builds the sprite you just created, frame by frame. When the motion stops, click on the Save Sprite button to display the SAVE sprite file dialog.

13. Specify a drive, directory, and filename for this sprite. Click on OK to save the file and return to the editor screen.

14. Repeat steps 1-13 for each of the remaining phrases that will form the moving list for this slide.

Now you're ready to create the two-line banner or title at the top of this slide:

Network Marketing
A D V A N T A G E S

In addition, you'll configure this text so it will stand up from a flat plane, looking as if someone has picked up a card that is lying on its back and stood it up on end, displaying the front of the card. To create this title sprite, we'll use the same techniques we used on Slide 2, but we'll select size 4 on the Size button and expand the size of the sprite window so that it reaches all the way across the editing screen and down to the middle of the third Tool icon. This title typed in the sprite editing window is shown in Figure 2.19.

Figure 2.19
Network
Marketing
Advantages in
Sprite Editor

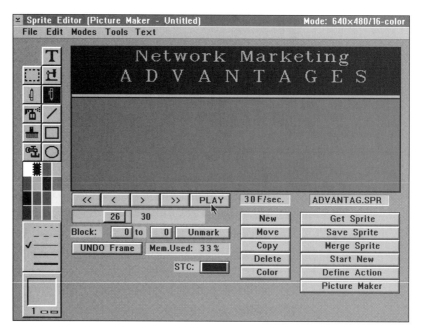

Also, when the Sprite Editor displays the Animation Effects window, click on the last effect to the right on the top row (a flat rectangle with an arrow).

Next, create a small square to be used as a bullet for the list:

1. Use the sprite editor's Start New command again, and select Picture from the list at the left of the screen.

2. Select the Appear from Point on Curved Line animation effect.

3. When the Sprite Editor first loads, select the white color bar at the bottom of the tool bar, then select the box drawing tool.

4. Position the pointer in the center of the drawing window and create a small square with the box tool.

5. Select the fill tool, then click on the Active Pattern Box (which looks like a small TV screen at the bottom of the tool bar) to set the fill color.

6. Move the pointer inside the small square you just drew. Refer to the magnified image to help you place the pointer. Click inside the square to fill it with white.

7. Click on the selector tool and use it to draw a dotted line around the small square. (Hint: Position the lower-right quadrant of the selector tool cross on the upper-left corner of the square, press the left mouse button, then draw the selector box around the square.)

8. Now use Edit Cut to copy the square to the cut buffer.

9. Use Start New to display the Start New Sprite dialog.

10. Click on Set Sprite Size to return to the sprite editing window with a dotted line around it.

11. Shrink the sprite editing window as small as possible. Press the left mouse button to set the size, then press the right mouse button to return to the Start New Sprite dialog.

12. Click on Picture from the list at the left of the Start New Sprite window.

13. Select the Appear from a Point on a Curved Line animation effect.

14. Click on Cut Buffer to specify the source of the picture for this sprite. The editing window is displayed, with the copied square inside a moving dotted line.

15. Press the left mouse button to accept the image, then press the right mouse button to return to the Start New Sprite dialog.

16. Click on OK. Watch as the Sprite Editor builds the sprite with its special effect.

17. Click on 10F/sec. and type **30**, then press **Enter**.

18. Click on Save Sprite and enter **BULLET** in the name field, then press **Enter**.

You need to design one more sprite and you're ready to use the Story Editor to build this animated slide.

To design a simple picture to separate the slide title from the bulleted list at the bottom:

1. Select Start New from the Sprite Editor screen. Click on User Created Sprite in the Start New Sprite dialog.

2. Use Set Sprite Size to drag the default Sprite editing window to the full width of the screen and narrow it to about the middle of the third Tool icon.

3. Select the pen tool and click on the red color bar at the bottom of the tool bar.

4. Select the line-drawing tool and position the pointer at the upper-left corner of the drawing window. Hold down the left mouse button and draw a straight line from the upper-left corner to the lower-right corner of this rectangle.

5. In a similar manner, draw another line from the upper-right corner to the lower-left corner of the rectangle so you have drawn a broad bow shape, as shown in Figure 2.20.

Figure 2.20
"X" Drawn to
Start Bow
Shape

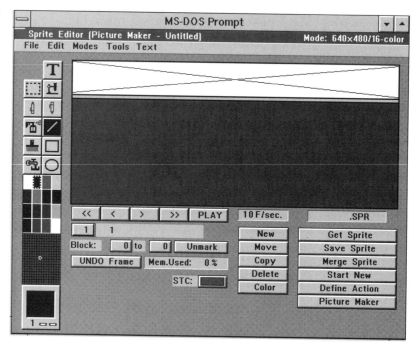

ls (left and right) of the bow by drawing a line
ft corner to the bottom-left corner, and another
p-right corner to the bottom-right corner.

ool and click once in each side of the bow
d fill with the red color previously selected.

blue background color and click once in the
dow above the bow and again below the
 is a red bow against a dark blue background.

elector tool and select the entire sprite you
 do this, place the pointer at the upper-left
image, hold down the mouse button, and
around the image.

place a copy of the image into the edit buffer.

New to display the Start New Sprite dialog.
w from a Point icon, then click on the Cut
 This will paste the image you just copied
back to the sprite editor screen, enabling the
ct you have selected.

nage with a production (retail) version of
 you can use the Define Actions button to
 actions for this custom drawing, just as you
did for the previous text sprites. Define Actions doesn't work
with this demonstration version, so use this "cut buffer"
workaround.

12. Click on the "10F/sec." field at the bottom of the sprite
    editor and enter **30** to speed up the line drawing process.

13. Click on STC (See Through Color) at the bottom of the Sprite
    Editor screen. The See Through Color dialog is displayed.

14. Click on the dark blue color bar at the bottom of the tool
    bar. Dark blue appears in the See Through Color window
    of the dialog.

15. Click on the Down Arrow at the upper left of the See
    Through Color dialog to close this window. Click on OK
    when the editor warns you that this will become the de-
    fault see-through color.

16. Use Save Sprite from the Sprite Editor screen to store the
    drawing under BOW.SPR.

Starting to Assemble the Show

You now have built all of the art required for this first show, a three-slide presentation with music and animation. Remember that the Storyboard Live! sampler is limited to 40 lines of instructions in the story editor. The commands for inserting these sprites and slides will just fill these command lines. In the next section, you'll learn how to assemble this show.

Return to the main Storyboard Live! menu with the File Exit command from the Sprite Editor screen and choose Electronic Presentation. The screen in Figure 2.21 should be displayed.

Figure 2.21
Main Electronic
Presentation
Screen

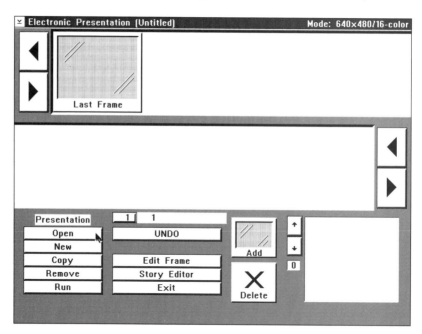

Use the tools you already have created to start building your Network Marketing presentation:

1. Click on New under the Presentation title at the bottom left of the Electronic Presentation screen to display the NEW presentation dialog shown in Figure 2.22.

2. Choose a drive and directory for the new presentation, then click on New to enter a filename. The .SH extension is added automatically to the filename.

Figure 2.22
NEW
Presentation
Dialog in
Electronic
Presentation

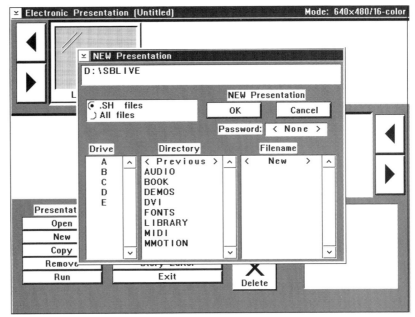

3. Press **Enter** after the name is entered and click on OK when the Update warning is displayed to return to the main Electronic Presentation screen.

4. Click on Edit Frame to display the Edit Frame dialog.

5. Click on Edit under the Foreground title on this dialog to display the Picture Maker screen.

6. Use File Get Picture to load Slide 1 that you created earlier as the title slide (for example, NET00001.PIC). You can either double click on the slide name to load it, or select it with a single click and then click on OK to load it. Either way, the slide is displayed in the Picture Maker edit window.

7. Use File Electronic Presentation to exit the Picture Maker. Click on OK when the Update Foreground? dialog is displayed.

8. Click on Exit on the Edit Frame dialog, which is displayed on the top of the title slide. The slide should appear in the first position on the Electronic Presentation screen, as shown in Figure 2.23.

9. Click on Edit Frame again, then click on the Right Arrow under the Edit Template button to advance the counter to Slide 2. The screen under the dialog will clear.

Figure 2.23
Title Network
Slide in
Electronic
Presentation

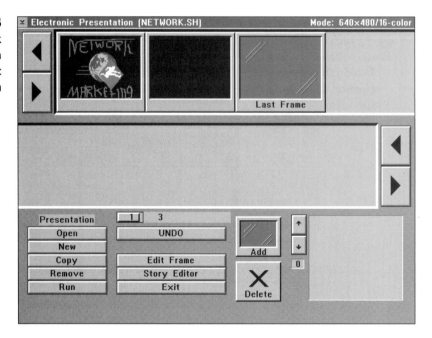

10. Click on Edit under Foreground to return to the Picture Maker screen. Use the same technique as before to load Slide 2 and return to the Electronic Presentation module. Click on the Left Arrow at the top of the screen to back up and display both of the slides you just installed. The screen should look like the one in Figure 2.24.

11. Click on Edit Frame again, then click on the Right Arrow under the Edit Template button to advance the counter to Slide 3. The screen under the dialog will clear.

12. Click on Edit Template on the Background Template side of the Edit Frame dialog. The Picture Maker screen is displayed.

13. Use File Get Picture to display the GET Picture file dialog. Click on the drive letter that represents your CD-ROM reader (or example, F), then select the IBM30000 subdirectory.

14. Choose WORK, then select DEMOS from the directory list in the middle of this dialog.

15. Select the BLUEBKGD.PIC file from the Filename list, then click on OK to return to the Picture Maker editor with the blue background file loaded.

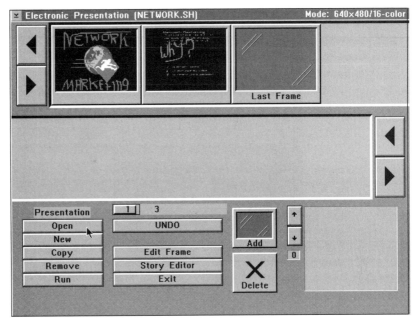

16. Use File Elec. Presentation to exit the Picture Maker. The SAVE Template dialog is displayed. Select the drive letter that represents where you're storing this Storyboard Live! presentation. Choose the proper directory, then click on New to display the filename prompt.

17. Enter **BLUEBKGD** at the prompt. The editor automatically adds the **.TEM** file extension to designate a template file. Click on OK to return to the Edit Frame dialog.

18. Click on Select Template to display the GET Template dialog. Choose the drive letter, directory, and BLUEBKGD.TEM file you just saved. Click on OK to return to the Edit Frame dialog. The background template you just selected appears under the dialog.

19. Click on Exit to return to the Electronic Presentation module. The blue background template you just loaded should appear as the last slide in the presentation.

20. Load the Story Editor by clicking on the Story Editor button at the bottom of the Electronic Presentation screen. You should see the screen shown in Figure 2.25.

Figure 2.25
Story Editor
Screen with
Code for
Two Slides

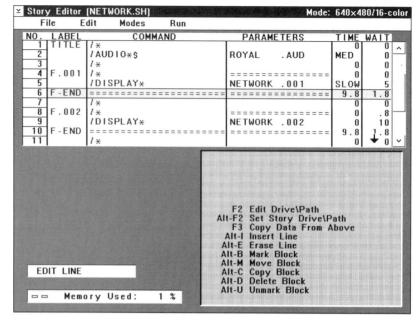

Notice that Electronic Presentation has automatically written a series of commands to control the presentation that you've built to this point. Each slide requires four lines on the program screen:

- A Frame start and Frame number command
- A display command
- A Frame End command
- A separating command line

During automatic generation (as opposed to writing the script yourself in the Story Editor), this type of separated instruction list helps you find each slide unit during editing, and because the red lines cannot be erased in the Story Editor, you can add effects or sound inside any slide definition and the slide components stay together as you move images to build the show.

The next slide is constructed of sprites that you designed with the sprite editor. You can't build a sprite slide inside Electronic Presentation.

To construct a sprite slide inside Story Editor, do the following:

1. Use the mouse or the Down Arrow to position the horizontal colored line over the "/*" comment symbol just above the "/*Story Last Line." This should be the first blue colored line on the screen.

2. Press **ALT+I** to insert a line in the show script. A blue comment line (/*) should appear.

3. Use the mouse to point to the command field on the line you just inserted. Press and hold the left mouse button to display a list of available commands (See Figure 2.26).

Figure 2.26
Story Editor
Command
Pulldown Box

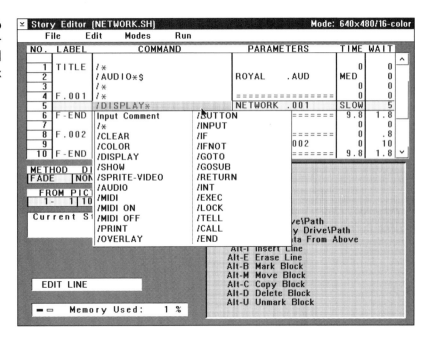

4. Select /SPRITE-VIDEO from the list and /SPRITE* will appear on the current command line.

5. Move the pointer to the PARAMETERS field of this same story line. Press and hold the left mouse button to bring up the parameters options shown in Figure 2.27.

6. Choose Get Existing Name and select the ADVANTAG.SPR file you created earlier.

Figure 2.27
Parameters
Pulldown List

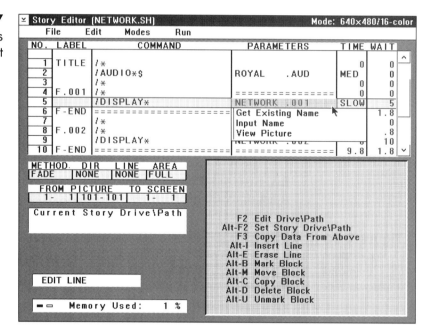

7. Move the pointer to the TIME field, then press and hold the
left mouse button to display the pulldown time choice list
shown in Figure 2.28.

Figure 2.28
TIME Pulldown
List from Story
Editor

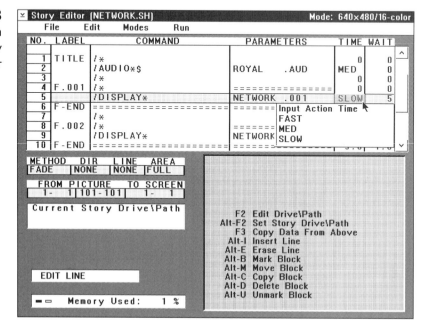

8. Select SLOW from this list. The default 0 should remain in the WAIT field of this line.

9. Next, move the pointer to the POSITION field at the bottom left of the screen. Hold down the left button to display the pulldown position menu shown in Figure 2.29.

Figure 2.29
Position
Pulldown Menu
in Story Editor

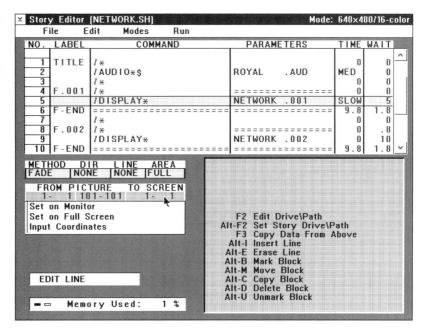

10. Select Set on Monitor. The editor clears the function key prompt window at the right side of the editor display and presents a blank screen with a dotted line showing the ADVANTAGE sprite you just inserted into the story.

11. Grab the box and move it to about the center of the monitor display (left to right) and at the top of the window. You want this sprite to play at the top of the screen when the story is run. When you release the mouse button, the position of the sprite is fixed and you're returned to the Story Editor screen. You'll enter and place the remaining sprites for this screen in the same way:

• Insert a line.

• Add the /SPRITE* command to the command line.

• Specify the filename and time.

• Use the POSITION monitor to place the sprite.

In addition to the sprites you created in the sprite editor earlier in this chapter, you'll be using the SPARKLE.SPR sprite included with the Storyboard Live! sampler.

To insert the bow sprite, do the following:

1. Insert a new line and specify the BOW.SPR sprite file you created earlier.
2. Use the POSITION feature to place the sprite in the upper-middle area of the screen. Precise placement is not important, but the remaining sprites will be placed relative to this one.

The following series of sprite placements is used to build the bulleted list. Each line of the list consists of three components:

- A sparkle
- A line of text
- A square bullet

To place the first item in the bulleted list:

1. Insert a new line and specify the SPARKLE.SPR sprite. You'll find this sprite in the CD-ROM directory \IBM30000\DEMO.
2. Position the Sparkle sprite to the left of the screen, on the line where the first bullet item will appear. The idea is to place the sparkle between the bullet and the first letter in the text. The Sparkle will rise from a point, flash and disappear, then you'll see the text, then the bullet.

Instead of placing the sprite on the monitor as you did in the previous step, you can try using screen coordinates. Select Input Position from the Position pulldown menu. Try a value of 49-311 for this sprite.

The Input Position selection uses pixels (screen dots) to specify coordinates on the screen. Pixel 0-0 is at the upper-left corner of the screen. The first number is the horizonal (X axis) position and the second number is the vertical (Y axis) position. While this sounds like precise positioning, it doesn't always work out that way because of variations in the way sprites were created. Unless you're *very* careful to start each sprite text line in precisely the same place in the sprite window, the text may not line up because the Input Position command places the sprite window, with the text inside it free to move around a little.

3. Specify FAST in the TIME field for this sprite.

4. Move down to the next line and press **ALT+I** to insert a new line.

5. Use the pulldown menu under COMMAND to place the CAPITAL.SPR sprite you created earlier.

6. Position the sprite to the right of the Sparkle sprite you just placed and on the same horizonal line. (Try position 57-311 if you want to use Input Position from the POSITION pulldown menu.)

7. Specify FAST in the TIME field for this sprite.

8. Insert another line under the CAPITAL sprite and specify the BULLET.SPR sprite. Position the bullet to the left of the first line of text. (Try a position of 25-311 for starters.)

Press **F4** to display the contents of a sprite on the monitor. Use **F5** to show previous sprites you have placed. This helps you move the current sprite to the proper location.

9. Specify FAST in the time field for this sprite.

Now enter the rest of the lines of text with sparkles and bullets. Remember the idea is to approximate the screen in Figure 2.14. You'll line up four bulleted lines of text on the left side of the screen, then place two more lines on the right side of the screen.

For each bulleted line, do the following:

1. Insert a new story line and specify the Sparkle sprite, position it, and specify FAST execution time in the TIME field.

2. Insert a new story line and specify the next sprite in the series. Position it under the previous text sprite.

> The text sprite files you designed previously will appear in this order:
>
> - Capital
> - Risk
> - Area
> - Sked
> - Profit
> - Help

3. Insert a new story line and specify the bullet sprite. Position it so that it appears under the previous bullet sprite and to the left of the last line of text.

After you enter the last sprite for this screen, you're ready to enhance the presentation with some music. First, you might want to see how the presentation looks up to this point. Use the mouse pointer or the cursor movement keys to return to the top of the story editor. Place the highlight bar over line #1 (TITLE). Use the Run Run Story command sequence to view the slide sequence to this point. Note that the Electronic Presentation module has specified that slides will change at the press of a key. To call up the next slide, slimply press any key. The final slide will remain on the screen until you press a key.

Adding Audio

One of the surprising and interesting enhancements that multimedia capability brings to the PC is sound: voice narration, music, and sound effects. You can't record new sound with the sampler version of Storyboard Live!, but the CD included with this book already has some sound files you can use.

We'll add two simple sound routines to this presentation, then show you how to add narration later if you decide to purchase a retail version of Storyboard Live!.

To add the first sound file to the presentation:

1. Position the Story Editor highlight bar over the first comment line (/*) after the line with the TITLE label at the top of the story file.

2. Press **ALT+I** to insert a new line, then pull down the COMMAND list.

3. Select /Audio*. The editor places the audio command on the command line.

4. Pull down the COMMAND list again and select Input Comment. This lets you add information to a command line that helps you interpret or document the story later.

5. Place a dollar sign ($) after the asterisk at the end of the AUDIO command. This is a special form of comment that tells the Story Teller module to start the specified audio file, then go on with the slides while the audio plays in the background. Without the dollar sign, the audio command plays the specified audio file with the slide display frozen on the last slide.

6. Pull down the command list in the PARAMETERS field and select Get Existing Name to display the File Manager dialog.

7. Click on the letter that represents the drive where your CD-ROM is installed, then choose the IBM30000 directory from the Directory list in the middle of the display.

8. Click on DEMO to display a list of .AUD files in the Filename list on the right of the display.

9. Select ROYAL.AUD and click on OK to return to the Story Editor screen. You don't need to change the TIME and WAIT defaults already displayed on the screen.

10. Press **ALT+B** to mark the line you just added. A dark box should appear over the line number at the left of the display.

11. Use the mouse pointer or the cursor keys to move the story down to the /DISPLAY* line that calls the BLUEBKGD.TEM template.

12. Press **ALT+C** to copy the line you just marked to the line just above the template display.

Now you have music to begin the show and to start the display of the sprite slide (Slide 3). In the next section you'll set the timing for the first two slides so that the initial music ends at the beginning of Slide 2, leaving room for your own narration.

The music then will pick up at the beginning of Slide 3 and end after a few moments, again leaving room for narration over this slide.

Storyboard Live! supports audio recording through a variety of audio cards that are normally used for multimedia systems. With the retail version of the product, you can input music or sound effects from a CD player, tape deck, or other source, and record live narration with a microphone attached to the audio card. This record audio feature is disabled in the sampler version of the product. However, we'll show you here how to capture additional audio for inclusion in this and other Storyboard Live! stories you might produce.

To record narration:

1. Select Modes from the Story Editor menu and choose Record Audio. The Record Audio Panel display shown in Figure 2.30 will appear.

Figure 2.30
Record Audio
Panel Display

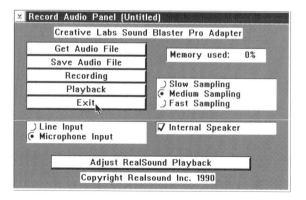

2. Choose a sampling rate. Medium is probably okay for voice files.

3. Make sure a microphone is plugged into the proper port on your sound card or that you have another audio source (such as a CD player, tape deck, and so on) connected and ready to play.

4. Select Recording from the button list, then press **Enter** to start recording. Press **Esc** to end recording.

> With a medium sampling rate, audio quality should be adequate for voice and you can record 20 to 30 seconds, depending on your system configuration. For higher quality (and shorter recording times), select Fast Sampling.

5. Speak into the microphone or turn on the recording source. Remember, you're limited to the amount of available memory, 15 to 25 seconds with most systems. It's best to record short takes that go with a single slide. That way, if you move the slide, the associated audio can go right with it.

6. After recording a sound segment, use Save Audio File to display the SAVE audio file dialog shown in Figure 2.31. A stored audio file will require 200K of storage, more or less, depending on length and the sampling rate you've chosen. Some audio sequences, on the other hand, can be stored in 25K or less for sound effects or very short narration segments.

Figure 2.31
SAVE audio file
Dialog from
Record Audio
Module

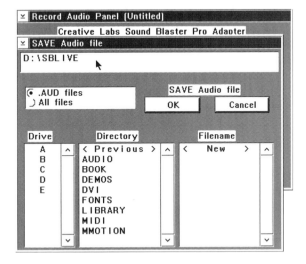

7. Specify a drive, directory, and filename to store the audio file.

By default, Storyboard Live! stores audio in the .AUD format, a format compatible with the Story Editor and Story Teller. You can use .WAV file formats in your stories (such as the files included with Microsoft Windows) if you load them first into the Record Audio module and save them as .AUD files. (Again, you can't do this with the sampler version of Storyboard Live!.)

Once your .AUD files are saved, you can incorporate them into your stories through the Story Editor, just as you did the audio files supplied with the Sampler CD-ROM.

Putting it All Together

Now we'll add a few final enhancements, and this "sampler" presentation will be complete.

To add the final enhancements:

1. Move the highlight bar over Slide 1 in the Story Editor, the /DISPLAY* statement that calls for NETWORK.001.

2. Click on the Method field at the lower-left side of the screen to pull down the display options shown in Figure 2.32.

Figure 2.32
METHOD
Pulldown Menu
in Story Editor

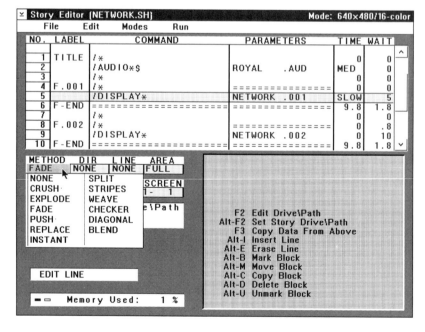

3. Choose FADE from this list and the word FADE appears in the METHOD field.

4. Click on the TIME field to the right of the /DISPLAY* line and select \SLOW from the pulldown list.

5. Click on the WAIT field on this same line and select Input Wait Delay. A blinking cursor appears in the WAIT field. Type **5** and press **Enter**.

6. Use the cursor movement keys or the mouse to highlight the Slide 2 display line.

7. Accept the defaults for this slide, except for WAIT. Pull down the wait menu, select Input Wait Delay and enter **10**, then press **Enter**.

8. Highlight the /DISPLAY* line that calls for Slide 3 (NET-WORK.003). This should be the last line in the program. Check the WAIT command on this line. If it's not already set to KEY (the Electronic Presentation default), use the pulldown menu to set it.

That's it! You now have produced a short multimedia presentation that includes graphics, text, animation, and music. To play the show, use the Story Teller module. (Or use Run Run Story from the Story Editor. Just make sure the cursor is at the first line of the story.)

If you want to try the Story Teller, return to the main Storyboard Live! menu screen and click on the Story Teller icon to display the prompt shown in Figure 2.33.

Enter the path and name of the story. When you press **Enter**, you'll see a brief Storyboard Live! opening screen, then the presentation you just created will play from beginning to end. The length of this show is about one minute.

The final slide will remain on the screen until you press any key on the keyboard. Then the main Storyboard Live! menu will be displayed.

You can use the basic techniques you've learned here to build any slide show with Storyboard Live!. As you can see, the utilities

Figure 2.33
Story Teller
Prompt

for music, animation, text, and graphics are built in. Even with the sampler version, you can create useful presentations and learn how to use the various modules that are part of this application.

Now that you've built one presentation from scratch with our step-by-step guide, why not design something simple of your own? Start with a simple design, rough out the screens, decide on graphics or music, then jump right in to build your own show.

Later in this book, we'll show you how to produce additional MPC presentations.

Designing Multimedia Applications

CONCEPT TO PRESENTATION

Designing presentations for multimedia is a lot like designing presentations in any other medium, and a little like nothing else you've ever experienced. Multimedia gives you a broad range of graphics, sound, and animation tools that allow you to create presentations you never would have dreamed of with conventional presentation media.

In addition, remember that by far the majority of multimedia presentations are accompanied by a human presenter. Even if you've used music and narration, you may still want to stand up and control the presentation, to answer questions, or to add personal comments during the show. The exception to this idea, of course, is standalone interactive training material. For business or sales presentations, however, the majority of multimedia presentations are designed to accompany a speaker.

With that in mind, part of your planning and design of a multimedia presentation should be to focus on how the human presenter and the multimedia presentation can work together.

In this chapter, we'll show you the basics of screen design and how to develop a presentation concept into a finished presentation.

General Design Considerations

First of all, if you doubt the power you have in your hands as a designer and presenter of multimedia applications, consider how we gather information:

- 10 percent from the words we hear
- 40 percent from the way the words are said
- 50 percent from what we see

That means that what the audience sees on the screen accounts for half of what they'll learn from your presentation. That doesn't mean you should downplay the importance of text and speech, but as you design any presentation, you definitely should be aware of the power of the visual image.

By the same token, however, we expect to "hear" something during a presentation as well, so what we see should be designed to supplement what is being said, either live or recorded. It sometimes is distracting—even irritating—to be presented with a lot of material to read while someone is talking at the same time. Either you tune out the words to concentrate on the visual, or you skim or overlook the visual to listen to what is being said.

When visual material accompanies narration or spoken material, the visual should be especially brief, it should be displayed first and backed up with words, or you should hear the words first and back up the words with the visual.

You can help make on-screen presentations shorter by forgetting some of the long-standing rules of language you were taught in school. A bulleted list, for example, doesn't always require a subject and verb. Instead of writing:

- Mechanical engineering requires complex math skills
- Mechanical engineering requires a thorough background in natural science and physics

You can write:

Mechanical Engineers Need:

∞ Math
∞ Natural Science
∞ Physics

The short, keywords help your audience focus on your main point and make it easier for them to remember your message. To increase the visual appeal of these lists, try using different symbols (such as the infinity sign used above) instead of the usual dots or "bullets." Remember, the idea is to help the viewers understand as much information as possible as quickly as possible, and to help them retain that information as long as possible. The more visual you can make the presentation, the more you will enhance it.

Some of the same design rules and guidelines you would use for desktop publishing or photographic composition also apply to multimedia presentations. After all, the individual components of a multimedia show are slides or pages, individual units that are linked together to form the whole.

The difference between multimedia screens and a printed page or a photograph, of course, is that you can use sound and motion in addition to layout, color, shape, and shading to get your message across. The key to a successful presentation is to use the tools at your disposal in a creative way that is appropriate to the audience you hope to reach and to the message you hope to convey.

Always Keep Your Audience in Mind

When creating a presentation, always keep in mind your ultimate goal: Do you want the audience to remember specific details, or is a general idea really the important consideration? For instance, in preparing a sales presentation, is it more important that you design it so the viewer will remember the technical specifications and statistics of the item you're trying to sell, or do you want to leave the audience with a concept or an overview of what the item can do for them or for their business?

There is no simple answer to that question, rather it depends on who your audience is, what you're selling, and what you want the audience to do or think or feel as a result of your presentation. If your audience is a group of upper-level personnel managers with non-technical backgrounds, you wouldn't be doing them (or yourself) any good by focusing your presentation on the electrical specifications of the computer monitors you want to sell; you would do better to focus on the fact that your monitor reduces eye fatigue and has very low radiation emissions.

If you want to leave the viewer with a concept, feeling, or idea:

- Use motion video and photographs
- Reduce the amount of on-screen text
- Show people using the product
- Show people who appear pleased or satisfied
- Emphasize *what* is being done over *how* it's being done

Remember, we retain information visually, as pictures, a lot easier than as text. So whenever you can convey you message visually, you have a better chance of retaining audience interest.

If you want to communicate factual details:

- Use text and charts
- Use no more than six lines per slide
- State and restate ideas, using different methods and terms
- Simplify screens
- Use photographs or art to help the viewer link raw data to the real world

The sample slide in Figure 3.1 is relatively simple and should be fairly easy for the viewer to understand, interpret, and remember.

Figure 3.1
Simple, Easy-to-
Interpret Slide

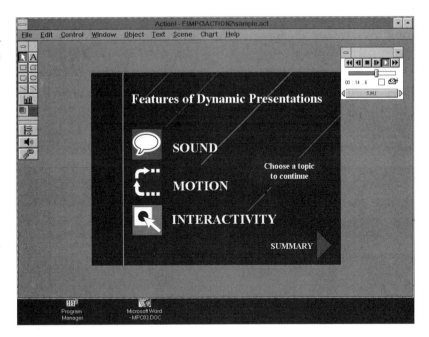

The sample slide in Figure 3.2, on the other hand, is too complex, has too much information on the screen, and would not be very easy for most viewers to understand.

Figure 3.2
Complex,
Difficult-to-
Interpret Slide

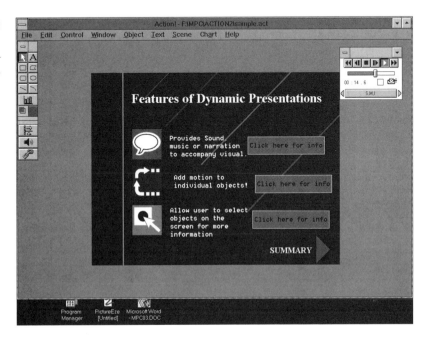

Another important concept, especially with a live presenter giving the presentation, is that you should design presentations so that they can be controlled randomly. For example, as you show a presentation, you should be aware of the audience's level of understanding. If the audience seems confused or (worse) bored, you should be able to back up the show, or branch to an entirely different segment. Also, there may be times during a presentation that members of the audience will ask questions. This could change the direction of the presentation completely. If you haven't designed your presentation to be flexible, to back up or jump to a specific location within the presentation, your presentation could easily fail.

Another good design technique to include in your presentations is the ability to compress or expand the information you present depending on audience needs. You might have a series of summary screens, for example, and include on each one a button that could branch to a more detailed description if necessary during the presentation.

For example, you might have one series of slides that uses very common terms for the concepts you're trying to convey. These slides would be enough for non-technical or inexperienced audiences. When you have to make the presentation to a more experienced audience, on the other hand, you could expand it with more technical information and details.

So be creative, look at the message you want to get across, consider the audience, and be aware of the broad range of presentation tools you have at your disposal as you work on your design. Although there are some general rules that apply to all types of presentation design, some rules are meant to be broken. And, the dynamic nature of the multimedia platform promotes experimentation. If you think of something that might work, try it. Then don't hesitate to listen to feedback from users and viewers of your finished product and make changes as necessary.

Designing Screens and Slides

Whether you're designing a printed page, a slide, or a computer display, the overall effect of your efforts is the *layout*. A layout is the arrangement of the elements that make up the page or screen. Some of the possible elements of a multimedia screen are:

- Text
- Graphics
- Photographs
- Boxes and other static objects
- Animated objects
- Motion video
- Color space (yes, space is one element of all designs!)

As you work on the screen layout, keep in mind one excellent rule of design: No single element of a layout is intended to stand on its own. Every element on the screen (or slide) should relate in some way to every other element. And in most cases, elements on one screen should relate to elements on other screens so that you're building a theme and presenting a consistent message.

If you change the typeface or type style used for a heading, for example, it may change how much information will fit on the page, and it may require a change in the type used for the rest of the screen. If you open up a screen with more colored space, you may not be able to fit all of the elements you had on the screen before. (See the section on fonts later in this chapter for more information on screen design using type.)

As you work on placement of the various elements on a screen, keep these ideas in mind:

- Each screen or slide should address a single concept or idea
- Screens should follow a logical progression, each building on the other
- In general, a simple design is best
- The viewer must be able to digest each screen quickly and easily
- For text screens, six lines are generally the maximum
- Use upper- and lowercase for most text, not ALL CAPS (Headings and titles may be set in all caps)

- Choose a color appropriate to the mood you want to convey
- Avoid using too many colors (five colors per screen maximum)
- Use photographs and/or motion video wherever possible

In addition, be aware of how most of us view a page, screen, or photograph. The scanning pattern usually is a reverse "S" that starts at the upper-left corner, moves to the middle toward the right side, zooms to the left about three-fourths of the way down, and exits on the lower right.

Obviously, you should place items you want to emphasize along the "reversed-S" scanning pattern for maximum visual impact. And, you can use other multimedia tools and techniques to help the viewer focus on a particular item or area of the screen.

Brief animation, for example, causes the eye to move to that area of the screen; we're naturally drawn to movement even if we aren't focused on that area at the time. This animation doesn't have to be cartoons; any type of movement can be used. Even flashing or changing colors will cause a viewer to look at that area. If you back up such an attention-getter with music, sound effects (for instance, a bell) coupled with narration to reinforce or amplify the message, the viewer is more likely to follow the presentation and retain the information than if you use a straight, static presentation.

Now let's talk about some specifics of screen design and show you some examples of these concepts.

Using Photographs

Earlier, we said that you should use photographs whenever possible to help the viewers relate the information being presented to the real world.

Look at the examples in Figures 3.3 and 3.4. Figure 3.3 shows a bulleted list against a plain background. Figure 3.4 shows the same list against a photograph.

The photographic background—even if you show only a hint of an item—helps make the text less abstract to the viewer. It also helps the viewer retain the information because, again, we remember things visually better than we do when a concept is presented as just plain text.

Figure 3.3
Bulleted List
with Plain
Background

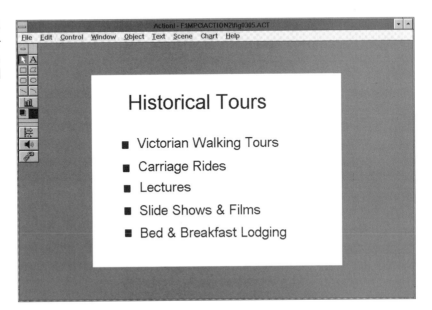

Figure 3.4
Bulleted List with
Photograph
Background

So, if your presentation includes a list of information about computers, for example, place the list on the screen over a picture of a computer.

By the same token, if your bulleted information has to do with sales information, place it over a photograph of something that suggests selling, such as a store interior, shopping mall, or cash register.

Using Graphics

If you don't have a photograph available, your next best choice is a graphics image: something you've drawn from scratch or maybe a clip art image. Where do you get photographs and other images for your presentations? There are many places to look, including:

- Company brochures, letterheads, business cards, or catalogs
- Annual reports, user manuals, sales aids, or engineering reports
- Art used by other members of your organization in previous presentations
- Product samples, company reports, or letters
- Clip art or software samples
- Custom-drawn art using a graphics package
- Videotape still frames

You can scan many of these images into the computer with a full page or hand-held scanner. Most readily available, reasonably priced scanners produce black and white images. Black and white scanners work okay for presentations if you can use colored text as the overlay, place the photograph inside a color border, or "colorize" the image with a transparent overlay.

If you want a color image, check your telephone book for a company that will scan your images, then save them in a .TIF, .PCX, or other file format compatible with your software package. Just be careful when using images from sources outside your company or that you have not been given permission to use. For instance, you can't legally scan many images from magazines or books and use them for your show, tempting though it may be.

Using Video

One really good source of still, color images for your presentations is videotape or a video camera fed directly into a video capture board. (See Chapter 1 on hardware, and Appendix D for more information on video capture technology.) Most video hardware includes some form of software driver to let you capture a still frame image, so all you need to do is set up your camera on a tripod, light the scene appropriately, and take a few seconds of tape. Then hook up your VCR to the video capture board, take a snapshot, and you're ready to go.

This technique lets you capture shots from physical images, such as computer keyboards or hardware, equipment used by your company, scenes of your town or area, and so on. Once the image is captured and stored in a graphics file format, you can use it as a background or as a picture inside a window, just as you would any other graphics image from your computer.

Visual material during a presentation is designed to augment the presentation, to add information to what the speaker is saying, or to help the audience retain or interpret what the speaker is saying. Don't use motion video, animation or other multimedia techniques simply because you can; use them because they're the most effective tools for different situations.

To help you decide whether you should use video, ask yourself how video will enhance your presentation. For instance, will it help tell the audience

- *Where* something is?
- *How* something works?
- *How much* is involved (cost, quantity, and so on)?
- *Who* is involved or affected?
- *When* you should take a particular action or use a particular tool?
- *Why* this information is important?

Again, remember that you design visual materials to catch a viewer's interest and to enhance what the speaker is saying. To that end, you can use the following techniques to enhance the attention-getting aspects of your slides.

As we mentioned earlier, you should use a photograph instead of a drawing whenever possible, because a photograph just naturally gets more attention and has more impact than a drawing. By the same token, if you can't use a photograph—or a photograph isn't appropriate or practical for what you're doing—then you should use a drawing instead. An illustration will still have more impact—that is, get more attention—than plain text.

In fact, there are a number of attention-getting concepts that you need to be aware of as you design slides for presentation, as shown in Table 3.1.

Table 3.1 Relative Impact of Presentation Screen Elements	
High Interest	**Low Interest**
Photos	Words
Color	Black and white
White (Blank) space	Solid copy
Bold type	Italic type
ALL CAPS	Lowercase
Large type	Small type
Wide lines	Thin lines
Large area	Small area
3D	2D

The information in Table 3.1 is just a guideline. Use it with other guidelines you learn in this chapter. For example, the table shows that ALL CAPS gets more attention than initial-capped text. However, you don't want a chart with all text in uppercase because it becomes too difficult to read. We're used to reading text in upper- and lowercase, so use all caps for headings, titles, and other text you want to use as an attention getter, then revert to normal initial caps for the rest of the text.

Using Text Charts as Multimedia Screens

Remember, too, that even though the number of tools and formats available for your multimedia productions is large and the choices varied, at least half of business-oriented presentation material is still text based. With multimedia, you can use narration and music to augment what is said on the screen, but it's still true that you'll likely be using a lot of text charts as part of your multimedia shows.

A *text chart* is simply a screen display, slide, or printout that you use for tables of organization and flow charts, timetables, sales presentations, and summaries, as shown in Figure 3.5. The name notwithstanding, a text chart may incorporate a variety of graphic elements—scanned images, graphs, and clip art—as well as grids, boxes, lines, and shading, along with basic text.

Figure 3.5
Sample Text
Chart

At its simplest level, a text chart may simply be a bulleted list. The advantage of the multimedia platform is that you can organize and present this text information in creative ways to catch and keep the viewer's attention and to improve the retention of the data.

Obviously, you can use number-based graphs (such as from a spreadsheet or graphing program, for example), but text charts have a free-form design that is particularly useful in the following ways:

- To present information that includes too many data types or too much information to present logically in a graph
- To show exact values instead of graphic approximations
- To show information that covers a very broad range between the highest and lowest numbers
- To show data when the exact amount is critical

The guidelines for designing a text-chart screen are generally the same as for any other multimedia screen:

- Pay attention to the typefaces and type sizes you choose
- Keep the amount of information on each chart relatively small
- Each screen should contain data that is closely related
- Highlight the benefits or results of the ideas you present
- Avoid generalities; be as specific as possible
- Keep each sentence or phrase as short as possible
- Keep charts (screens) in a series consistent with the same combination of fonts, similar size, and layout ratios
- Use both upper- and lowercase characters, not all uppercase
- Drop extra or unnecessary words, even if incomplete sentences result
- Generally, you should avoid the use of hyphens, which might break up the flow of data

Using Color

Color may well be the single most important element of screen design. Compared to a black and white image, such as an overhead projector slide prepared with a standard, black-type printer, for example, color images

- Accelerate learning, retention, and recall by nearly 80 percent
- Improve comprehension more than 70 percent
- Increase viewers' willingness to read up to 80 percent
- Improve selling efficiency by as much as 85 percent

So if color has this much power, you definitely should use it, but more important, you should use it appropriately. As mentioned earlier, it's important not to place too many colors on a single slide or screen. In general, five colors should be the maximum, but most of your screens probably will use even fewer colors, unless you're including a full-color photograph or drawn image. (Obviously, if you're using a full-color image as part of the screen, you'll quickly surpass the five-color guideline. That's okay.)

Another way to look at color is to determine what the overall message of the screen or presentation is, then choose a color appropriate to that message. For example, a recent study by the Wagner Institute for Color Research in Santa Barbara, California, showed how people react to different colors in interior design, as shown in Table 3.2.

Table 3.2 Colors and the Emotions They Suggest

Color	Emotion
Red	An emotional color that can actually make a person's heart beat faster. Denotes excitement and may mean "stop" or "danger," depending on the viewer and context. It also takes longer for the eye to interpret red than any other color.
Dark Blue	Stable, calming, trustworthy, mature. Can encourage fantasy, but also has a calming effect, so don't use blue if you want the audience excited and upbeat.
Light Blue	Youthful, masculine, cool.
Green	Growth, positive, organic, go. Can help people feel comfortable in unfamiliar places. Choose shades carefully, however because many of us carry a prejudice against "institutional" green—the green of classrooms and chalk boards.
White	Pure, clean, honest, sophisticated, refined, delicate. Used properly with other colors, it can be useful in attracting an "upscale" audience.
Black	Serious, heavy, death. Use black carefully, but it can be useful, particularly for some backgrounds.
Gray	Integrity, exclusive, neutral, cool, mature. A color that creative people feel comfortable being around.

continued

Table 3.2 Colors and the Emotions They Suggest (Continued)	
Color	**Emotion**
Brown	Wholesome, organic, unpretentious.
Yellow	Emotional, positive, caution. It is interpreted by the eye faster than any other color. Good to draw attention to a slide or screen area, but can also incite anger or irritation.
Gold	Conservative, stable, elegant.
Orange	Emotional, positive, organic. Also considered a neutral color that can help the viewer adapt to other colors. Orange and blue in combination denote strength.
Purple	Youthful, contemporary.
Pink	Youthful, feminine, warm.
Pastels	Youthful, swift, feminine, sensitive.
Metallic	Elegant, lasting, wealthy.

In addition, different colors usually are associated with specific feelings or moods:

Cool Colors   Cyan, Blue

Warm Colors   Yellow, Red

Magenta and green, on the other hand, are transitional colors that can take on qualities of either warm or cool, though magenta is basically a warm color while green is a cool one.

As you design slides, you should generally use dark colors for backgrounds and lighter colors for text and illustrations, because the eye is naturally drawn to the lighter areas in the foreground. This is the same concept used by photographers and painters to focus attention within a scene. Photographers sometimes adjust brightness in the darkroom to change the focus of a photograph during printing. By "printing down" (making darker) areas of the picture that should receive less attention, they help the viewer focus on the more important areas of a picture. Notice especially portraits printed by professional photographers. The faces—already lighter than the surrounding features—sometimes are made extra light to force attention on them. The same concept holds true when designing multimedia slides. A dark background with light foreground helps keep the viewer focused on what is most important.

The Tektronix company, a leader in color printer technology, advises that from a viewer perspective the most popular colors for backgrounds, in order, are:

1. Dark blue
2. Black
3. Gray
4. Brown
5. Red
6. Green
7. Purple

Also, if you design a chart that arranges items by color, or that uses color to code or flag certain concepts, you should consider arranging the items in the order the colors appear in the natural spectrum:

1. Red
2. Orange
3. Yellow
4. Green
5. Blue
6. Indigo
7. Violet

And, your presentations should consist of logical groupings of color. You should use the same range of colors within a logical section of your presentation, for example, and use colors that are close together on the color chart. If you switch color schemes too often or too suddenly, it's jarring to the audience.

Using Fonts

In the presentations you create, the type of characters you use are an important part of how your message is perceived. Not only does the typeface you select help convey information, it also conveys a mood or style.

Here are definitions for some of the terminology used to discuss text.

Typeface: A distinctive shape and design or a design style of type that makes a collection of letters recognizable. Typefaces are generally identified by name, such as Times Roman, Helvetica, Palatino, and Century Schoolbook. Figure 3.6 shows some common typefaces.

Figure 3.6
Four Different
Typefaces

This is Times Roman

This is Helevtica

This is Palatino

This is New Century Schoolbook

Point size (or type size): The size of the type you use is measured in *points*. One point is equal to 1/72 of an inch, so that 72-point type is about one inch tall. In most typefaces, a 12-point type is standard for many printed pages and also is a readable on-screen size. A 30- or 50-point size is appropriate for titles and headings or for a bulleted list when viewed from a farther-than-normal distance from the screen. Figure 3.7 shows some different point sizes.

Figure 3.7
Point Sizes

This is 12-point type
This is 14-point type
This is 18-point type
This is 24-point type
This is 30-point type

Type style and weight: Most typefaces can be presented in different styles and stroke weights, such as bold, italic, shadow, or bold italic.

Font: A collection of all of the characters available for a particular typeface and style. For example, Times Roman Italic, Palatino Bold, or Helvetica Bold Italic.

Serif type: Type that includes finishing strokes at the end of main strokes, as shown in Figure 3.8. Most typefaces use serifs, and serif type usually is easier to read than typefaces without serifs (sans serif type). Roman typefaces have serifs.

Sans serif type: Type without serifs, as shown in Figure 3.8. Helvetica is a popular san serif type.

Figure 3.8
Serif and
Sans Serif Type

Roman is a serif typeface
Helvetica is a sans serif typeface

Notice the difference between *typeface* and *font*. A typeface is a named shape or design of character, whereas a font is a collection of all of the available characters in a particular typeface in a specific style.

Although many multimedia authoring tools incorporate a wide range of text styles, sizes, and colors, the general guideline is to work with a limited number of fonts and styles within any given presentation. Moreover, it's best to stick with the same type style for the same positions across all slides.

For example, if you have a series of slides that includes a title or header line on each one, all of the title text should use the same font and (usually) the same font size. Likewise, captions for the images on these slides should all use the same size and font, running text or bulleted lists should be the same, and so on.

You should use no more than two or three different fonts on a screen: one basic type style for *body copy* (the text used in the middle of the screen for descriptions or lists), and one or two *accent faces* (such as italic or bold) that might be used for captions or emphasis. These accent faces could be an extended or condensed version of the basic body type, or they could use a related, new font. By *related* we mean type of the same general style. You don't want body copy of clean, modern Helvetica type, for example, mixed with large titles drawn in florid Old English.

As a general rule, sans serif fonts are a good choice for presentations over serif fonts because serifs tend to disappear or blur, particularly if you're projecting the image.

And, of course, you must be concerned about the size of the type you use. The most general rule on size is "Can the audience read it?" You can find this out by testing the presentation on co-workers or friends in an environment similar or identical to the environment to be used for the presentation.

In addition, you should know something about the location of your presentations as you design screens. In general, a good rule of thumb is that the maximum viewing distance from a presentation screen is six times the screen diameter. So, in our 30-by-40-inch example, you should plan the presentation so that no one in the audience must sit further than 20 feet (40 inches times 6 = 240 inches, divided by 12 equals 20 feet). If you're making the presentations on a standard 14-inch PC screen, on the other hand, you should avoid having anyone in the viewing audience sit further than about 7 feet away (14 inches times 6 equals 84 inches, divided by 12 equals 7 feet).

Test these guidelines by simply pushing your chair away from the desk where you're working on your PC. By the time you get six or seven feet away from the screen, reading anything other than fairly large type becomes difficult. And, you can make the process easier through the use of color, accent shapes, and so on.

Using Motion Video

Many of today's multimedia software packages support motion video, an excellent way to enhance a presentation. Most of this software supports motion video within a small window on the screen, and this small window can be part of an overall screen design. A motion video window from Storyboard Live! is shown in Figure 3.9.

One reason for using a small window within a screen display is storage limitations. Standard, full-motion video presents information at a rate of 30 frames (screens) per second. Since each of these screens is a graphics image, storage requirements for this amount of information at full speed on a full screen can be staggering.

To get around this limitation, some full-motion video limits the size of the display screen and the resolution of the display. For

Figure 3.9
Storyboard Live!
Full Motion
Video Screen
Shot

many types of video, these limitations are not serious. After all, being able to see realtime, full-motion video as part of a presentation or to highlight a presentation, probably is worth a slight reduction in image quality.

Whatever the limitations, if your presentation package supports it and you have the hardware and any additional software you need, use motion video. As we said earlier, we remember pictures more than words. Therefore, anytime you can use video as part of a presentation, you have increased the likelihood that the audience will remember the message you're trying to convey.

Remember, too, the video component of a given slide doesn't have to carry the majority of the information. Just as you can use a background with a still photograph, you can place motion video behind a text or graphics window as a way of helping the viewer focus on a topic or to help the audience relate the data you're presenting to something in the real world. (Use this technique carefully, however, as we all like movies and you don't want to pull the audience entirely away from what you're saying or what you may be presenting on the screen.)

On the other hand, you can open a motion video window and let the person or the action in the sequence tell the whole story while the live presenter simply waits until the end. Such sequences should be short for a couple of reasons. First, full motion video requires a lot of storage space, so if you do very much of it during a presentation you may find yourself needing a very large hard disk. Second, a motion video sequence is there to augment or enhance the presentation, not *to be* the presentation. Use it for variety and to enhance a presentation, not to show a movie.

For more information on how you can process your own motion video, and some hardware and software requirements, refer to Appendix D.

Designing a Multimedia Show

Designing a multimedia show is an individual process, one that has as many variations as there are people doing it. However, here are some suggestions that may ease the process a little for you.

Garrison Keillor, the affable narrator of a National Public Radio show, always said he just started talking until he thought of something to say. This approach can work when your audience has a lot of time, can relax, and there is no particular message that needs to be communicated. Unfortunately, too many speeches and presentations are designed just this way.

Obviously, a better approach is to plan carefully all aspects of your show, from what you want to say and what you want the audience to learn or do as a result of what you say, all the way to what type of room you'll use and how you'll dress. And you shouldn't be using multimedia just for its own sake. "If you don't have anything to say, don't say it," is also a good rule.

Making a presentation is a little like flying an airplane: While you're doing it there is so much going on that if any one thing goes wrong, it could endanger the whole show. If, like flying, however, you have planned adequately in the beginning, then one or two mishaps along the way won't throw you off course or cause you to "crash and burn."

Here are the steps for producing a well-constructed presentation:

- Brainstorm
- Create an outline
- Make a storyboard
- Write a script
- Build the presentation
- Test and debug the presentation

We'll discuss each of these processes in the following sections of this chapter.

Brainstorming

As you first begin to think about designing a presentation, put on your reporter's hat and ask yourself (or your client) the classic reporter's questions:

- Who?
- What?
- When?
- Where?
- Why?
- How?

These general questions can take more specific forms, such as:

- Who is my audience?
- What do they think of my subject?
- What do they expect to get from my presentation?
- What do I want to accomplish: educate, motivate, inform? What should they feel, know, or do differently after the presentation?
- Under what conditions will my presentation be delivered?
- When and how often will the presentation be delivered?
- Where will the presentation be delivered?

- Why am I giving this presentation?
- Why would anyone come to see this presentation?
- How important is it to achieve the goals of my presentation?
- How can I most effectively achieve my goals with the resources available?

The answers to some of these questions will be immediately obvious. For example, your supervisor may tell you to prepare a show on a specific topic, perhaps, and tell you in general what to say and what should be accomplished, or the group or organization for whom you are preparing the presentation may answer some questions for you.

Other questions may not be so obvious, such as what does the audience already think or know about the subject, or how will you be most effective in achieving your goals and what resources do you have at your disposal. One tried-and-true technique to answer these questions, and others you probably haven't thought of, is *brainstorming*.

Although brainstorming is an excellent planning tool, it has been trivialized to the point that most of us don't use it effectively. Conducted properly, however, brainstorming can help you to understand aspects of yourself, your job, and even discover things you didn't know you knew.

Brainstorming most often is associated with a group effort, and it can be effective in that context. But group brainstorming should be preceded by considerable individual effort. It's the inward-looking aspects of brainstorming—discovering something about yourself.

Beginning Brainstorming

Basically, the brainstorming process works like this:

1. Arrange for 10 to 20 minutes of uninterrupted time.
2. Use a notepad or word processor and write a topic word or phrase at the top of the first page, such as **Network Marketing**.
3. Spend the next 10 to 20 minutes thinking about the topic.

4. Write down every word or phrase that comes to mind. Don't edit, judge, or qualify what you write down.

5. When you have to force the ideas or 20 minutes have passed, stop the session.

6. Don't try to consciously think about the topic for several hours; 8 to 24 hours is a good break time.

7. Start another session by reading your previous work quickly.

8. Repeat steps 1 through 7 until you have to force topics from the beginning and the sessions get very short.

When you're brainstorming, write down everything that pops into your head, no matter how silly or irrelevant it seems at the time. The important thing is to get a lot of ideas down; later you can go back and edit them, keeping some and throwing away others.

During this brainstorming process, which can take anywhere from several days to a few weeks, you should get into the habit of carrying a pen and a small notepad wherever you go. It's also a good idea to leave this pad next to your bed at night. If you have one, a small tape recorder also is a good tool to use during this process because you can note ideas whenever and wherever they occur, even while driving.

> Never put off an idea that rises out of your subconscious, unbidden, while you're brainstorming a project. If you wait to write it down or record it, the fundamental concept might be lost.

One interesting and useful aspect of this type of regular, organized thinking is that your subconscious mind becomes active, processing the thoughts you set in motion during each new session.

Relax and be creative. Don't worry about order at this point, but leave room under each item for some subtopics. Figure 3.10 shows the result of one brainstorming session about a network marketing presentation.

Figure 3.10
"Brainstorming"
List of Net-
working Topics

Network Marketing
Brainstorming Session #1

Selling
Helping others
Leverage
More time
Independent business
Flexible hours
Low capital
Exchange ideas
Limited risk
Wide geographical area
Savings
Profit
Little training required
Worldwide (global) nature
Thousands of products possible
Travel
Large growth potential
Good support system in place
Reduced or no competition
Full or part time

When brainstorming, write now, critique later.

Taking Brainstorming to Stage 2

Once you have a basic list of (perhaps) unrelated ideas, you can begin to organize a little. It's still too early to throw away anything from the list. All you want to do now is group the items, or expand the list for further brainstorming. If you're trying to pull information from your subconscious mind, try expanding each topic:

1. Write each topic you have generated so far on a separate page or screen.

2. Repeat steps 1 through 8 from the previous section for each new topic.

Depending on the complexity of what you're trying to accomplish, you may need to conduct several more iterations of Stage 2 until all of the topics are sufficiently expanded.

Brainstorming: Moving to Stage 3

By this stage in the brainstorming process you should have several (maybe dozens) of pages of notes about different topics. During this stage of brainstorming you'll begin editing the lists, making decisions about what ideas and concepts fit within the general limits of the current project, and which ones are obviously beyond the scope of it.

> As you edit your brainstorming notes, don't actually throw anything away. You may find that a particular page of ideas may help you later in the process or may have to do with something totally different that you may work on later.

Begin by reading the major headings at the top of each brainstorming sheet you've prepared. If you discover entire topics that don't seem to fit the current project, lay them aside.

Now arrange the major topics in order of importance.

Highlight the really important ideas under each major topic (use a highlight pen or boldface on your word processor). Finally, extract the important subtopics into a list organized by order of importance or, if appropriate, in a logical order for processing into an outline or procedure list.

At this stage in the brainstorming process, the material you have could take several forms, depending on your own personality, the level at which you started, and the type of project you're working on.

In all likelihood, the end product will be a list of important topics or goals that you hope to present or accomplish with the current multimedia presentation. Now ask yourself the following questions:

- Which of these ideas or concepts is most important?
- How will I present the ideas most effectively?
- In what order should they appear?
- What resources do I have to help me present them?

At this stage of the creative process, you may want to bring other people into the loop. Call a meeting of others involved with the project, make an informal presentation that shows what you have accomplished to this point, including your goals for the presentation, and ask for creative input.

Whether you're primarily responsible for the project and you're just asking for a little friendly help at this point, or you're part of a team charged with designing the presentation, be sure to give the others involved a definite deadline by which you want their feedback. Ideally, this should be no more than a few days from the time you make your initial presentation to them. In addition, make the following points clear:

1. The form of feedback you wish: written report, telephone call, another committee meeting, sample screens, and so on.
2. The date, time, and place where input should be provided.
3. The ultimate goal of the project and the nature of your peers' involvement.
4. How the rest of the project will proceed and whether you'll want additional help in the future.

Once you're satisfied with the brainstorming process, you're ready to outline the presentation. Don't try to outline a presentation until you have at least done some form of brainstorming. Remember, brainstorming is the creative part of the design process. An outline is an organizational tool only. It will help you put in the proper order the creative data you've already collected.

Creating an Outline

Most of us were exposed to outlining at some time during our education, and, if you're part of the majority, you probably hated it. If you're like most people, you handed in outlines when the teacher asked for them, but you wrote the paper first.

Whatever preconceived notions you may have about outlining, try to set them aside, then try it one more time. Outlining is a useful tool that augments the creative process.

The purpose of an outline is:

- To help organize
- To highlight areas that may be more important than others
- To highlight ideas or concepts that should be touched only lightly
- To discover ideas or concepts that should be dropped

By writing an outline you're giving a concrete structure to your ideas, but an outline is not carved in stone. Be open to new ideas throughout the writing and design process, and change your outline whenever necessary.

Depending on how your organization is structured, you may want to use the outline to get feedback from your co-workers on the ideas you plan to cover and the order you plan to present them.

While there are some classic outline forms from which to choose, you can pretty much design your own outlining process. Remember, however, that the outline is an organizational tool, so the more organized the outline is, the better it can do its job for you. The formality of your outline style should vary directly with the number of people you expect to read it. If your outline is simply for your own reference, a way to guide you toward a storyboard design, then adhering to strict outline format is less important. If, on the other hand, you expect to distribute the outline to several other members of your design committee or other experts in your company, a more formal approach may be needed.

Here are some outlining guidelines we suggest you follow:

1. Use a consistent numbering system that ranges from high to low level. The classic form is Roman numerals at the highest level, followed by capital alphabetic, then Arabic numbers, and so on. Your word processor can provide a workable numbering system.
2. Provide at least two entries at each level (no *A* without a corresponding *B*, no *1* without an accompanying *2*).
3. Use consistent style, single words and phrases (topical outline), or sentences (sentence outline) at each level.

4. Use parallel headings and subheadings so that the same type of material is placed in similar levels.

5. Use consistent wording among entries at the same level.

6. Use main headings that represent slide topics to make storyboard development easier.

7. Use headings that convey sufficient information for other readers to understand.

Figure 3.11 shows part of an outline for the sample show on network marketing described in Chapter 2. Obviously this is not the only format, but it's a good "middle-of-the-road" design.

Figure 3.11
Sample Show Outline— Network Marketing

Preliminary Outline
Network Marketing Presentation

I.   Title
A. Network Marketing
B. Single frame graphic—"Global" theme

II. Introduction
A. Definition of Network Marketing
B. Reasons people are attracted to Network Marketing

III. Advantages
A. Animated bulleted list
B. Narration with music

IV. Traditional vs Network Marketing
A. Traditional Marketing flow diagram
B. Franchise Marketing flow diagram
C. Network Marketing flow diagram

V. Products and Services
A. Graphics annd motion video "buttons"
     1. Home Tech
     2. Health & Fitness
     3. Gifts & Novelty
     4. Fashion
     5. Business
     6. Home Supplies
B. Series of slides linked to each button
     1. Picture of typical item
     2. Narration of product examples
     3. Name brand emphasis

If you're using a word processor (and you should be!), then you don't have to be too careful about item placement as you convert your brainstorming notes into outline form. Once you have the format established and you have entered all of the points you want to cover, you can cut and paste your data to arrange it in the proper order.

If you follow these brainstorming and outlining steps properly, then when it comes to building the storyboard, the hard work is done. All you really need to do is use the main outline headings as slide titles and fill in the description from the subheadings on each slide.

If you're designing an interactive presentation—more difficult than a straight self-running or presenter-directed show, but increasingly popular in training and education applications—then you may want to conduct a flow charting step between the outline and the storyboard. A flow chart shows graphically any branches or decision points that occur in the show. In an interactive application, the user/viewer can change the direction of the presentation at some points as the result of prompts or other stimuli such as sound, movement, color change, and so on. A simple flow chart is shown in Figure 3.12.

Figure 3.12
Sample
Presentation
Flow Chart

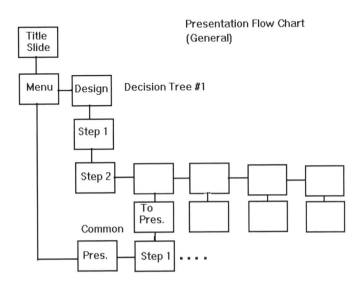

Making the Storyboard

Once you're satisfied with the outline and flow chart (if necessary), you're ready to make a storyboard. Think of a storyboard as a graphical representation of the outline. You can construct a storyboard by hand on a series of pages, you can use a drawing tool on your computer, or you can start building the application directly in the presentation package you plan to use.

For all but the simplest shows, however, the best approach is to rough out the story line on paper. You can use plain white computer paper, an easel with large sheets, a legal pad, or whatever tools you're comfortable using. The idea is to use the outline as a basis for drawing a simple representation of each slide you'll have in the program. Don't worry about your drawing skills; this is not a test or an art competition. You merely want to present the basic idea of the show to better visualize the presentation.

Think of a multimedia presentation as a series of slides, modules, or events, some of them placed sequentially (end to end), and some of them lying parallel. One of these lines contains the images (slides) you'll use during the presentation. Associated with each slide is another unit that represents music, sound, or narration. In addition, you can specify a special effect (fade, wipe, and so on) as the transition between slides.

The sample storyboard fragment in Figure 3.13 shows this concept. Any art such as drawings or photographs is shown, plus placement of text, windows, and other special effects. You can note on the drawing what sound, if any, will be associated with the slide.

The first storyboard after the outline can serve as a "doodling" session, a chance for you to put in primitive visual form the outline you've developed. As with other steps in the design process, you may have to go through this procedure several times to refine the design, locate problems, add new ideas, and get input from others.

The good news about storyboarding is that it can be a fun process. It's not difficult or complicated, and a good storyboard makes designing the final show in your presentation software a lot easier.

Figure 3.13
Storyboard
Fragment for
Network
Marketing

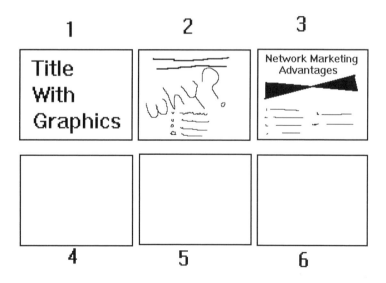

As you work with your storyboard design you'll have accomplished a number of important things. You will have:

- Established the order of the slides
- Determined the number of slides
- Settled on the general design of each slide
- Decided what special effects you'll use (sound, video, wipes, and so on)
- Determined what resources are required to produce the slides
- Given other team members a vehicle for reviewing the presentation and making changes if necessary
- Provided an archival copy of the information

As you work in these areas—particularly sound, other artwork, and resources—you may want to brainstorm again by writing artwork and sound ideas next to each topic. Again, don't worry if your ideas seem strange (or difficult) at the time—write them down! Later, what seemed like a bad idea may be the unique angle you were looking for, or it may make you think of an even better way to do something.

As you refine the storyboard, you can add more and more information, making the process of building the actual application in a multimedia software package even easier. You may wish to include notes on the filenames for any graphics or scanned images, for example, or jot down a list of resources and their locations beside each slide drawing.

If your presentation is relatively simple with only a few slides, your storyboard will likely include every slide that will appear in the final production. If yours is a more complicated presentation, however, the storyboard—at least the initial one—may show only the first slide or two in a multi-slide series so you can track modules of information.

And as you work on the storyboard, you may modify your outline, re-arranging slides, adding new material, or deleting some information. The visual process is a good polishing step and helps you to see how a show shapes up.

Remember throughout the design process that you're trying to tell a story, make a point, sell an idea, change an opinion, or whatever. How you do this depends on the audience, the material being presented, and your own personality.

In general, there are a few recognized ways of telling a story. For example, you can begin by generalizing, becoming more and more specific as the presentation unfolds, until you've given your audience all of the desired information:

The computer may seem like a new idea, but the conceptual design for machines we use today is over 100 years old...

On the other hand, you can start with some piece of important information well into the story, then bring the audience up to date a little at a time:

Today's desktop PC can process information to the tune of about 112 million instructions per second, speed and power that...

Consider these ways of organizing information for your presentation:

Deductive organization: Moves from the general to the specific.

Inductive organization: Moves from specific to general.

Chronological organization: Starts at the beginning, describing a sequence of events in the order they occurred.

Process Organization: Presents the steps involved in a process or procedure where each step must occur in a given order.

Agenda Organization: Presents information in a random order, frequently without logic. However, to be successful, the audience must be told what the order is going to be.

You can design other ways to organize a presentation that are combinations of these. In fact, it's difficult and rare to see a "clean" organization that follows strictly one of these presentation designs.

Which one should you use?

As with any creative endeavor, the answer is not a simple one. It's more important for you to know the audience, to understand what end result is desired, and to select a combination of tools and arrangement of elements to achieve these goals. During and after design, use viewer feedback and testing to determine how you need to refine and improve the show.

And, as with outlining, writing, movie making, and other creative endeavors, accept the fact that your carefully planned design is bound to change when you begin the actual production. While the outline and storyboard are excellent organizational tools, they shouldn't overshadow your thinking as you work on the script and prepare the slides for the presentation.

Writing a Script

A multimedia presentation script is just what the name implies. Like a movie script or the script for a play, the presentation script provides a textual representation of all of the elements of the final show. Whereas the storyboard is a visual representation of all or part of the show elements, everything that will be part of the presentation will appear in a script, including:

- Slide description
- Text and how it will be presented
- Slide or scene number
- Duration
- Total running time (if self-running)

- Narration (if any)
- Sound effects
- Music
- Graphics elements
- Motion video

A portion of the script for the Network Marketing presentation is shown in Figure 3.14.

Figure 3.14
Network Marketing Script Fragment

```
Network Marketing Presentation
Working/Design Script-Preliminary
Version 1.3

AUDIO                          VIDEO
                               |
FADE UP: MUSIC                 SLOW FADE UP FROM BLACK
FILE:  IBM30000\ROYAL.AUD      SLIDE#1: TITLE
                               (NET00001.PIC)
ANNCR: Network Marketing is
one of the hottest and
newest concepts for
distributing goods and
services.

MUSIC OUT                      SLIDE#2: INTRODUCTION
                               (NET00002.PIC)
ANNCR: With so many
traditional marketing
avenues available, why
Network Marketing? Here are
just a few reasons...but the
benefits of Network
Marketing TO YOU go far
beyond this list.

                               SLIDE#3: ADVANTAGES
MUSIC: Pick up ROYAL.AUD       (Sprite-Built in Story
SOUND: DING.WAV (Coordinate    Editor)
with Sparkle.SPR)

ANNCR: There are many
```

Like storyboarding, scripting leaves a lot of room for you to develop your own format and style. As you evolve a script format, keep these ideas in mind:

- Who will use the script?
- Are several people working on the production?
- How complex is the production?
- How will the presentation be produced?

The answers to such questions as these will help you determine how serious you need to be about designing a complete and consistent script style. Here are some guidelines or suggestions to help you develop your own style:

1. Use a split-page format where the left side of the page includes visual instructions and the right side holds audio information.
2. Number the scenes or slides associated with each module of text and instructions.
3. Include filenames or other location information where possible.
4. Write instructions in all uppercase, voice over (narration) in upper- and lowercase.

Remember, too, that while you want to include a lot of detail in a working script, you also want to strive for clarity and an uncluttered appearance. That helps those who may be unfamiliar with the show to help you during production or during the proofing and testing process. Just as you want to achieve an open, uncluttered feel to each of the slides you design, your script that will be used to produce the presentation should also feel open and accessible.

When the script and storyboard are completed and you're satisfied with the order of the slides, the content, and the mood of the presentation, you're ready to begin building the show.

Building the Presentation

The precise process involved in building a multimedia presentation depends to a large degree on the software you're using. We show in some detail how to build three presentations in this book.

The general process, however, is the same for all software. When you bring a detailed outline, a storyboard, and a script to the production table, you already have accomplished much of the work in building a presentation. Using these reference tools, you can follow the production process:

1. Construct individual slides or screens by creating titles and adding text or graphics elements.
2. Specify the order in which they will appear.

3. Set the duration or control (how the slide will change).
4. Add sound, music, or narration as required.

Testing and Debugging Your Presentation

After the elements of the presentation are in place, you can conduct some testing to make sure everything functions as you intended, and that the program produces the desired effect.

You'll do a certain amount of testing and debugging as the program is built, of course. As each element is finished—motion video, animation, bulleted list, or sound or music—you likely will play that individual slide to ensure that the technical features work as they were designed.

After these individual components are assembled, you'll need to test the entire program. If this is a one-time presentation to a small group and intended as a small informational effort, then you can likely view the show yourself and decide whether it achieves its goal.

If the presentation is something that will be used for multiple audiences and you expect some definite results from it, such as a sales or promotional program for your company, then the testing process needs to be somewhat more involved.

We recommend that you get as many people involved in the testing and debugging process as possible. It may be true that during the creative and design stages you want as much individual freedom as possible so as not to become sidetracked or confused. But when the program is finished (a *final beta* or *prerelease* version, in computer jargon), it's time to gather outside opinions.

If the show is for internal viewing, as with training or educational material, then you can use co-workers to view and critique the presentation. You should schedule two or more showings to different audiences at different times and evaluate their feedback carefully. As much as possible, you should foster an atmosphere of cooperation, of working together on a project that is important to everyone in the company.

Test audiences should feel free to tell you honestly how they reacted to your work, and you should be prepared to separate their comments and criticisms from personalities. Try to elicit honest opinions and use them in conjunction with your production expertise and what you know about the goals of the production to draw your own conclusions about the quality and value of the product.

One way to help test viewers open up is to prepare a questionnaire for them to fill out after they've seen the show. However, you have to be careful how you construct the questions in such a survey, making sure they're not weighted in any direction, for example. You should also avoid questions that force the viewer to make a "black or white," "yes or no" decision, such as:

- Have you ever seen a more professional presentation?
- List three reasons why the audience will adopt our viewpoint after seeing this presentation.
- Do you believe that XYZ Corp. should be using quality multimedia presentations such as this one?

Well, you get the idea. At the same time, however, don't be afraid to inject some humor into your questions. This can allow the audience to say some negative things about the program without feeling they'll hurt your feelings or suffer consequences:

This is a good tool for our company because (check all that apply):

  [ ] Information is clear
  [ ] Entertaining
  [ ] Correct company perspective
  [ ] Professional production
  [ ] Are you serious? This is terrible because_____
_____.

Another technique we've used to make a critical audience relax during a session is to make the presentation during a lunch break or over special refreshments during an afternoon break.

There's something about food that creates a relaxed atmosphere and brings a group together.

After you have received feedback, make whatever changes in the production you think should be made based on the comments received, then schedule at least one more showing to see if the problems were corrected. Again, through personal contact, memos, or a pre-show presentation, make it plain that you appreciate everyone's involvement, and that you've made changes in the show based on their previous comments. However, you should also make it clear that the previous comments were taken under advisement and the resulting changes were made on the basis of a variety of input, including input from other professionals.

Of course the final testing is done in the field, before a live audience. So always be aware of audience reaction during a presentation. And, if this show or another similar one will be used repeatedly, you may want to devise a questionnaire for each audience. Such regular evaluations over time can help you polish and refine a program, removing any unclear or unnecessary components.

Building Multimedia Presentations with Action!

THE BASICS

Another good choice for multimedia presentations is Macromedia Action!. While it has many of the same features as IBM's Storyboard Live!, Action!'s design and user interface are updated, and the program is easier to conceptualize and use. Plus, it has the familiar Windows look, as shown in Figure 4.1.

Like Storyboard Live!, Action! presentations consist of individual slides, or *scenes*, positioned in the order you want them to appear. These scenes can include a variety of *objects*, including:

- Text
- Charts
- Sound
- Animation
- Motion video

121

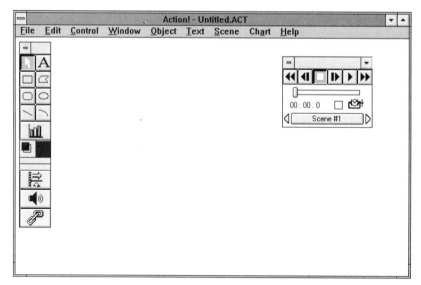

In addition, you can add motion to objects that are normally static, such as text and charts. This feature lets you make your presentations more interesting and visually exciting.

You can also create interactive objects, such as buttons or graphics images, that let the user control the direction and flow of the presentation. This is especially useful for training or education presentations, where you want the user to be able to go at his or her own pace, selecting what areas to cover in more detail and what areas need to be repeated.

In this chapter, you'll see how Action! is designed, and how to use the Action! tools to create your own presentations. Then, in Chapter 5 you'll learn how to build a practical presentation from beginning to end.

Getting Started with Action!

Each Action! scene is composed of one or more objects, which you can either draw from scratch inside Action!, using the Tool Palette utility, or import from a number of other sources, including:

- External paint or drawing programs
- Charting and graphing applications
- Scanned images
- Digitized sound
- CD-based sound
- Digitized motion video

In addition, Action! comes with a series of pre-designed templates that serve as a starting place for your own material. These samples are carefully designed to take advantage of color, fonts, shapes, and size for maximum impact, and provide an excellent way to begin designing your own presentations.

Also, you can save the screens you create for one application and use them as templates for future presentations. This is useful when you need to produce, say, a monthly sales report with the same general information and format, but with different data.

Action! templates include text and graphics objects, motion programming, and transitions such as fades (a slow ending of one scene coupled with a slow beginning of the next) and wipes (canceling one scene and starting the next by moving a line or other shape across the screen). To create your own presentations, all you have to do is modify each scene in your template to put in the text and graphics you want, reducing design and development time significantly.

You can use Action! to add motion to images you create, making them more visually exciting. For example, you can make each component of a bar or pie chart zip across the screen into place on command, or have each line of a bulleted list move across the screen with accompanying sound effects or music.

In fact, one of Action!'s biggest strengths is its ability to transform relatively ordinary objects into visually powerful, attention-getting presentations.

The objects you include in Action! presentations are placed on a *Timeline*. A Timeline shows you the order in which objects appear in a scene, or where a particular scene appears within a show. Each object on the Timeline appears as a bar, as shown in Figure 4.2. The length of each bar shows the duration of the object's appearance. This is one way you can edit a scene: Simply lengthen or shorten one or more Timeline bars that represent objects you want to change. Obviously, as an object's length of appearance changes, the content of a slide or slides, over time, changes because objects disappear at different intervals. Remember, Action! scenes are more like movies than static slides.

Figure 4.2
Sample Action!
Timeline

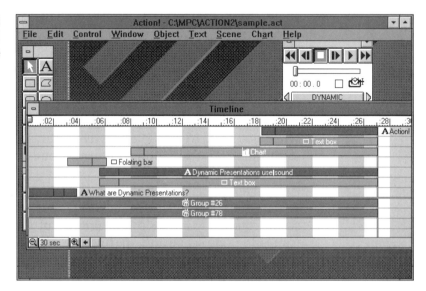

Everything that is part of a scene appears on this Timeline, including sound effects, narration, music, animation, and so on. Numbers at the top of the Timeline show elapsed time in seconds. You can watch the playback head as it moves through the show, and you can grab the playback head and move it anywhere along the Timeline to begin or resume playing wherever you wish.

Action! Tools and Techniques

Action! consists of several separate software components for tasks that range from object design, to scene placement, to program presentation.

To load Action! from the Ultimedia Tools Series CD-ROM, do the following:

1. Make the logical drive that represents your CD-ROM reader the current drive (for example, type **E:**, then press **Enter**).
2. Type **UTSDOS** and press **Enter**.
3. From the main Ultimedia Tools screen, select the Product Selector button.
4. Click on the Action! button on the right of the display.
5. Click on Working Demonstration within the Action! demo window to launch the program.

When you first start Action! the program opens with a blank Presentation Window, shown in Figure 4.3.

Figure 4.3
Opening the Action! Presentation Window

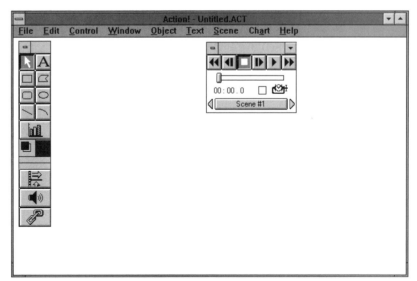

Once you've designed your presentation, as we discussed in Chapter 3, you are ready to create an Action! presentation.

To create a presentation in Action!, do the following:

1. Create or import the individual objects you will use in the presentation. These objects will be placed on individual

screens, or scenes, in Action!, because the program supports motion and sound.

2. Add support material, such as sound or motion.

3. Arrange the scenes into the proper order for the presentation. This is really an editing process, since you will most likely build the presentation in the order you want scenes to appear in the first place.

4. Fine-tune object and scene timing.

We'll discuss each of these steps in the next section.

Creating Objects

An Action! *object* is anything the program can display and present as part of a scene. Objects are created (or imported) in the Action! Presentation Window. You'll probably create the majority of scene objects with the *Tool Palette*, a series of drawing and import tools easily accessible from the Tool Palette displayed to the left of the presentation window. (For more information on the Tool Palette, see the separate section (Tool Palette, pages 164 and 182) later in this chapter.)

The tools on the Tool Palette have five basic functions:

1. Pointing
2. Entering text
3. Drawing objects
4. Importing objects
5. Setting colors and other attributes

To create an object, use the File New command to start with a clean screen in the Presentation Window. Then select one of the object creation tools from the Tool Palette. Each screen usually is composed of multiple objects; some or all of those objects include enhanced attributes such as motion or sound.

All of the objects taken together on a screen comprise a scene. A completed presentation consists of a series of scenes arranged in the proper order.

Suppose you want to create a title screen with some text and a graphics image, like the one in Figure 4.4.

Figure 4.4
Sample Title
Screen in
Action!

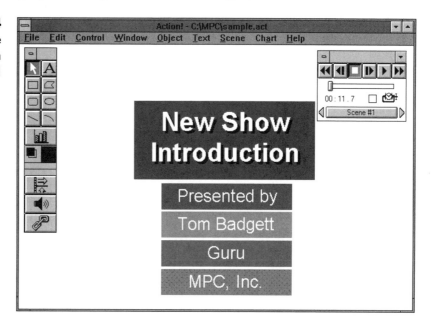

We designed this scene using one of Action!'s templates. Templates—those supplied with Action! or ones you create yourself—make creating scenes a lot easier and faster.

Here's how to create this screen, made up of several individual objects with some enhancements:

1. Use File New to begin with a clean screen.
2. Use File Load Template to display the dialog shown in Figure 4.5.

Figure 4.5
File Load
Template Dialog

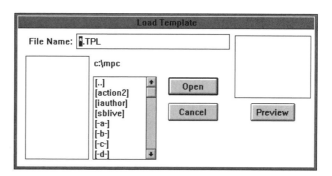

3. Choose **12_INTRO.TBL** from the list of files. The Apply Template dialog shown in Figure 4.6 is displayed.

Figure 4.6
Apply Template
Dialog

4. Click on OK to accept the defaults on this dialog. A solid black screen is displayed.

5. Click on the Compressed View icon on the Control Panel to display all of the objects in this scene, as shown in Figure 4.7.

Figure 4.7
Compressed
View of
12_INTRO.TBL
Template

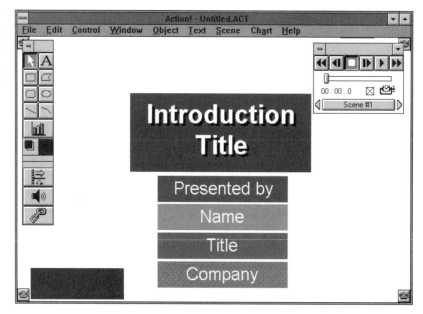

6. Select the Introduction Title object on this screen.

7. From the main menu, select <u>O</u>bject and choose <u>P</u>romote to Scene. Handles appear around the text object.

8. Double click inside the box around the Introduction Title object. Text mode is selected and you can enter the new title.

9. Click anywhere on the Presentation Window outside the Title object to deselect it. Your new title becomes part of the scene.

10. Select the Name object.

11. Using Object Promote to Scene again, enter your name in the same way you edited the Introduction Title object.

12. Repeat steps 6 through 11 for Title and Company.

13. Use File Save As to save your work.

Now you have an interesting, moving title scene for a new production. To see how the scene looks in action, click on the Play button in the Control Panel. The screen clears and for the next 12 seconds Action! builds the introduction screen, object by object.

This template doesn't include any music or narration, but you could enhance this scene even further by adding music or voice files of your own. We'll show you how in the next section.

Adding Support Material

Because this scene was created from a template, the objects that make up the scene already have some enhancements added to them, such as motion.

To add motion to these objects, do the following:

1. Select Control and choose Scene View.

2. Double click on the Introduction Title object to display the Edit Object dialog, shown in Figure 4.8.

Notice that the Transition field specifies that this object will enter the scene "Center Out, Horizontal." That means the text will grow from a point, appearing on the screen slowly instead of appearing suddenly as a complete image.

The introduction title is placed on a colored rectangle as the background. This background also has action of its own.

To specify the background used, do the following:

1. Select Control, then choose Template View.

Figure 4.8
Edit Object
Dialog with
Introduction
Object

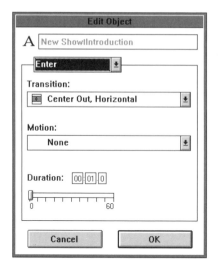

2. Double click one of the outer edges of the colored box behind the title text. The Edit Object dialog for this object is
   displayed.

You can see from the dialog that this object's Transition is "Center Out, Vertical." This is similar to the transition for the text,
except that it moves vertically instead of horizontally.

Notice that neither the introduction text nor the background for
this text has any motion specified with it. But what about all of
the apparent motion that *is* occurring on this opening scene?

There is motion, in the form of blocks of color that move through
the scene while the text and text background blocks are generated.

**To view the Edit Object dialog for one of these blocks, do the
following:**

1. Choose Template view (the "T" icon should be at each of the
   four corners of the Presentation Window).
2. Click on the Rewind button on the Control Panel. A black
   screen should be displayed.
3. On the Control Panel, click on the Step Forward button three
   times. The screen shown in Figure 4.9 should be displayed.

Figure 4.9
Partial Template
Introduction
Screen

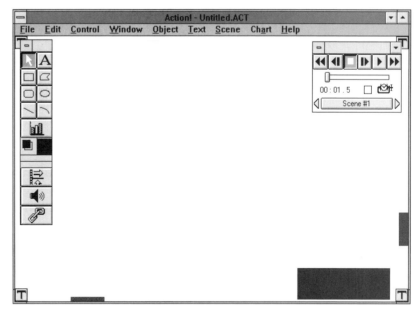

4. Double click on the red rectangle at the lower-right corner of the screen to display that object's object editor, shown in Figure 4.10.

Figure 4.10
Edit Object for
Template's Red
Rectangle

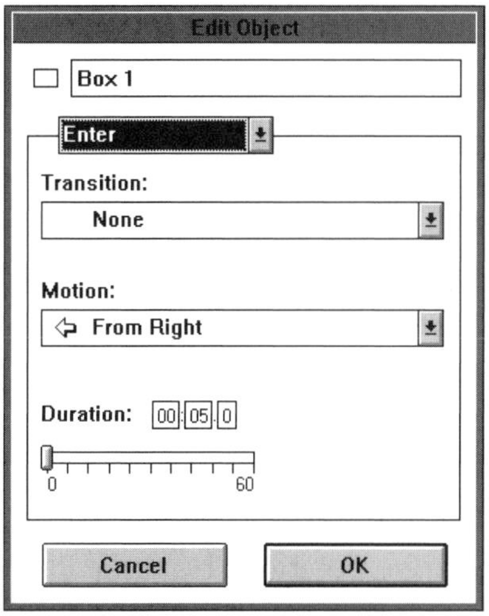

Notice that there are no Transition: actions specified for this object, but in the Motion: field you should see a left-facing arrow and the words, "From Right." This message indicates the object will move into the scene from right to left.

You can add this type of motion to any object you define on the Action! Presentation Window screen. Simply double click on the object to open its own Edit Object dialog, and fill in the blanks. In most cases, you can use a pulldown list by clicking on the Down arrow to the right of the data entry field.

You can modify other objects in this scene in the same way. Simply scroll through the scene with the step forward button until you see an object you want to change. Double click on the object, and its own Edit Object dialog will show you the current settings. This single stepping also is an excellent way to slow down the action in a scene so you can be sure of exactly what is happening.

Fine Tuning and Debugging Action!

In the case of this single scene, no real fine tuning should be required because we used a template provided by Action! (another good reason for using templates).

When you design your own scenes—or make slight changes to any of the scenes you create with the templates provided—you can make use of several more Action! features, including:

1. The Timeline
2. The Scene Sorter
3. The Content List

Each of these Action! components provides a different view of your presentation, allowing you to see what is happening and make changes, if necessary.

The Timeline

The Timeline lets you view all of the objects in a scene in their relative positions by time. Each object is represented by a horizontal bar with a title, as shown in Figure 4.11.

The length of the bar indicates the object's duration in the scene. Its vertical positioning on the Timeline indicates the type of object. By default, the Timeline is displayed as in Figure 4.11.

Figure 4.11
Basic Timeline
Display, Partial
Screen

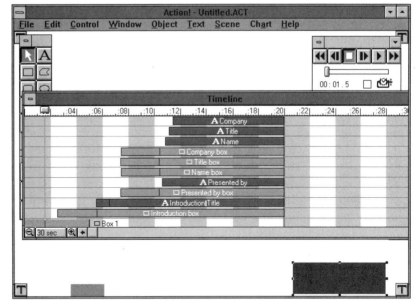

However, it's like any other Windows screen, so you can expand it to full-screen display by clicking on the arrow in the upper-right corner of the display, as shown in Figure 4.12.

Figure 4.12
Full-Screen
Timeline Display

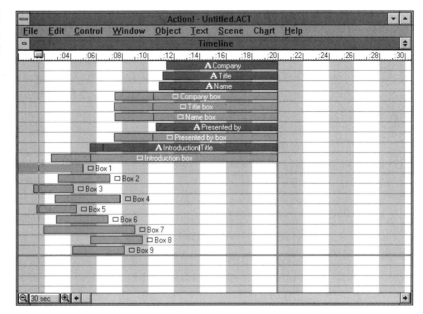

This expanded display shows every element in the scene and its placement along the Timeline. Notice the series of nine boxes at the lower-left corner of this display. These are the moving rectangles that zip through the scene while the Name and Title boxes are being built. These boxes are temporary and are not visible at the end of the scene; you can tell this by noticing where each box enters and when it ends.

You can look at the Timeline and the scene action at the same time. Simply shrink the Timeline back to its original size by clicking on the double-ended arrow at the top-right corner of the screen. Now click the Play button on the Control Panel (or use the Control Play command). Watch the Timeline pointer (playback head) move across the Timeline display while the screen changes. Notice that at about 12 seconds into the scene, the screen is stable and the show is essentially over.

Notice, also, that the Company, Title, and Name text lines don't appear at the same time. You can synchronize these items by grabbing the line that represents the Company text and extending it so it is the same length as the other two. Or, you can adjust all of them, causing more of a staggering effect as the text appears.

As you can see, the Timeline is a basic representation of the action in a scene, merely showing when each object appears and how long it stays. What you don't see on the Timeline is information about what kind of transitions are built into each object, or the type of motion attributes they carry. You can learn more of this type of data with other Action! features.

To close the Timeline, press **Alt+F4**, or select the Window menu item and choose Timeline to toggle the Timeline off. (You can actually display all of the features we are discussing in this section—Timeline, Scene Sorter, and the Content List—simultaneously, but the screen becomes rather cluttered if you do.)

The Scene Sorter

Like the Timeline, the Scene Sorter offers you another way to view your presentation. Whereas the Timeline is most useful for a scene-level view of your presentation, the Scene Sorter provides a wider view, representing the entire show.

When you load the Scene Sorter, Action! displays an icon to represent each scene in the presentation. In our sample presentation, there is only one scene so far, so the Scene Sorter display looks like the one in Figure 4.13.

Figure 4.13
Scene Sorter
with One Scene

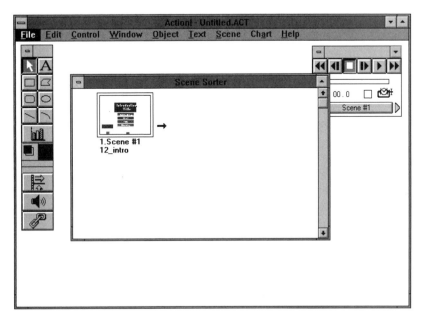

At this point in our presentation, the Scene Sorter has little value. If you load a presentation that includes several scenes, such as the ACT2DEMO.ACP shipped with your CD-ROM sampler, then the Scene Sorter takes on more importance, as you can see in Figure 4.14.

The illustration in Figure 4.14 is expanded over the default display. We did this simply by grabbing an edge of the display and dragging it outward and upward to display all or most of the presentation.

Once you have a presentation displayed in this format, you can re-arrange the scenes any way you wish simply by grabbing a scene icon and moving it where you want it. Obviously, you'll usually create a presentation in order, one scene at a time. So you'll move scenes carefully to avoid producing a presentation

Figure 4.14
Scene Sorter
with Multiple
Scenes

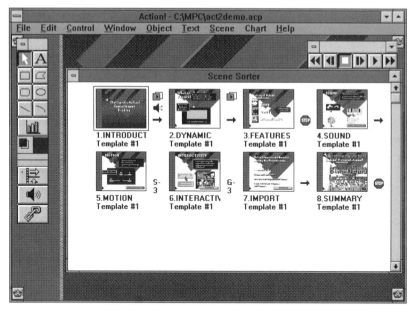

that doesn't work. But being able to get this "bird's eye" view of your presentation makes it much easier to visualize how scenes fit together—or why they don't—so you can make any necessary changes.

The Content List

The Content List gives you still another view of your presentation. Like the Scene Sorter, the Content List covers the whole presentation, but with this view, you also have access to the individual components of each scene.

Figure 4.15 shows the Content List for ACT2DEMO.ACP, which is available on your CD sampler disk. (We've also expanded this display by grabbing a couple of the edges and pulling them outward.)

This view of a relatively simple application shows you just how complex a single scene can be. As you can see in the INTRO-DUCTION slide, for example, this scene is composed of 13 separate objects, including lines, text, sound, and bars.

Figure 4.15
Content List with
ACT2DEMO.ACP
Loaded

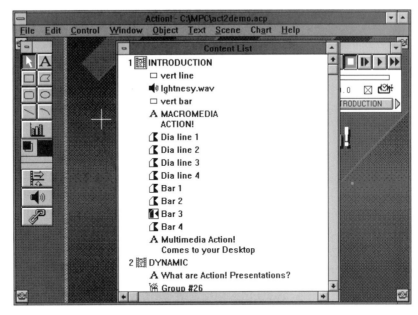

Now, use the scroll bars to view the content of scene four, the SOUND scene. This one consists of 18 objects, two of which are groups of two or more objects.

The Content List itself is much like an outline. Double click on the toggle button beside any scene number and the object list is compressed to show only the scene title. Double click again on the icon and the list returns.

When the object list under a scene name is compressed, you can grab a scene name and drag the entire screen to another location. When the scene is positioned at a location where you can drop it, a wide black line appears across the window to indicate where the scene will appear if you drop it there. Release the mouse button, and the scene is moved to the new location, along with all of its objects.

You can move any object that appears under a scene name in the same way. Just move the mouse button over the object name, press the left mouse button, and drag the object to a new location. You can move objects within the current scene, or between scenes.

Presenting and Distributing Action! Shows

Once you have a presentation designed, created, edited, and fine-tuned, what do you do with it?

By far the majority of multimedia presentations today are given right on a PC, frequently with the PC connected to a large-screen monitor. Professional presenters prefer a 27-inch monitor because the image is large enough to be seen from a reasonable distance, yet remains sharp and clear. For larger audiences, you can use projection devices that produce really large displays, but the quality of the images may not be as high.

Action! supports PC-based playback of presentations in two ways: First, you can simply load a presentation into the Action! software, select Control, and choose Play to watch the show. Second, you can use the Action! player to distribute presentations that will run on any PC with Windows 3.1 or later.

To create a file that can be played without the full Action! software, just save the presentation in the appropriate format. Here's how:

1. Select File and choose Save As to display the Save Presentation dialog. Pull down the File Type: list, as shown in Figure 4.16.

Figure 4.16
File Save As Save
Presentation
File Type:
Pulldown List

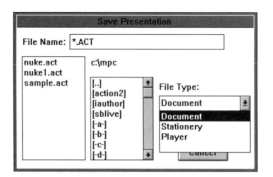

2. Choose "Player" from this list, and Action! automatically sets the filename extension to .ACP. Type a path and filename and the presentation is stored in Player format.

The Player feature isnt supplied with the Ultimedia Tools Series CD-ROM. However, it is part of the retail version of Action!.

3. To play the presentation on a PC not equipped with Action!, simply copy the presentation file (the *.ACP file) to a diskette along with the Action! multimedia player files (PLAYACT.EXE and MMPLAYER.DLL). You can execute the player file from within Windows; the screen will look similar to the main action screen, but with fewer choices, as shown in Figure 4.17.

Figure 4.17
Action! Player Screen with TEST.ACP Loaded

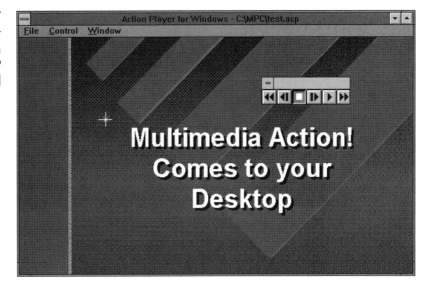

There are other ways to present your PC-based multimedia show, of course. One way is to copy the whole show to video tape.

All you need to copy a presentation to videotape is a compatible video I/O card, such as Intel's ActionMedia II. Action! calls the process "printing to video," and you do it like this:

1. Connect the VCR to your video output card on the computer.

2. Insert a blank tape.

3. Use File Print to Video to display the Print to Video dialog, shown in Figure 4.18.

4. Click on Print to Video.

Figure 4.18
Print to Video
Dialog

You could print your presentation to paper if you wanted to create a "leave behind" or manual for your audience to reference, or as a reminder of the presentation they've seen. This should not be considered a substitute for the actual presentation, of course, because you lose color, motion, and sound with a paper version of your show.

Using Action! Menus and Commands

The basic Action! screen is the Presentation Window, shown blank in Figure 4.19 with its components labeled.

This screen contains four basic components:

1. Title Bar
2. Menu Bar
3. Tool Palette
4. Control Panel

We'll discuss each of these basic components and their subsystems in the following section.

Title Bar

The Action! Title Bar, as with other Windows products, simply holds the name of the current file you are working with in the Presentation Window. When you first load Action!, the Title Bar

Figure 4.19
Blank
Presentation
Window Screen
with Labels

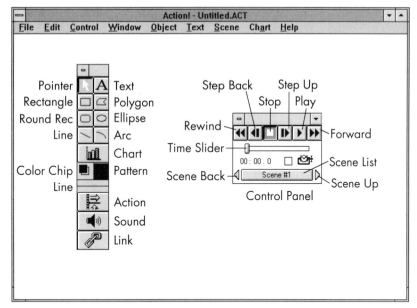

displays the default title, UNTITLED.ACT, indicating that the current file has not yet been saved under a new name.

Once you save the current file (using File Save As or File Save), the path and filename for it are displayed on the Title Bar.

Menu Bar

The Action! Menu Bar should be familiar to anyone with Microsoft Windows experience.

The Action! Menu Bar contains nine selections:

1. File
2. Edit
3. Control
4. Window
5. Object
6. Text
7. Scene

8. Chart

9. Help

The Menu Bar structure helps simplify potentially complex programs such as Action! by hiding much of the underlying structure. In this section, we provide a reference to each of the menu choices on the Menu Bar.

File

As a Microsoft Windows product, Action! includes menu items familiar to Windows users. The File menu is one of these "constants," providing the following choices:

1. New
2. Open
3. Load Template
4. Save
5. Save As
6. Save Template As
7. Import
8. Import Presentation
9. Export
10. Printer Setup
11. Print
12. Print to Video
13. Exit

Many of these choices are the same ones you'd find in any Windows-compatible package, while others are unique to Action!. We'll discuss all of them in the following section.

New

The Action! New command is the same as with other Windows products. It instructs Action! to create a new file. Since you can have only one Action! presentation file open at a time, when you select New, the current file is cleared from memory. If you have not saved the file since it was changed, Action! asks if you want to save the current file.

Open

The Open command displays the familiar Open File dialog to let you open an existing Action! presentation. The program automatically lists only files with .AC? and .STA extensions that are in the current directory. You can select a different drive and directory as you would with other Windows products.

Load Template

Action! includes a number of template files to help you design your own scenes quickly and easily. The Load Template command displays another form of the open dialog that lists only template files. A sample Load Template dialog is shown in Figure 4.20.

Figure 4.20
Load Template
Dialog

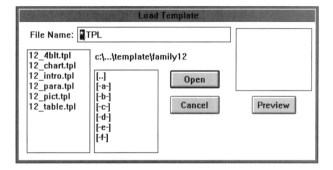

Action! displays only .TPL files when you load this dialog.

Save

The File Save command simply saves the current file, replacing the version that already exists on disk. If you have not previously saved the current file, Action! displays the Save As dialog instead.

Save As

You use the Save As command to save a file for the first time or to save an existing file under a new filename. You might want to do this to generate a backup of the file you are working with to preserve an original version so you can make changes, or you might want to save the file to a new directory. Action! automatically includes a .ACT extension to the files you are about to save.

Save Template As

The Save Template As command displays a version of the Save As dialog with the .TPL extension already included. Any existing template files in the current template directory will be displayed as well. You can select an existing template name or supply a new one to hold the current Template file. Again, you might want to use this command to store an existing template to a new file after you have modified it. This lets you maintain an existing version—one of the templates supplied with the Action! software, for example—while saving a version you have edited.

Import

The File Import command displays the Import dialog, shown in Figure 4.21.

Figure 4.21
File Import
Dialog

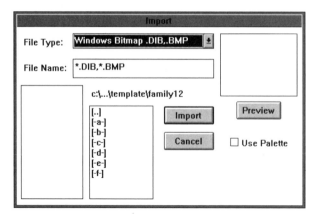

Use this command to import existing files in different formats. The default import format is .DIB or .BMP graphics files. Use the Down arrow to the right of the File Type: field to display a list of supported formats. This pulldown list is shown in Figure 4.22.

When you select a graphics format and click on Preview, you'll see a small image in the Preview window. If you've selected an audio file, Action! displays a speaker icon in the Preview window and plays the file through your sound board.

Figure 4.22
File Type:
Pulldown List
from Import
Menu

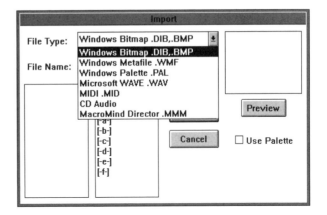

Import Presentation

Use the File Import Presentation command to access scenes and objects created in other applications. When you use this command, Action! displays the Import Presentation dialog shown in Figure 4.23.

Figure 4.23
File Import
Presentation
Dialog

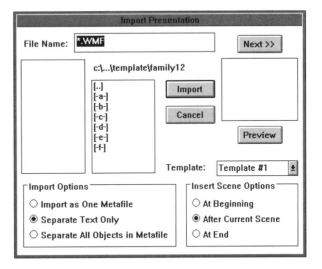

Action! supports a number of presentation formats, including:

- Lotus Freelance
- Harvard Graphics
- Aldus Persuasion
- Microsoft PowerPoint

Click on the Preview button to view a file before you import it. You can select multiple files in the list on the left side of the dialog, then use the Next>> button at the top of the dialog to step through the selected files, previewing each one in turn.

You can use information from other presentations as complete files that contain all of the individual components, or you can separate objects from the original presentation format, importing them into Action! so you have more control over their placement and use.

For example, you can click on the Separate Text Only button under Import Options on this dialog to tell Action! to extract only the text from the selected file. Or, you can separate all of the objects by clicking on the Separate All Objects in Metafile button. A metafile is a collection of individual objects saved and managed as a single unit. When you separate objects in this way from the source metafile, you can apply the usual Action! attributes to them, including motion and sound. Unless you separate the objects during file import, you can't manipulate them individually inside Action!.

Action! expects to import presentations or presentation objects from .WMF metafile format. Therefore, to access these files from within Action!, you must first export them from the source application in .WMF format. Use whatever exporting or saving features are available within the source program to create the .WMF file that Action! needs.

You can try this import feature for yourself using files available on the Ultimedia Tools CD-ROM:

1. From the Import Presentation dialog (shown in Figure 4.21), click on the Parent Directory symbol (the three dots at the top of the file list window) to return to the root directory on the CD-ROM.

2. Use the scroll bar to find the MON20000 subdirectory and select it.

3. Select the DEMO subdirectory from this directory. You should see three .WMF files names: IBMCD01.WMF, IBMCD02.WMF, and IBMCD03.WMF.

4. Click on the Separate All Objects in Metafile button.
5. Double click on the IBMCD01.WMF file.

Action! loads a screen capture image that has had lines and text added to it to label the various portions of the screen. This is a small image without a lot of detail. You can select the image and drag one or more sides outward to enlarge the picture.

Experiment with selecting various objects inside the image and dragging them onto the Action! Presentation window. You can drag text and arrows off of the metafile image, for example, and display them in another part of the Presentation Window. (If an object you drag off of the metafile seems to disappear, click on the color tool and establish another color for the object so that it's a different color than the background of the Presentation window.)

If you double click on an object within the metafile, Action! displays the Edit Object dialog so you can set the transition, motion, and duration for each individual component of the imported metafile.

Export

The File Export command displays the Export dialog, shown in Figure 4.24.

Figure 4.24
File Export
Dialog

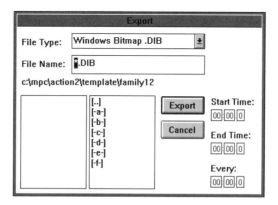

Use this command to export Action! presentation files into either Windows Bitmap (.DIB) format, or to Metafile (.WMF) format.

This feature lets you select and save "snapshots" of the current scene to print as part of the documentation for your presentation or to import into other presentations.

Notice the Start Time:, End Time:, and Every: fields that are part of this dialog. Remember that Action! presentations are composed of scenes; each scene may contain multiple objects that appear at various times along the Timeline. To specify when the export feature is to make the snapshot of the scene, enter the start time and end time for the snapshot.

The Every: field specifies how often a snapshot is to be made. You could, for example, specify a start time of 0 (the beginning of the scene), and enter 00:05:0 in the Every: field to tell Action to make and save a snapshot file every five seconds while the scene is playing.

If you're making multiple snapshots, action uses the first five characters of the specified filename, adding a numeric extension to denote the following filenames. If you specify a filename of FILENAME.DIB in the File Name: field, for example, the first snapshot will be stored in FILENAME.DIB, the second filename will be stored in FILEN001.DIB, the third field will be stored in FILEN002.DIB, and so on.

Printer Setup

Use the Printer Setup command to access the Windows Printer Setup dialog. Use this dialog to select a new printer, choose landscape or portrait printing, specify the number of copies to print, and more.

Print

The Print command displays the Print dialog shown in Figure 4.25.

From this dialog, you can specify the number of copies, which scenes from the presentation to print (all or a range of scenes), and what part of the presentation you want to print. You can print only one of these components at a time.

Figure 4.25
File Print Dialog

In addition, you can specify how many scenes to place on a page—from one to four—by entering a value in the Scenes per Page: field of this dialog.

Print to Video

As the name implies, you can use this command to print a presentation to video. When you select the Print to Video command, the dialog shown in Figure 4.26 is displayed.

Figure 4.26
Print to Video
Dialog

To use this feature, you must have a video I/O board such as the Intel ActionMedia II with a tape recorder attached to the output port.

When you use this command with the Ultimedia Tools sampler version of Action!, the software automatically places the Action! logo at the top of the screen, and it will appear throughout the video image you create. The commercial version of Action! does not include this logo.

E__xit

Select the E__xit command to close the current presentation file and exit Action!. You're then returned to the Windows Presentation Manager.

Edit

The Edit menu from the main Action! menu is almost identical to any other Windows application, though a few of the subcommands are unique to Action!. The complete list of Edit subcommands is:

1. Undo
2. Cut
3. Copy
4. Paste
5. Paste Slide
6. Delete
7. Select All
8. Paste Special
9. Clear Special
10. Duplicate
11. Edit Object
12. Edit Arc/Poly
13. Snap to Grid
14. Preferences

Each of the Edit menu commands is described in the following section.

U__ndo (Alt+Backspace)

The U__ndo command reverses the most recent editing step. If you delete a block of text, for example, the text is restored when you use U__ndo, providing you use the U__ndo command *immediately* after you delete the text. If you move a block of text, the U__ndo command puts it back in its previous location.

> The Undo command changes, depending on your most recent action. When you first enter data on the Presentation Screen, for example, the Undo command is displayed. If you use Undo, however, the command becomes Undo Undo (to reverse the Undo operation), then the command becomes Redo, which is a toggle, switching between the most recent action and the one before that. This feature is useful in playing "what if" with a presentation object.

Cut (Shift+Del)

The Cut command deletes a selection from the Edit screen and places it on the Windows Clipboard. You can restore the deleted information to a new or the same location using the Edit Paste command.

Copy (Ctrl+Ins)

The Copy command works like the Cut command except that the original material is not deleted.

Paste (Shift+Ins)

The Paste command copies information stored on the Clipboard to the screen at the location of the insertion point. Use Paste in combination with Copy or Cut to copy and move information within a screen or from one file to another. Once data is on the Clipboard, it remains until you execute another Cut or Copy operation, or you exit Windows.

Paste Slide

Choosing this option opens the Paste Slide dialog, shown in Figure 4.27. Use this command to copy slide information already on the Clipboard into the current presentation screen.

You can paste Clipboard slide data as a single metafile, or as individual objects. Use the Paste Options buttons to select how the information from the Clipboard will be copied to the current file.

You can also specify where the data will be placed by selecting the appropriate button under the Insert Scene Options heading.

Figure 4.27
Paste Slide
Dialog

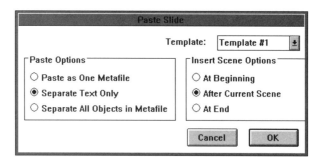

Delete (Del)

The Delete command removes any selected data from the presentation screen. The information removed *is not* placed on the Clipboard, so you can't use Paste to restore data that has been deleted. You *can*, however, use the Undo command to restore the most recent deletion.

Select All

As its name implies, Select All selects all of the objects in the current scene. Use this command when you want to make global changes to a scene. For example, you might wish to copy or delete all objects.

Paste Special

This command opens the Paste Special dialog, shown in Figure 4.28.

Figure 4.28
Paste Special
Dialog

Use Paste Special with Cut and Copy to paste objects along with certain attributes you specify. For example, the Time: option in the Paste Special dialog lets you specify when you want the pasted object to appear in the presentation. When you specify

"From Offset," the object is pasted with the same time interval ahead of it as it had in the original or source slide. If the object was copied from a scene, say, 33 seconds into the presentation, then when you paste it with "From Offset" selected, it will be placed 33 seconds into the destination presentation from the present location of the playback head.

If you paste an object with a 33-second offset into a presentation with the playback head positioned at zero, the object will appear 33 seconds from the beginning of the scene. If the playback head in the current scene is set to 10 seconds, on the other hand, then the object will be placed 43 seconds into the scene (33 seconds from the current playback head location).

The "From Now" selection, on the other hand, tells Action! to insert the object into the destination presentation at the present time without any offset.

The Attributes buttons determine which attributes are copied with the object. When you select All, all of the pasted object's attributes are copied into the destination scene, including any timing attributes, transitions, motions, sounds, and links. When you select the static button, on the other hand, only static attributes—those that don't change over time—are moved with the copied or cut object. Static attributes include such things as color and content. Note that the hold content of an object is transferred even when the static button is selected.

Clear Special

Clear Special lets you clear the time attributes from a selected object. This selection displays the additional selections shown in Figure 4.29.

When you select a Dynamic clear, an object is stripped of its dynamic time attributes such as transitions, motions, sounds, and links, but the static attributes such as color and hold duration are not affected.

Beginning to Now clears time-related material from the current playback position to the beginning of the scene. This selection can clear all of an object's Enter, Hold, and Exit information,

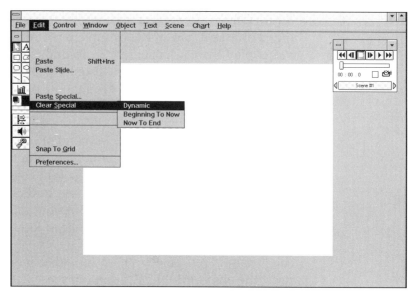

Figure 4.29
Clear Special
Pulldown
Choices

depending on the position of the playback head when you issue the command.

Now to End works the same as Beginning to Now, but it works from the current position of the playback head to the end of that object's time. This shortens an object's playback time so that it ends at the current location of the playback head.

Duplicate (Ctrl+D)

Duplicate is used to copy selected objects, which are then offset slightly from the originals in the Presentation window. This is a useful command when you want to present a series of objects slightly offset from each other.

For example, the "before" image in Figure 4.30 shows the original object. Figure 4.31 shows the same object after having been duplicated several times to produce a cascading effect.

Although duplicated objects such as these may appear as one object, they actually are duplicates of the original, so you can select each component of such a combined object and move, delete, edit, or copy it.

Figure 4.30
Object Prior to
Duplicating

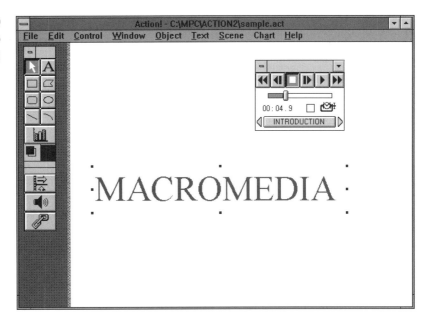

Figure 4.31
After the Object
Has Been
Duplicated
Several Times

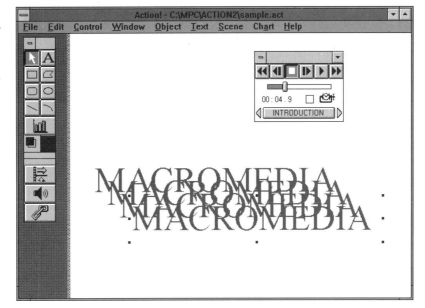

Edit Object

Use the Edit Object command to open the Edit Object dialog and edit an object's attributes, as shown in Figure 4.32.

Figure 4.32
Edit Object
Dialog

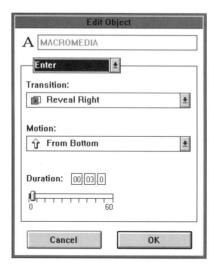

Use this command to edit an object's attributes. You don't have to go through the Edit menu to access this editor. Simply double click on an object to open its object editor.

You can select a group of objects and change any shared attributes in one operation. Don't worry about changing the wrong thing. If one or more objects in the selected group or range don't share the attribute being changed, then nothing happens to those objects.

You can use this grouping of objects feature to change the font or the type size for all selected objects, for example.

Although you can use the Object Editor for any objects displayed in Action!, the procedure for each type of object is slightly different, and the features you are allowed to edit with the Editor dialog changes from object type to object type.

For the most part, these differences are obvious. For example, the editable characteristics for a sound file would be different from those for a .BMP bitmapped graphics file. And, the attributes available for a text object are different from the attributes for a drawing.

The basic procedure, however, is the same. Use the pulldown menus located to the right of most fields in the dialog to display available choices, as shown in Figure 4.33. Make the necessary changes and click on OK to end the edit.

Figure 4.33
Edit Object
Dialog with
Pulldown Menus

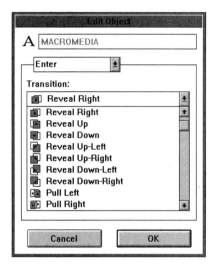

If you change your mind while editing an object, simply click on the Cancel button to close the Object Editor without making any changes.

Edit Arc/Poly

Use this command to edit a selected arc or polygon. This menu item changes, depending on the object you've selected. However, if neither an arc nor a polygon is selected, the command is grayed.

To use the command, click on a polygon or an arc. Action! places handles at the points of the figure being edited. Drag these handles to move the object or to change its size.

If you want to change the basic shape of the arc or polygon, on the other hand, you must use the Edit command, which changes the positions of the handles.

Snap to Grid

Snap to Grid is a toggle. When it is active, a check mark appears beside this command in the edit pulldown menu. When this command is toggled on, an invisible grid is overlaid on the presentation window, letting you align objects precisely when you create, reposition, or resize them.

If you need precise control over the position of an object, on the other hand, you should turn off this option.

Preferences

You can use the Preferences command to set a number of Action! operational parameters. The choices are presented in a dialog, like the one shown in Figure 4.34.

Figure 4.34
Edit Preferences
Dialog

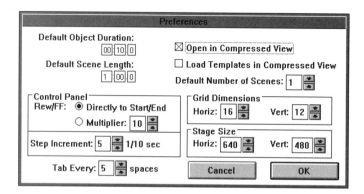

Any changes you make to the settings on this screen become the defaults Action! uses when you start it up.

Control

The Control menu duplicates some of the features available continuously on the graphics Control Panel displayed on the Action! screen. The commands available on this menu include:

- Rewind
- Backstep
- Stop
- Step
- Play
- Fast Forward
- Play Presentation

- Zoom In
- Zoom Out
- Set Loop
- Set Pause
- Scene View
- Template View
- Compressed View

You can decide whether to use the graphics Control Panel or the pulldown Control menu to access the commands that are duplicated. Generally, it's easier to use the graphics interface because it looks like a VCR or tape recorder control panel, making it easier to operate.

We'll discuss each of these commands briefly in the following section.

Rewind (Ctrl+1)

The Rewind command moves the playback head to the beginning of the scene. You can set the rewind speed with the Preferences dialog, which you select from the Edit menu.

Backstep (Ctrl+2)

The Backstep selection skips back through a scene in small increments. You can adjust the step increment with the Preferences dialog; the default is 10 milliseconds.

This command is useful when you need to step slowly through a scene to debug it or to adjust object positioning.

Stop (Ctrl+3)

The Stop command halts the playback of a scene and freezes the playback position at the current location.

Step (Ctrl+4)

The Step command skips through a scene in small increments. The default step increment is 50 milliseconds, which you can change with the Preferences dialog.

Play (Ctrl+5)

The Play command plays a scene from the current position of the playback head.

Fast Forward (Ctrl+6)

Fast Forward rapidly advances a scene to the end (the default) or moves forward a specified number of times faster than the scene's normal playing time. You can set the playing time in the Preferences dialog.

Play Presentation (Ctrl+Enter)

Play Presentation shows the entire presentation (all scenes) in full-screen mode. When you choose this selection, the screen is cleared of all menus, palettes, and other windows. You can use **Ctrl+3** to stop the presentation at any time.

Zoom In

Zoom In changes the scale in which a scene displays on the Timeline. You can adjust the Timeline from 10 seconds to 30 minutes. Use Zoom In to concentrate on a smaller portion of the Timeline at a larger scale.

Zoom Out

Use Zoom Out to expand the Timeline display so you can see more of the Timeline at once.

Set Loop

Use a loop to play a specified sequence over and over. When you select the Set Loop command, the Set Loop dialog shown in Figure 4.35 is displayed.

Figure 4.35
Set Loop Dialog

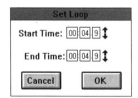

Specify the scene start and end time to determine which portion of a scene you want to play over and over.

Set Pause

Use the Set Pause command to specify the length of a pause you'll insert in the Timeline. Enter a number in the Set Pause dialog shown in Figure 4.36.

Figure 4.36
Set Pause
Dialog

To insert a pause, locate where you want the pause to occur. Press the Stop button at the proper location, then set the length of the pause in the Set Pause dialog. The Pause symbol is inserted in the Timeline at the location of the playback head.

When Action! encounters a Pause command, everything in the scene freezes temporarily.

Scene View

Scene View lets you view scene objects and the template on which they are placed. This is the "natural" view of the scene, the view that will be seen during the presentation.

Template View

Template View grays out scene objects, making them unable to be moved or edited. Use Template View to create or edit the template objects in the scene.

Compressed View

Compressed View shows all scene and template objects in a scene in their hold positions. When you view a scene in Scene View, what you see on the screen depends on the position of the playback head. In Compressed View, you can see all template and scene objects in their final position in the scene.

Window

The Window menu provides six submenu choices:

1. Timeline
2. Scene Sorter

3. Content List
4. Control Panel
5. Tool Palette
6. Full Screen

These toggle commands control what you see on the screen and how this information is displayed. When any of these toggles is enabled, a check mark appears on the Control menu beside each enabled entry. Each of these choices is discussed in the section below.

Timeline

Timeline is used to display or remove the Timeline. A scene that includes a Timeline display is shown in Figure 4.37.

Figure 4.37
Scene with
Timeline Display
Enabled

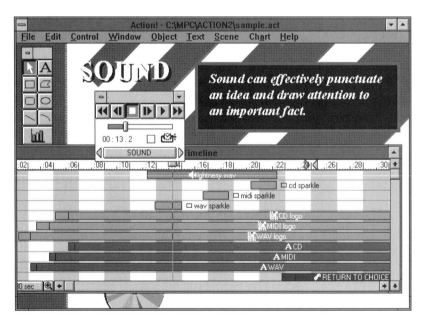

The Timeline is used to show the relationship among the various components of a scene or presentation. Each object in the scene is represented by a bar that shows the placement relative to the beginning and end of the Timeline and with other objects. The length of the object's bar shows its duration.

Scene Sorter

The Scene Sorter option displays a representative icon for each scene in the presentation. As you can see from the sample in Figure 4.38, the Scene Sorter also shows the title, the template used with each scene, and each scene's relative position in the presentation.

Figure 4.38
Scene Sorter
Display

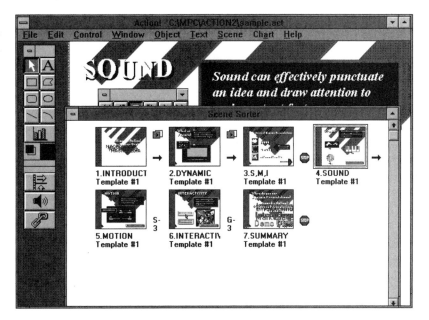

You can use the scroll bars on the right of the Scene Sorter window to step through the presentation, displaying all of the scenes and objects in the show.

Content List

The Content List option displays a text and icon outline of your presentation. Objects are arranged in order by start time and the scenes are arranged sequentially. A sample Content List window is shown in Figure 4.39.

Use the Content List as a convenient way to name objects and scenes, edit text, move objects, or add new objects to a scene.

Control Panel

By default, Action! displays a Control Panel on the screen that lets you control the playback of a scene by clicking on VCR-type

Figure 4.39
Sample Content
List Window
Display

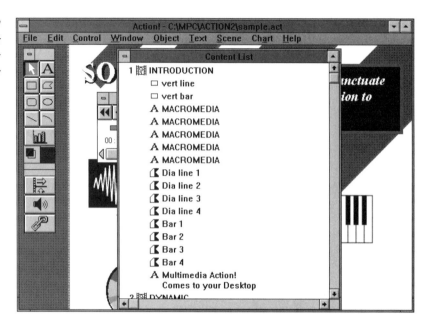

buttons. You can remove the Control Panel display by clicking on the Control Panel to deselect and remove it from the presentation screen.

Figure 4.40 shows the Control Panel with its controls labeled.

Figure 4.40
Control Panel
with Labels

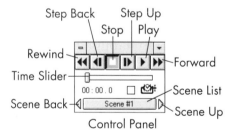

Tool Palette

The Tool Palette is displayed by default to show you the tools you can use to create your own objects. Click on the Tool Palette command if you want to deselect and remove it from the presentation screen.

Figure 4.41 shows the Tool Palette with its features labeled.

Figure 4.41
Tool Palette with
Labels

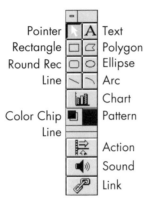

Pointer | Text
Rectangle | Polygon
Round Rec | Ellipse
Line | Arc
| Chart
Color Chip | Pattern
Line
| Action
| Sound
| Link

Full Screen

By default, Action! presentations and screens are displayed in a window smaller than full screen. The presentation window is surrounded by the Menu Bar, the Tool Palette, the Control Panel, and perhaps other objects. When you select Full Screen, you can see the full screen of a scene. Only the Menu Bar is removed in Full Screen mode, however. If you want to see a scene in a full, uncluttered screen, you'll need to close any other open windows, including the Tool Palette, Control Panel, or whatever you have open. Figures 4.42 and 4.43 show how a sample presentation screen looks in normal mode and in Full Screen mode.

Figure 4.42
Sample
Presentation
Screen in
Normal Mode

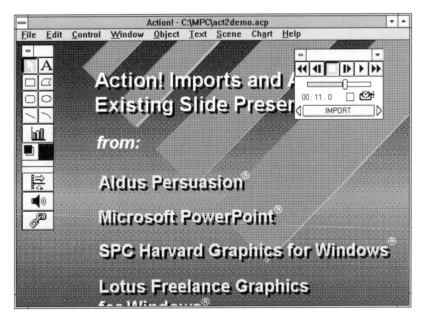

Figure 4.43
Sample
Presentation
Screen in Full
Screen Mode

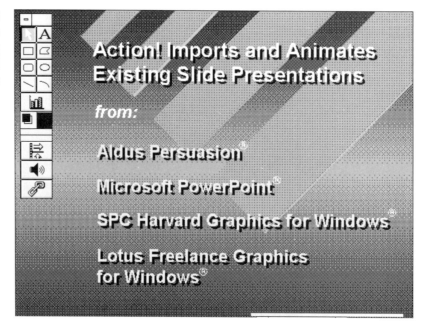

In Full Screen mode, you can restore the main Menu Bar by pressing **Esc**.

Object

The Object menu lets you create a new object on the Presentation Screen, and supports other object manipulations, including:

1. New Object
2. Group
3. Ungroup
4. Explode Metafile
5. Align Objects
6. Synchronize Objects
7. Bring to Front
8. Send to Back
9. Move Forward
10. Move Back
11. Hide Template Objects

12. Hide Scene Objects

13. Promote to Scene

New Object

When you select this command, Action! displays the New Object pulldown menu shown in Figure 4.44.

Figure 4.44
New Object
Pulldown Menu

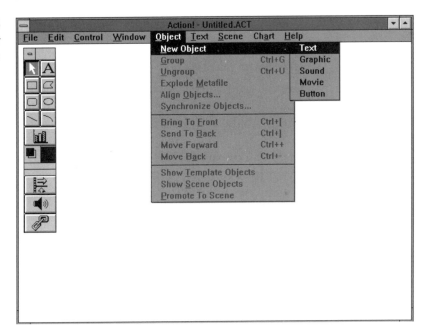

When you select one of these choices, Action! creates a "dummy" object or placeholder that you can move around the presentation window, size, and edit.

Group (Ctrl+G)

The Group command combines multiple selected objects into a group that you can manipulate as a unit. Unless you have more than one object selected on the presentation window, the Group command is grayed out and not accessible.

To specify a group, press and hold the **Shift** key, click on the first object, click on the second object, and so on. You can also specify a group by drawing a selection box around them. After selecting the multiple objects, issue the Object Group command, or press **Ctrl+G**, and Action! links the selected objects. Now when you click on any of these objects, all are selected as a group. You can move, edit, size, or delete them as a group. Grouped objects share the same transitions, and grouped objects appear as a single object in the Timeline.

To change a group back to single objects, use the Ungroup command (see below).

Ungroup (Ctrl+U)

Use the Ungroup command to separate previously grouped objects. When you ungroup objects, they revert to their original form with their own attributes; group attributes no longer apply.

After you ungroup objects, they remain selected together. If you try to move one, they all move. To complete the ungrouping, click anywhere in the presentation window away from the objects to deselect them all. Then you can select the objects individually again.

Explode Metafile

Many graphics files used in Action! and other multimedia and graphics products actually consist of many individual components. When you create a slide in a drawing package, for example, the slide may contain several text objects, drawings, clip art, and other components. Once combined, these objects form a single "metafile."

You can import this metafile into Action! as a single unit, then use the Explode Metafile command to separate it into individual components. In Action! you may want to control individual objects from metafiles so you can add motion or other attributes to them. The Explode Metafile command does this for you.

Align Objects

To align two or more objects, first select the objects by drawing a selection box around them or by holding down the **Shift** key and clicking on each object. Select Align Objects to display the dialog shown in Figure 4.45.

Figure 4.45
Align Objects
Dialog

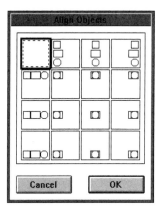

This dialog contains 16 windows that represent different object alignments. Click on the window you want, then click on OK. Action! automatically arranges the selected objects into the new alignment pattern. To reverse the alignment, use the Edit Undo command.

Synchronize Objects

This option is only available when the Timeline is activated.

Use the Synchronize Objects command to synchronize the enter times of objects in a scene. To use the command, display the Timeline (Window Timeline), select two or more objects to be synchronized, then select Synchronize Objects. The dialog shown in Figure 4.46 is displayed.

Figure 4.46
Synchronize
Objects Dialog

You have several options for synchronizing objects in this dialog:

- Start all objects together
- Start each object when previous object starts

- Start each object when previous object holds
- Start each object when previous object exits
- Start each object when previous object ends

Select the type of synchronizing you want, then click on OK.

Bring to _Front (Ctrl+[)

Action! lets you create a variety of objects to include in a scene or presentation. Unless you choose otherwise, the latest object you create or move is on top of everything else.

If you want to display a background object on top of everything else, simply select the object, then use the Bring to _Front command to display the entire object, pushing other objects under it.

You can even move template objects to the front of all other objects. This might be useful if you're using a template button object, for example, and you want the button always to be on top of everything in the scene. Simply select the object, enter the template view (_Control _Template View), and select the Bring to _Front command.

Send to _Back (Ctrl+])

The Send to _Back command does the opposite of the Bring to _Front command. When you select an object that is in the front of a scene, then select Send to _Back, the object moves behind all other objects in the scene, promoting the next object in line to the front.

Move Fo_rward (Ctrl++)

This command works similarly to the Bring to _Front command, except that it moves the selected object one level at a time. Suppose there are five objects stacked on a scene. If you select the rear-most object and then press **Ctrl++**, the selected object moves up one layer to position four. Press **Ctrl++** again and it moves to level three, and so on.

Move B_ack (Ctrl+-)

The Move B_ack command works like Move Fo_rward, except that it moves the selected object back in the scene stack one level.

Hide Template Objects

Hide Template Objects is a toggle that shows and hides template objects in your scene.

Hide Scene Objects

Hide Scene Objects is a toggle that shows and hides template objects in your scene.

Promote to Scene

Use the Promote to Scene command to copy a template object into a scene, making it a scene object instead of a template object. Once you promote a template object to scene status, any changes you make to it are valid only for the current scene, leaving the original template object unchanged.

Text

The text menu contains five options for changing attributes for text in your scene:

1. Font
2. Size
3. Style
4. Alignment
5. Border

Use these commands first to set the attributes of the next text you type. Or, you can select a previously-entered text object, then use one of the text commands to have it affect the existing text.

Font

The Font command lets you choose from a list of 15 fonts supported by Action!. When a font is active, a check mark is displayed beside the selected font.

Figure 4.47 shows the pulldown menu that is displayed when you select the Font command.

Figure 4.47
Text Font
Pulldown Menu

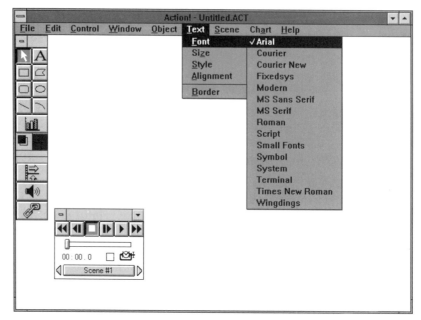

Size

The Size command lets you adjust the size of the font you specified with the Text Font command. Like the Font command, the Size command displays a pulldown menu, as shown in Figure 4.48.

Figure 4.48
Text Size
Pulldown Menu

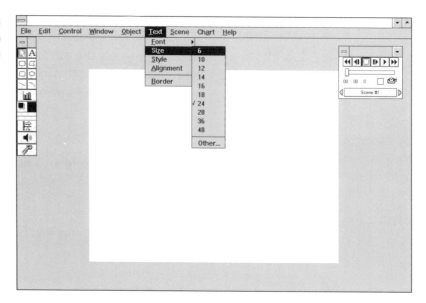

The pulldown menu lets you choose sizes from 6 points to 48 points. If you want to use a smaller or larger font, select Other from this menu to display the Other Size dialog.

Style

The Style command lets you specify plain, bold, italic, or underline attributes for selected text. Select these attributes from the pulldown menu that is displayed when you select the Style command, as shown in Figure 4.49.

Figure 4.49
Text Style
Pulldown Menu

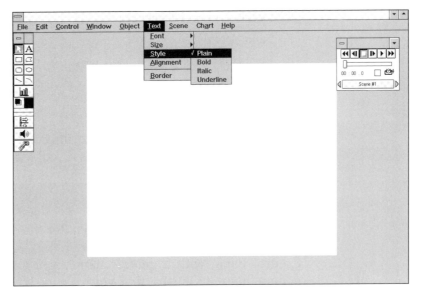

Alignment

The Alignment command lets you specify placement of text within the presentation window. Choose from Left (the default), Center, or Right alignment from the pulldown menu.

Border

The Border command displays a menu of five line widths and the None selection. To use this command, select the text first, then choose an option from the pulldown menu.

Scene

Use this menu to create, edit, move between, and list scene objects. Remember that a scene is the basic element of an Action!

presentation. A scene is a slide with enhanced attributes such as motion or sound. And a scene usually consists of multiple objects, each with unique attributes. Use the Scene menu to manage Action! scenes. The basic commands under this menu are:

1. New Scene
2. Insert Scene
3. Edit Scene
4. Edit Template
5. Set Background
6. Delete Unused Template
7. Next Scene
8. Previous Scene
9. Set Preview
10. Scene List

Some of these choices produce additional menus or dialogs. Each command under this menu is discussed briefly in the following section.

New Scene

This command inserts a new scene after the current scene. The new scene appears in the Scene Sorter, the Content List, and the Control Panel with a generic name. You should change this generic name to ensure that your scenes have unique names. Use Edit Scene, discussed later in this section, to enter a new scene name.

Insert Scene

Use the Insert Scene command to insert one or more scenes, or to place the scene(s) you insert somewhere other than after the current scene. When you choose this command, the Insert Scene dialog is displayed, as shown in Figure 4.50.

You can also use this dialog to specify a template for the inserted scene(s).

Figure 4.50
Scene Insert
Scene Dialog

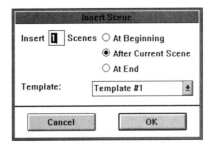

Edit Scene

Use Edit Scene to display the dialog shown in Figure 4.51.

Figure 4.51
Scene Edit
Scene Dialog

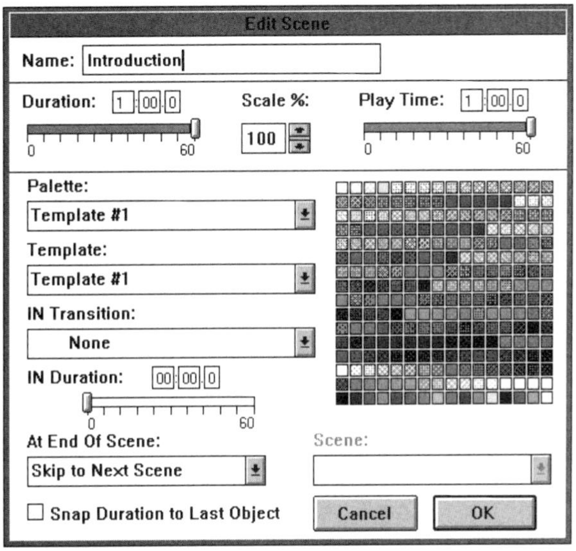

From this dialog, you can change the scene name, set the duration and play time, specify palette and template, establish transitions, and specify what to do when this scene ends.

Edit Template

The Edit Template command displays the dialog shown in Figure 4.52.

You can use this dialog to establish a new template name, set the palette, and specify a transition effect.

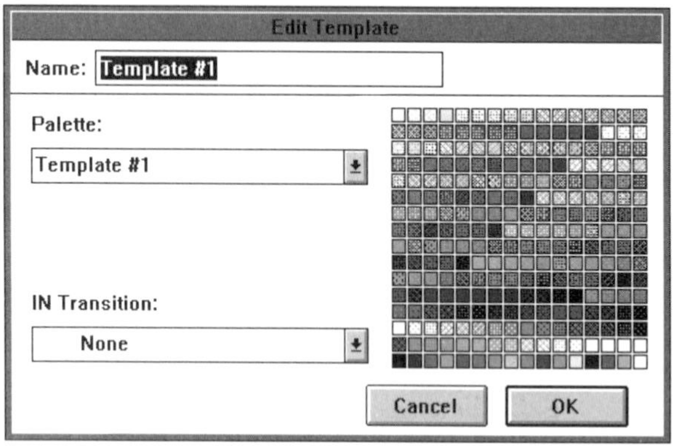

Figure 4.52
Scene Edit
Template Dialog

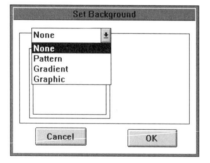

Set Background

Use the Set Background command to select a background pattern from the dialog shown in Figure 4.53.

Figure 4.53
Scene Set
Background
Dialog

You have four choices from this dialog: None, Pattern, Gradient, and Graphic. The None choice leaves the scene with a plain background.

The Pattern choice lets you choose a plain colored background, or one of the other 64 pattern choices displayed from the separate pop-up pattern box available in this dialog.

The gradient choice displays a colored background that ranges from light to dark. This type of background is popular in multimedia presentations to show depth or to suggest transitions. When you choose gradient from this dialog, you then have a choice from another pulldown menu that specifies how the colors will be arranged:

- Top to Bottom
- Bottom to Top
- Left to Right
- Right to Left
- Shape Burst
- Sun Burst

With Shape Burst and Sun Burst, colors "explode" from a center point, outward, in a graphics shape or sun pattern.

When you choose a graphic background, Action! displays a Load button to let you load a specific graphics file to serve as a background. You can use this feature to load a photograph or scanned image over which you can place a show title, menu, or other list.

_Delete Unused Template

When you choose this menu item, Action! displays the Delete Unused Template dialog shown in Figure 4.54.

Figure 4.54
Scene Delete
Unused Template
Dialog

Enter a template name or use the pulldown list to display templates available for deletion. An unused template results when:

1. The last scene that uses it is deleted
2. A new template is assigned to a scene
3. You choose Apply Later from the Apply Template dialog

Ne_xt Scene

The Ne_xt Scene command advances the display to the next available scene in the presentation. You can also display the next (or any) scene by pulling down the scene list on the Control Panel or by clicking on the Right or Left arrows on the Control Panel scene bar.

Previous Scene

Previous Scene displays the scene previous to the current scene. You can also use the Control Panel for this task.

Set Preview

The Set Preview command establishes the present display as the image used to represent the current scene in the Preview box, Scene Sorter, and the Import dialog. The display you specify here is shown in all of these facilities to help you remember what is contained in this scene.

Scene List

The Scene List command displays a pulldown list that shows all of the scenes in the current presentation. You can jump to any scene in the list by clicking on it.

Chart

The Chart menu is available only when you've selected a chart. When you choose this menu, the following selections are made available:

1. Gallery
2. Data Window
3. Data Motion
4. Chart Options
5. Axis Options
6. Perspective

Gallery

The Gallery command displays the Chart Gallery, shown in Figure 4.55.

From this dialog, you can specify a chart type and format, and tell Action! to plot the specified chart.

Data Window

The Data Window display, shown in Figure 4.56, lets you use a spreadsheet format to edit chart data and text.

Figure 4.55
Chart Gallery
Dialog

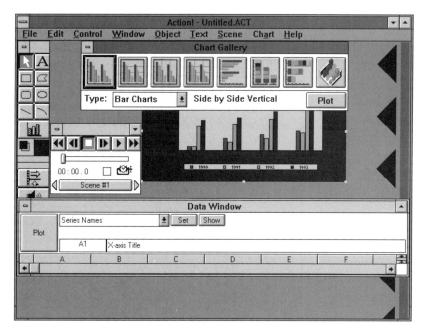

Figure 4.56
Chart Data
Window Dialog

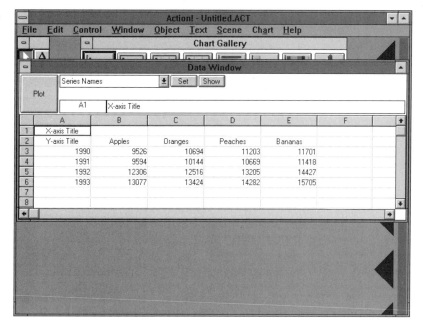

After you change information on this screen, you can click on the Plot button to have Action! plot a new chart based on the data in this window.

Data Motion

The Data Motion command lets you set Enter, Hold, and Exit phases for data objects in a chart. You can set these criteria for a series of objects, for categories of objects, or for a series or category as a whole group.

To set these attributes, you use a series of dialogs under the Data Motion command.

Chart Options

Use the Chart Options command to define how chart data is labeled and laid out. You do this from the dialog shown in Figure 4.57.

Figure 4.57
Chart Chart
Options Dialog

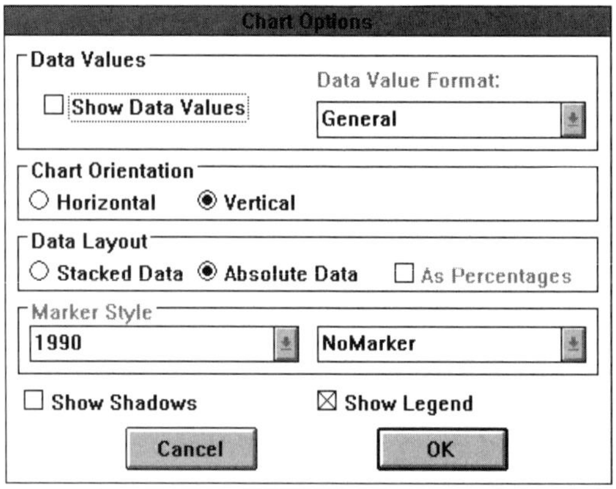

Notice that the specific content of this dialog changes with the type of chart you've selected.

Among the options you can set with this dialog are:

1. Chart Orientation
2. Layout
3. Data Marker Style

Axis Options

The Axis Options dialog lets you define the X and Y axes for bar, line, and area charts from the dialog shown in Figure 4.58.

Figure 4.58
Chart Axis
Options Dialog

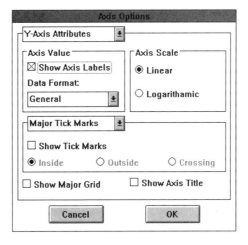

Perspective

The Perspective command lets you choose from among 16 different views or perspectives for your charts. The Perspective dialog is shown in Figure 4.59.

Figure 4.59
Chart
Perspective
Dialog

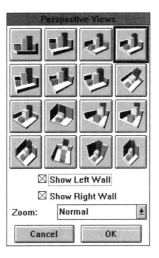

To specify a particular perspective for the selected chart, simply click on the icon that represents the view you want to use.

Help

As with other Windows applications, the Help command lets you search for topics or display descriptions of individual menu items. This is a good place to turn if you have more questions about Action!'s features.

Tool Palette

The Tool Palette (shown in Figure 4.41) displays 15 icons that represent tools you can use to create or manage objects on the presentation window.

The function of most of these tools is probably self explanatory. The default tool—the pointer—is used to select objects, to make menu choices, or to draw a selector box around one or more objects on the presentation screen. This tool is selected automatically for you when Action! loads and anytime you finish using another of the Tool Palette tools.

You use the seven tools at the top of the Tool Palette to enter text (Text tool) or to draw a variety of figures. Use these tools as you would any Windows-type drawing package to create boxes, circles, polygons, lines, arcs, or text.

The Chart tool in the middle of the Tool Palette is used to create new charts or to modify existing charts. Use this tool by clicking on the icon to activate it. Then draw a box on the presentation window to specify the size and location of the new chart.

When you release the mouse button after drawing the box, a sample chart is displayed and the Chart Gallery is displayed above it; the Data Window on which the chart is based is displayed below it. This beginning chart screen is shown in Figure 4.60.

Use the spreadsheet format in the Data Window to change data values and titles for your own chart. Then select the chart type and orientation by selecting the chart type you want from the Chart Gallery display. Click on Plot on the Chart Gallery display to change the sample chart to the new one you have created.

Figure 4.60
Sample Chart
with Chart
Gallery Display

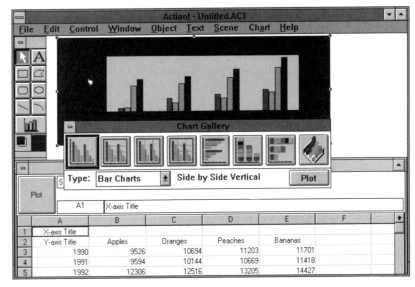

The Color Chip icon under the Chart icon lets you choose a color from a pop-up display of colors. One such color chip display is shown in Figure 4.61.

Figure 4.61
Color Chip Pop-
Up Choices
from the Tool

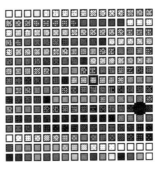

Select the color you want to use; any objects you create thereafter will use that color. In addition, you can change the basic color of existing objects by first selecting them, then choosing another color.

Beside the Color Chip icon is the Pattern Sample icon. Use this icon to change the pattern of the current or selected object from a wide range of choices. The patterns available change, depending on the color you select with the color chip display.

Use the Line Sample tool to set the width of the line used to draw presentation objects. You can select the line width tool to specify the line width of new objects, or you can select an existing object, then choose a line width for it.

The Action tool opens the Import dialog shown in Figure 4.62 when no object is selected. Use this dialog to import motion video in the MacroMind Director (.MMM) format.

Figure 4.62
Import Dialog
with Action Tool

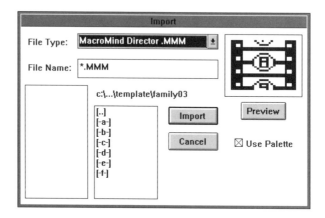

Click on Preview to display a small image of the selected action file before you import it.

If you select an object before choosing the Action tool, the Apply Action dialog shown in Figure 4.63 is displayed.

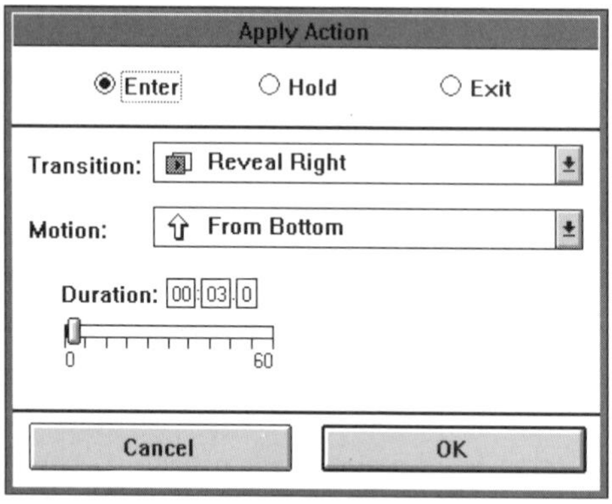

Figure 4.63
Apply Action
Dialog from
Action Tool

Use this dialog to specify actions for the selected object.

The Sound tool works like the Action tool. If you use it without selecting an object, the Import dialog shown in Figure 4.64 is displayed. You can import files in Wave (.WAV), MIDI (.MID) or CD Audio format. Use the pulldown menu beside the File Type: field to choose the audio type. Use the Preview button to listen to a selected file before you actually import it.

Figure 4.64
Import Dialog

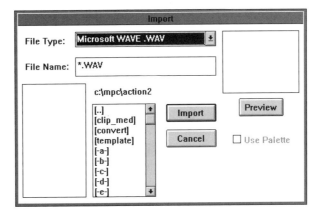

The Link tool lets you apply a link to any object in your presentation. Why use a link? To make the object act as a button, linking the scene to another location that you specify.

To use the Link tool, click on the tool, then click on the object in the presentation window you want to link. The Create Link dialog shown in Figure 4.65 is displayed.

Figure 4.65
Create Link
Dialog with
Pulldown List

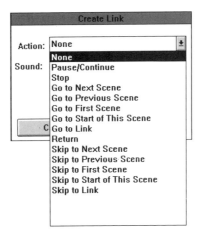

Use the pulldown list at the right of the Action: field to specify what action you want to occur when the object is clicked.

You can also specify a sound to accompany the action by selecting a sound type and source from the pulldown list in the Sound: field. When you select a sound type, Action! displays the Import dialog so you can specify a path and filename for the sound source.

You don't have to use an existing object for a link. You can also use the link tool to create a button anywhere in the presentation.

To create a button, select the Link tool, then click anywhere in the presentation window to open the Create Button dialog shown in Figure 4.66.

Figure 4.66
Link Create
Button Dialog

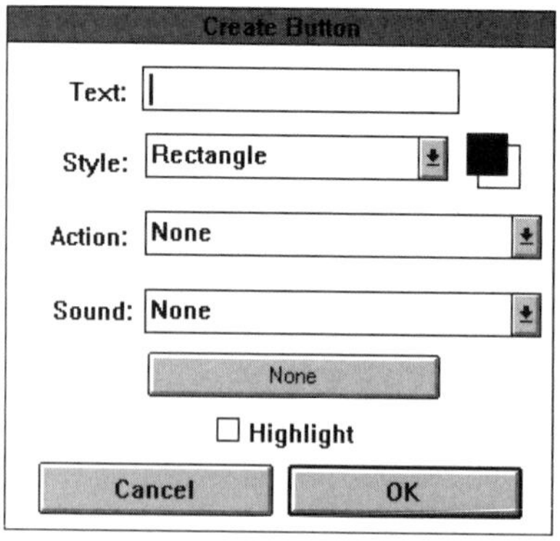

Use the pulldown menus at the right of each field to specify the button style, the action, and what sound file you want to play with it. Enter the text to accompany the button, then click on OK to create the button.

If you specified Go to link as the action, a second dialog will display, prompting you to click on the next object in the link path.

Control Panel

The Control Panel (shown in Figure 4.40) is a useful tool that is displayed at the upper-right corner of the presentation window by default. (You can turn off the Control Panel display by selecting Window and choosing Control Panel to toggle the Control Panel display off.)

Look at the Play controls. The Stop button's function should be obvious.

To the right and left of the Stop button are the buttons Play, Step Forward, Fast Forward, Rewind, and Step Backward. (These controls are explained in more detail in the discussion of the Control menu earlier in this chapter, which duplicates many of the functions of the graphics Control Panel.)

Beneath the Control buttons is the "Time Slider," which you can use to advance the playback head in the scene to a time displayed in the digital time readout on the next line. Use the slider to advance the current scene to any time you wish to view or edit it.

You can use the Control Panel to toggle Compressed View on and off. (For more information on Compressed View, see the Compressed View section earlier in this chapter.) To turn on Compressed View, simply click in the Compressed View square or on the Compressed View symbol to the right of it. Again, this is a toggle, so you can enable or disable Compressed View by clicking in these areas. When Compressed View is turned on, you'll see a Compressed View icon at all four corners of the presentation window.

Notice the view of the Control Panel in Figure 4.67.

Figure 4.67
Control Panel
with Pulldown
Scene List

You can use the Control Panel to display all the scenes in a presentation, then jump to these scenes by simply clicking on the one you want from the pulldown list.

Alternately, you can use the Control Panel to step through a presentation scene-by-scene by clicking on the right-facing arrow to the right of the Scene List bar. To step backwards through the scenes, click on the left-facing arrow to the left of the Scene List bar.

Finally, if you want to display only the minimum part of the Control Panel, click on the down-facing arrow in the upper-right corner of the Control Panel display. The Control Panel will shrink so that only the Play bar is displayed. (See Figure 4.68)

Figure 4.68
Control Panel
with Only Play
Bar Visible

Restore the full Control Panel display by clicking on the arrow again.

Building Multimedia Presentations with Action!

HANDS ON

In Chapter 4, you got an overview of Action! features, and if you tried some hands-on experiments, you know how some of these features work. In this chapter, we'll show you how to use Action! to build an interactive, animated presentation.

You'll design this application from scratch, using the Action! drawing tools to design a series of images, interactive buttons, and text.

In the following sections, we'll recap some of Action!'s features and remind you how to design a presentation. Then, we'll show you step by step how to create the images, links, text, and motion.

The presentation you'll build in this chapter is an educational, or self-teaching, application that describes and demonstrates the basic operation of a nuclear power plant. We'll build the basic presentation around the graphics image shown in Figure 5.1.

Figure 5.1
Completed
Power Plant
Graphic

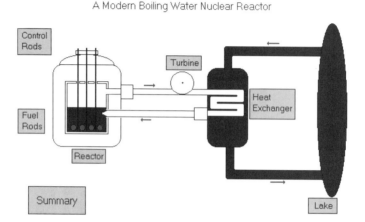

And, yes, you *will* draw this image and all of its components before we're through with this chapter. Don't worry—we'll show you exactly how to do it.

Action! Summary

If you skipped the detailed description of Action! and its features in Chapter 4, you may want to go back and check them out. In case you're really anxious to get started, here's a brief summary of Action!, what it is, and what it does.

Action! is a powerful multimedia development tool that offers a relatively simple user interface. Action! supports the following features:

- Drawing tools
- Charting tools
- Text tools
- Digitized and CD sound

- Motion video (version 2.5 and later)
- Graphics with special effects
- Interactive design
- Presentation tools
- A run-time player module

The evaluation version of Action! provided with this book (on the Ultimedia Tools Series CD-ROM) includes nearly all of the features of the commercial version of the software. There are some differences, however:

- Any presentations you design with the sampler will include an Action! logo overlay at the upper center of the screen, as mentioned in Chapter 4. This is a way of letting you experiment with a full-featured version of Action!, yet limiting your actual application of the presentations you create with it. If you decide to purchase the retail version of the product, you can select this logo object and delete it from your scenes.
- While the commercial version of Action! is supplied with 13 template files, the sampler you have with this book includes only six.
- As this book is written, the current version of Action! is 2.5, whereas the version on the sampler CD-ROM is 2.0. There are some significant enhancements in 2.5 over 2.0, so if you decide to purchase Action!, make sure you are getting the latest version.

In addition, neither the version supplied with the Ultimedia Tools Series CD-ROM, nor the commercial version 2.5 is designed for Windows for Workgroups. Although most features seem to work properly with Workgroups, we also uncovered some strange problems relating to file saving and retrieval that might have been caused by Workgroups. Action! technical support personnel caution against using Windows for Workgroups with Action!.

In the next section, we'll discuss briefly how our sample presentation was designed. For more information on presentation design, see Chapter 3.

Designing the Action! Application

While each presentation design and construction is unique, there are some general steps that everyone using Action! will follow. (We provide more detail on these steps in Chapter 4.)

Some of the general steps you follow when designing and constructing a presentation include the following:

1. Plan and design the presentation.
2. Create or import the individual objects.
3. Arrange the objects into scenes (or slides).
4. Add support material such as sound or motion.
5. Arrange the scenes into the proper order for the presentation.
6. Fine-tune object and scene timing.

As you plan and design the presentation, you must determine the following information:

1. Identify the audience.
2. Decide what the presentation will do.
3. Determine what the audience should do or feel as a result of your presentation.
4. Specify the presentation format: interactive, presenter supported, self-running, and so on.
5. Determine what resources you have available to help you accomplish this design.

The sample application in this chapter is designed for a nontechnical audience, and we determined that it would be a standalone interactive presentation. This is the type of application that might be installed at a kiosk in a school, library, or museum.

Because this is an educational presentation, it's important to have a clear introduction to the topic, but then the people viewing the presentation must be able to explore the information at their own pace, and in a manner that makes sense to them. This way they'll retain the information better and enjoy the presentation more.

The target audience is people with no technical background, so the text and graphics must work together to communicate the relatively complicated workings of a nuclear power plant in clear, everyday language.

The presentation we'll design will display an opening screen with some general information, then show a simple nuclear power plant drawing with some interactive buttons so a viewer can obtain additional information about the various components of the system.

Building the Application

Each Action! application consists of objects (text, graphics, sound, and video) arranged into scenes or slides. A series of scenes is strung together to form the finished presentation.

We've designed this sample application to be divided into ten scenes. Each scene contains several objects, most of which you'll construct using tools within Action!. If you follow the steps in this chapter, you'll build a file called NUKE.ACT that you can run through Action! or with the PLAYACT.EXE player utility supplied on your Ultimedia Tools Series CD-ROM. (This player file and its associated MMPLAYER.DLL file are located in the \MAC10001\WORK subdirectory on your Ultimedia Tools Series CD-ROM disk.)

The basic scenes for this application are:

Scene	Description
1	Opening/Introduction
2	General Description
3	Interactive Screen
4	Control Rods
5	Fuel Rods
6	Reactor Info
7	Turbine
8	Heat Exchanger
9	Lake
10	Summary

Each of these scenes contains multiple objects. We'll show you each of them as we design the scenes. Don't worry; we provide step-by-step instructions so you can build your own version of this application in Action!, then use it as a basis for your own designs.

Building the Initial Screens

To make this presentation as easy as possible to produce, we'll use as many facilities as possible from the ones supplied with Action!. What we don't have as part of the Ultimedia Tools Series CD-ROM, we'll design using Action! tools.

Opening/Introduction

The first scene, the opening and introduction, will be built around the same template we used in Chapter 4. (See the step-by-step instructions in Chapter 4 if you need help changing this template for the NUKE presentation.)

The finished scene looks like the screen in Figure 5.2.

Figure 5.2
Opening/
Introduction
Scene: NUKE

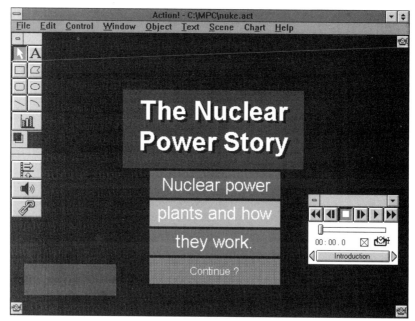

Here's how to create this opening scene:

1. Use File Load Template to load the supplied template file.
2. Change to compressed view by clicking on the compressed view icon in the Control Panel.
3. Select the "Introduction Title" text.
4. Use Object Promote to Scene to move the text from the Template to the scene.
5. Double click on the "Introduction Title" text to place it in text edit mode.
6. Change the text to "The Nuclear Power Story."
7. Change the text in "Presented by," Name," "Title," and "Company" in the same way. Notice that you don't have to use "Presented by," "Name," or any of the other information types. You can use these existing text areas for whatever text you want to use on your opening screen.

When you finish editing, the screen should look like the one in Figure 5.2. Now we're going to make one more modification to this template-based scene by creating a linked button object. This makes the presentation interactive so that the user can click on the final button on the screen (Continue?) to go to the next scene.

With Action! you can create buttons to use for transitions, or you can create links with current objects, making them function like buttons.

To create links with current objects:

1. Use Text Size to change the size of the Continue? button text to 14 points.
2. Select the Link tool from the Tool Palette and click on the Continue? button. The Create Link dialog shown in Figure 5.3 is displayed.
3. Pull down the Action: menu and choose Go to Next Scene.
4. Click on OK to accept this setting.

The first scene is now complete.

Figure 5.3
Create Link
Dialog for
Continue?
Object

You should save the file to avoid losing data and to establish a filename for future saves:

1. Use File Save As to display the Save As dialog.
2. Specify a filename and click on OK to save the file.

Your final task for the first scene is to provide it a name other than the default Scene #1. For this relatively simple application, this is not a particularly important step, but as you build more complicated presentations, you should get in the habit of giving each scene a descriptive name.

This is important because as you move scenes around with the Scene Sorter, the names remain the same even though the order changes. So, if you were to move Scene #1 to a new location, it's name would be confusing since it's no longer the first scene.

You also should get in the habit of naming the objects you create for your scenes. Otherwise, Action! names them sequentially as Object#1, Object#2, and so on.

Here's how to change the scene name:

1. Use Scene Edit Scene to display the Edit Scene dialog shown in Figure 5.4.
2. The Name: field is highlighted. Type a new name, such as **Introduction**.

In addition, we want to change the default scene length and what action will take place when the scene is finished. By default, all Action! scenes last one minute and the presentation automatically steps to the next scene when the current scene ends.

Figure 5.4
Edit Scene
Dialog

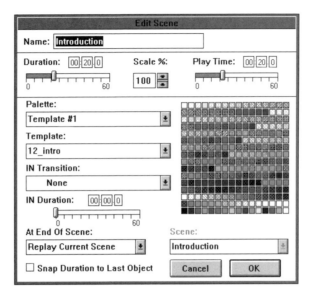

We want the user to control when the next scene begins, and we want to keep some action on the screen if no one is interacting with the computer. Here's how:

1. Use the slider bar under Duration: to set the duration time to 20 seconds (or click in the digital fields and enter 20 from the keyboard).

   We used the Timeline to determine how long to make the duration. The Timeline shows existing objects, when they appear, and when they disappear. All of the objects in this scene are shown on the Timeline as ending at 20 seconds. Therefore, by limiting the scene duration to 20 seconds, there will be no blank screen time waiting for the scene to recycle.

2. Pull down the menu for the At End of Scene: field and choose Replay Current Scene.

This will cause the scene execution to repeat if the user doesn't click on the Continue? button at the end of this scene. This keeps the screen active to attract attention or to show users that the computer is active and waiting for input.

Why not play this scene once at this point to get an idea of how it looks so far?

To play your presentation:

1. Click on the Play button on the Control Panel to start the scene.

   The scene will play, then restart, in a continuous loop.

2. To stop the scene, click on the Control Panel Stop button.

You now have a basic scene, based on a template supplied with the Action! software. In the next steps, we'll add a few more enhancements to the scene to create more interest for the viewer and to show you how to change the attributes for various objects.

First, we'll add some sound:

1. Click on Rewind on the Control Panel.
2. Click on Play on the Control Panel.
3. As soon as the first red box appears from the right side at the bottom of the screen, click on the Stop button on the Control Panel to freeze the scene.
4. Select the red box, then use Object Promote to Scene to move this object to scene status.
5. Double click on the box to display the Edit Object dialog shown in Figure 5.5.

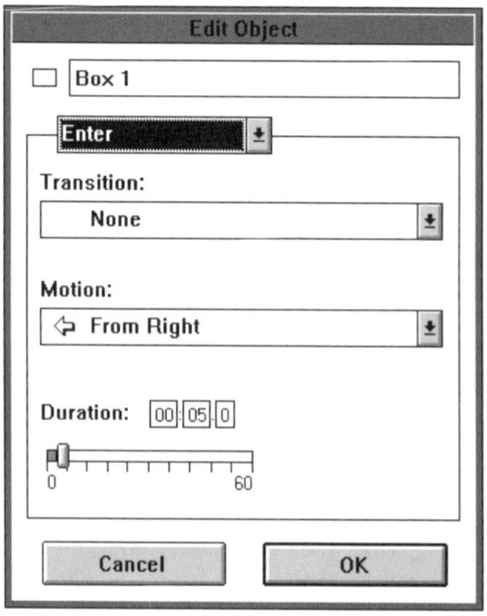

Figure 5.5
Edit Object
Dialog for Box

6. Pull down the attribute box and choose Sound. The Edit Object dialog looks like the one in Figure 5.6.

Figure 5.6
Edit Object
Dialog with
Sound Attribute

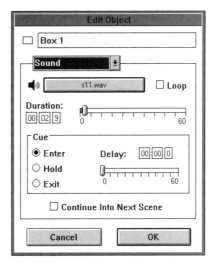

7. Click on the sound filename bar (it says "None" at this point) to display the Sound Import dialog.

8. In the File Name: field, type **\VIS10000\DEMO\S11.WAV** and click on Import. The filename S11.WAV appears in the filename box, and a speaker sound icon appears beside this field.

> If you want to hear what this sound is, click on Preview before clicking on OK.

9. Click on OK to accept the change.

You have associated a Wave sound file from another application on the CD-ROM with the BOX1 object of the Action! template. This is an attention-getting, fanfare-type sound that serves to open the show. Now, we want to add some music to the body of this scene.

To add music to the scene:

1. Click on the Control Panel Play button and wait until the large red template box under the main title is displayed.

2. Click on Stop to freeze the scene.

3. Select the red box.

4. Use Object Promote to Scene to promote this object to scene status.

5. Double click on the red box to display its Edit Object dialog. You are going to attach a sound file to this object as well.

6. Select Sound in the attribute box.

7. Click on the filename button below the attribute box.

8. In the File Name field of the Import dialog, type **\VIS10000\DEMO\S33.WAV** and click on Import.

9. Click on the Loop box beside the filename on the Edit Object dialog to enable sound looping.

10. Use the slider bar to set the duration of this sound to 17 seconds.

    This makes the sound continue in a loop to the end of the scene. The opening sound (associated with BOX1) runs about 3 seconds; we make this sound run 17 seconds to fill out the remaining time for this 20-second scene.

11. Click on Enter to enable the sound as soon as the object enters the scene.

12. Click on OK to set the changes.

You should now save the presentation again. Use File Save to store your work to the existing NUKE.ACT file you created earlier.

Play the scene again to see how effective the addition of sound can be. Again, you have started with a "canned" template that was fairly complicated looking with its moving boxes and type, and enhanced it with additional attributes.

Once you spend a little time on a product such as Action!, you'll begin to understand its design and how to use it effectively. Continue with the steps below to learn even more.

Now we want to add one more enhancement: some motion to the **Continue?** text to attract the viewer's attention.

To add motion to text:

1. Click on the Control Panel Play button to start the presentation.
2. Click on the Control Panel Stop button to freeze the display when the Continue? box is displayed.
3. Double click on Continue? to display its Edit Object dialog.
4. Pull down the Attribute menu and select Hold. You'll specify what happens to the object once it's in position and holding in the scene.
5. Pull down the Light Effect menu and select Shimmer Right.
6. Click on OK to accept the changes.
7. Save the scene with File Save.

Scene #1 is complete. When you play this scene you should hear a fanfare-type sound as the first box enters the screen, then a slight pause just before the main title box is displayed. As this box grows into full size, an upbeat music bridge is played.

When all of the text and boxes are displayed, you'll see a left-to-right movement in the Continue? box. Action! calls this "shimmer right" movement. It serves to draw attention to the user interactive box.

You're now ready to work on Scene #2.

General Description

At this point, the presentation consists of only one scene.

To add another scene:

1. Use Scene New Scene to add another scene to the presentation and make the new scene the current one.

Action! clears the screen and the scene count on the Control Panel changes to Scene #2. We'll use another supplied Action! template to build a general description screen.

To load another template:

1. Use File Load Template to display the Load Template dialog.

2. Click on the parent directory symbol (..) until the root CD-ROM directory is displayed. Use the scroll bars to find the MAC10001 directory, then select it.

3. Choose the Work directory from this directory to display a list of six template (*.TPL) files. Double click on the 12_PARA.TBL file.

Action! displays a solid black screen. You're looking at the template at time zero. To view the template contents, click on the compressed view icon on the Control Panel. The screen should look like the one in Figure 5.7.

Figure 5.7
Scene #2 with
Template
12_PARA.TBL

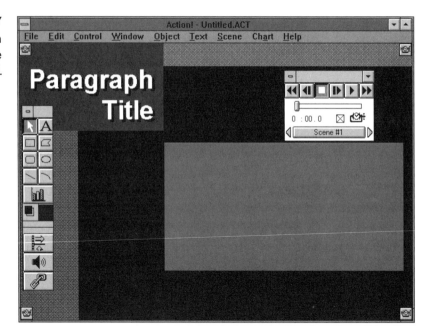

The first step in editing this template for our presentation is to change the text in Paragraph Title. Do this like you did in the previous scene by promoting the text to scene status, then double clicking on the object so you can edit it. Enter a title in this window, such as:

Nuclear Power Plant Basics

This text will be too big to fit in the box, so select all of the text and reduce the font size to 24 points:

To change the font size:

1. Select Text and choose Size.
2. Click on 24 to set the size.

   The text should now fit into the window.
3. Click anywhere outside the text window to set the text. The display should look like the one in Figure 5.8.

Figure 5.8
Scene #2
Nuclear Power
Plant Basics

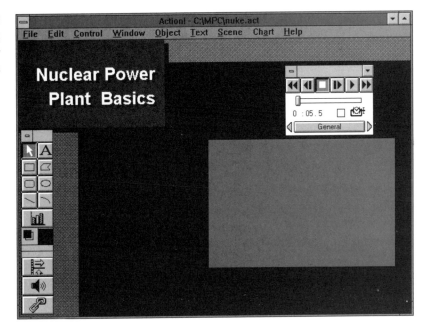

There also is a block of text beneath the green square in the middle of the screen.

You can view this text by sending the green box to the background:

1. Select the box and use Object Promote to Scene.
2. Grab the green box and move it downward slightly to reveal the text behind it.
3. Select the text and promote it to scene status.
4. Grab the green box and move it back up in line with the text.

Now you're ready to replace the existing text with some general text about power plants and this demonstration:

1. Double click on the text to select it and place Action! in the text edit mode.

2. Select all of the text and press **Del** to erase the dummy template text.

3. Type the following text in the window:

   A nuclear power plant consists of three major components: a reactor, a heat exchanger and a turbine. The reactor generates heat from nuclear fission. The heat is used to make steam to turn a turbine.

4. Click anywhere in the presentation window outside the text window. The screen should look like Figure 5.9.

Figure 5.9
Next Text
Screen Finished:
Scene #2

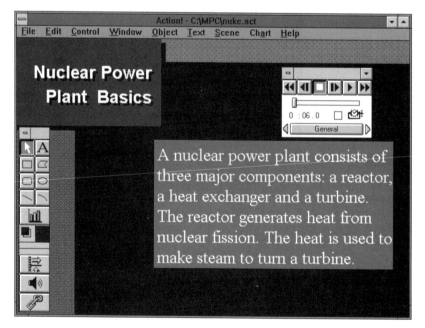

Now we need to add a button to this scene to let the user control when to go to the next scene.

1. Use Object New Object and select Button from the pulldown menu.

   Action! displays a large rectangle on the screen with a "Button" title. We'll position this button on the screen, resize it, and name it "Continue?."

2. Click on the Compressed View icon on the Control Panel to return to scene view.

3. Grab the button and move it to the lower-right corner of the screen.

4. Select the button, then grab one of the handles to shrink the button box to a smaller size. Adjust the size until it fits properly in the lower-right corner of the screen.

5. Double click on the button box to display its Edit Object dialog box.

6. Change the name from "Button" to "Continue?."

7. Pull down the menu in the Light Effect: field and choose Shimmer Right.

So far we've accepted the Action! defaults for the button background color. You can change this to anything you want by selecting the button and then choosing the color you want to use from the pop-up display from the color chips on the Tool Palette.

8. Click on OK to accept the changes.

9. Use Window Timeline to display the Timeline. Notice that the Button box is on the first line and scheduled to appear from time zero.

10. Grab the bar that represents the button box and move it along the Timeline until the left edge of the box is at the 10 second line.

11. Grab one of the handles on the right side of the button box bar and shrink the bar until its right edge lines up with the right edges of the other objects at 15 seconds. The Timeline should look like the one in Figure 5.10.

12. Use Scene Edit Scene to display the Edit Scene dialog.

13. Change the name from "Scene #2" to "General."

14. Use the slider bar to change the duration from one minute to 15 seconds.

15. Pull down the At End Of Scene: menu and choose Replay Current Scene.

16. Click on OK.

Figure 5.10
Timeline for
Scene #2 Button

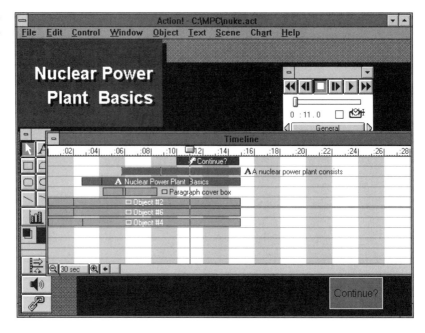

Now let's add another sound file so we have background music during this scene:

1. Click on the compressed view icon on the Control Panel to switch to compressed view.

2. Select the red box that holds the scene title.

3. Choose Object Promote to Scene. This moves the selected object from template to scene status.

4. Double click on the red box to display its Edit Object dialog.

5. Choose Sound from the pulldown attributes menu.

6. Click on the filename bar (now labeled "none") to display the Import dialog.

7. Select the VIS10000 directory and choose the DEMO subdirectory.

8. Double click on the filename S44.WAV.

9. Click on the Loop box so the sound will continue throughout the scene.

10. Click on the button beside Enter so the sound will start when the object first enters the scene.

11. Click on OK to accept the changes.

12. Use File Save to store the new version of the file.

> If the text in the red title box at the upper left of the screen seems to disappear at this point, it's because we've promoted the box to the front in the scene. Use Object Send to Back to place the box behind the text.

The way we've set up the presentation, it will cycle through this scene forever (or at least until someone shuts off the power). So let's add one more little touch to catch our users' attention and ask them for some input.

When the Continue button appears, we'll make a little sparkling noise to draw the viewer's attention to the button:

1. Play the scene until the Continue button appears at the bottom right of the screen, then choose Stop on the Control Panel.
2. Double click on the button to display its Edit Object dialog.
3. Pull down the attribute menu and select sound.
4. Choose SLIDIN.WAV from the MAC10000\DEMO subdirectory on your CD-ROM disk.
5. Click on Enter in the Cue area of this dialog.
6. Click on OK to accept the changes.
7. Save the file.

Run the scene again. You should get music throughout the scene until the button appears, then you will hear a brief sparkling sound with the button. After a few seconds, the scene repeats itself.

We'll now insert another scene and start drawing the next figures.

Interactive Screen

The Interactive Screen is the one that contains the completed drawing of the power plant with labels of the various components, as shown in Figure 5.11. These labels are set up as buttons, which the user can click on to get more information about a specific component.

We'll build this scene using a number of individual objects, which we'll also use for later scenes called by the user.

Figure 5.11
Completed
Nuclear Power
Plant Scene #3

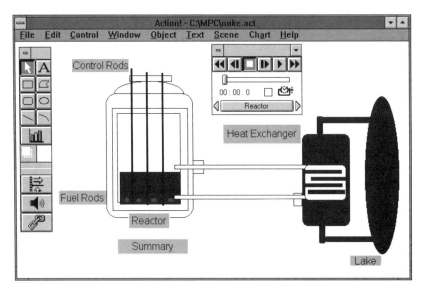

To begin building this scene, we'll first construct the module on the left, labeled Reactor.

First, we must insert a new scene in the presentation:

1. Use Scene New Scene. The scene bar should say "Scene #3."

   Draw the reactor component of this image using Tool Palette tools, as follows:

2. Click on the top-left corner of the color chip on the Tool Palette to pop up the color palette, then choose a white color to provide a transparent fill.

3. Click on the bottom-right corner of the color chip on the Tool Palette to pop up the color palette. Choose a black color to provide a black outline.

4. Select the square drawing tool and build a small, vertically oriented rectangle at the left side of the screen to represent the interior of the reactor.

5. Use the same tool to construct another rectangle just outside the first one. You should have two concentric rectangles with a small space between the two.

6. Select the Rounded Rectangle tool and draw a rounded, vertically oriented rectangle outside of the existing concentric

square rectangles. Leave about ½-inch of clearance between the largest square rectangle and the new rounded rectangle figure. You should have an image something like the one in Figure 5.12.

Figure 5.12
Beginnings of Reactor Image

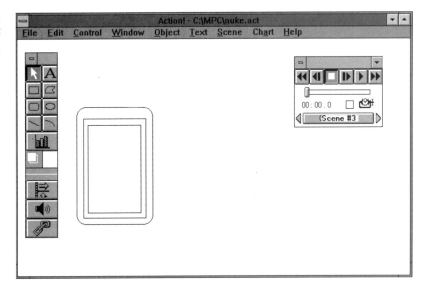

Now we'll add a thin rectangle at the top of the reactor to represent the housing for the motors that move the control rods up and down:

1. Select the arc tool from the Tool Palette. Position the crosshairs about ¼-inch above the top line of the rounded rectangle about half way between the left and right edges of this horizontal line.

2. Hold down the left mouse button and move the pointer to the left and down to where the crosshairs rest on the horizontal line just before the line starts to curve downward.

3. Release the mouse button. You should have half an arc like the one shown in Figure 5.13.

4. Repeat Step 3, starting an arc at the tip of the existing arc and drawing to the right corner of the rounded rectangle.

5. Select the square rectangle tool and build a small, thin rectangle on top of the arc you just finished. Your drawing should now look like the one in Figure 5.14.

Figure 5.13
Reactor Drawing
with Half an Arc
on Top

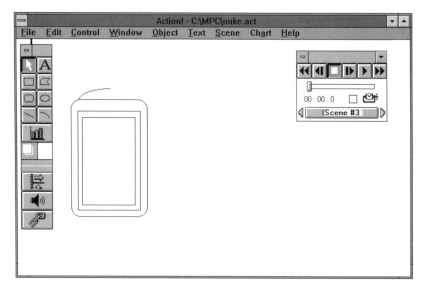

Figure 5.14
Reactor with Arc
and Rectangle
On Top

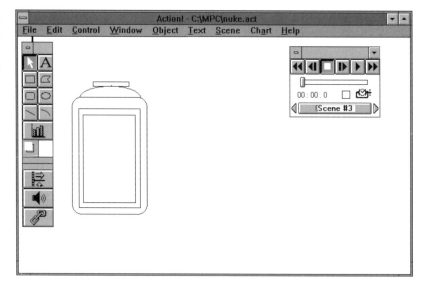

**Now we'll draw the blue box to represent the water that will
be boiled in the reactor and sent as steam to the turbine:**

1. Click on the color chip and select deep blue from the pop-up color squares.

2. Select the square box drawing tool and build a small box inside the series of concentric boxes. The box should be about half the size of the innermost box you drew previously.

The next task is to draw four small, red-filled circles to represent the hot fuel rods at the bottom of the reactor.

You want to place the small circles so there is room for the control rods that will be added in the next section:

1. Click on the line color chip and choose a bright red color for the lines in your objects.
2. Click on the fill color chip and choose the same bright red color.
3. Select the circle drawing tool and use it to build four small filled circles at the bottom of the reactor. Your drawing should look like the one in Figure 5.15.

Figure 5.15
Reactor with
Boxes, Water,
and Heated
Reactor

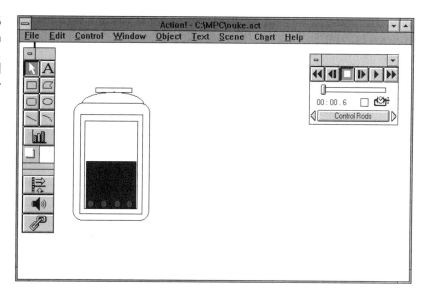

Next, we'll draw the control rods. They consist of three relatively thick vertical lines:

1. Select the line color chip and choose a black color from the pop-up samples.
2. Click on the line symbol on the Tool Palette and choose the third line.
3. Select the line drawing tool from the Tool Palette and use it to draw a vertical line from the top of the reactor figure down to the bottom of the innermost reactor box. This line

should fall between the left-most red circle and the one next to it on the right.

4. Draw two more vertical lines in the same way, placing them between the red circles, as shown in Figure 5.16.

Start drawing the control rod lines at the bottom and move to the top of the reactor. That way you can be sure the control rods will be lined up properly with the fuel rods at the bottom of the reactor.

Figure 5.16
Reactor with
Control Rods

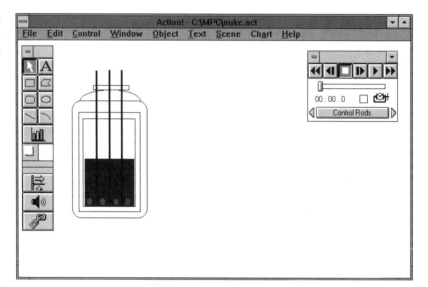

Now we're ready to start building a scene around this first part of the reactor drawing. We'll make the reactor appear slowly, its individual components drawn from the center out in a square pattern. By choosing the center-out option, you have focused the viewer on the internal components of the reaction—the important parts—and hinted at the density of the reactor's core.

As you design motion for your Action! screens, try to link the motion with the idea you are trying to convey:

1. First, save the show at this point with the File Save command.

2. Now draw a selection box around all of the reactor components

you have drawn up to this point. To do this, select the Pointer tool and use it to drag a box around the entire image.

3. Use Object Group to group these objects.
4. Double click on the group to display the Edit Object dialog for this group.
5. Change the name of the group from "Group #1" to "Group #1—Reactor."
6. Click on Transition to display the transition choices in this dialog.
7. Choose Center Out, Square from the list.
8. Slow down the drawing of this object by dragging the duration bar to 5 seconds.
9. Click on OK to accept the changes.

Next, we'll construct buttons with titles that describe the major components of the reactor assembly:

1. Use Object New Object to display the New Object pulldown menu.
2. Choose Button from the list. Action! displays a large rectangle labeled "Button."
3. Double click on the button to display its Edit Object dialog.
4. Change the name to "Control Rods."
5. Grab a corner handle on this selected button and shrink the button box so it is just large enough to hold the title.
6. Drag the button to a position above and to the left of the reactor drawing.
7. Use the same technique to create two more buttons: "Reactor" and "Fuel Rods." Place the Reactor button at the bottom of the reactor graphic. Place the Fuel Rods button to the lower left of the reactor. Your drawing should look like the one in Figure 5.17.

Action! defaults to a light yellow color for buttons. You can change the color to anything you want by selecting the button box and choosing a different fill color from the fill color chip on the Tool Palette.

Figure 5.17
Reactor with
Three Buttons

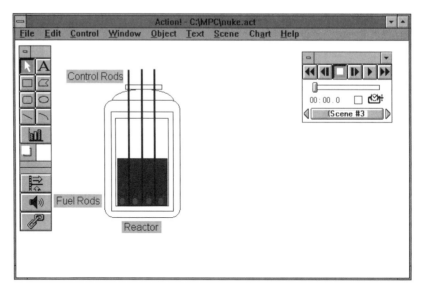

Now we'll set up this scene so that after it's finished, if there is
no input from a viewer after a set amount of time, the presentation will restart with the Introduction. Remember, we're assuming that you're building a stand-alone, kiosk-type application.

**You can adjust these parameters to suit your own needs for
this sample or your own applications:**

1. Use Scene Edit Scene to display the Edit Scene dialog.
2. Change the scene name to "Reactor."
3. Change the scene duration to 2:00:00.
4. Change the End of Scene: field to "Go to Scene."
5. Choose "Introduction" from the pulldown list in the Scene:
   field.

The next step is to create three new scenes and link them to the
buttons we just created so that when a user clicks on one of the
buttons, another scene is displayed to provide more information on the selected topic. This amount of flexibility in the way
information is displayed throughout the presentation will help
our audience learn at their own pace.

To create additional scenes:

1. Use Scene Insert Scene to display the Insert Scene dialog.
2. Change the "1" to "3" in the Insert Scenes: field of this dialog. Click on OK to accept the After Current Scene and template defaults.
3. Advance to Scene #4 by clicking on the Right Arrow on the scene name bar of the Control Panel.
4. Use Scene Edit Scene to display the Edit Scene dialog.
5. Change the name of this scene to "Control Rods."
6. Use the slider bar to change the scene duration to 0:30.
7. Change the At End Of Scene: field to "Go to Scene."
8. Change the Scene: field to "Reactor."
9. Click on OK to close the dialog.
10. Repeat these steps for Scenes #5 and #6, changing Scene #5 to "Fuel Rods," and Scene #6 to "Reactor Info." Change the At End Of Scene: field to "Go To Scene," and the Scene: field to "Reactor."

Now that you've created scenes for the button links, it's time to create those links:

To create links to the new scenes:

1. Click the Left Arrow on the scene name bar of the Control Panel to return to the Reactor scene created earlier. (You can also pull down the Scene Name list and select the scene to go directly to it.) The screen will be blank.
2. Use the slider on the Control Panel to advance the scene to 10 seconds. All buttons and the reactor graphic should be displayed.
3. Select the link tool from the Tool Palette.
4. Move the pointer (which now looks like the link tool) over the Control Rods button and click once to display the Create Link dialog shown in Figure 5.18.
5. Select Go to Link from the pulldown menu on the Action: field of this dialog.
6. Click on Highlight in this dialog. This tells Action! to highlight the button when a user selects it.

Figure 5.18
Create Link
Dialog for
Control Rods
Button

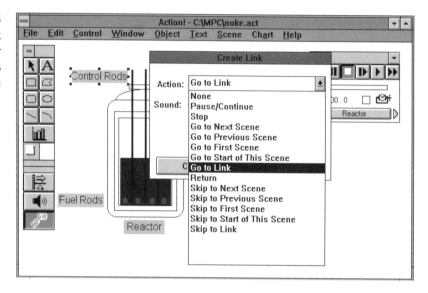

7. Click on OK. Action! displays the Link dialog, which instructs you to "Go to destination and click Link."

8. Pull down the scene name list from the bar on the Control Panel.

9. Choose Control Rods from the list. Action! jumps to Scene #4 (Control Rods).

10. Click on Link in the Link dialog. Action! returns you to the Reactor scene. The link has been created.

11. Repeat steps 3-10 for the remaining buttons, creating a link between the Fuel Rods button and the Fuel Rods scene, and another link between the Reactor button and the Reactor Info scene.

Okay! Can you guess the next step in constructing this presentation? Right! We've created linked buttons that point to three new scenes—Control Rods, Fuel Rods, and Reactor Info—but we haven't put anything in those scenes yet. That's the next step.

Control Rods

We'll show you step by step how to construct the Control Rods scene, then suggest how you might construct new scenes for the other two topics.

Here's how to construct the Control Rods scene:

1. Click anywhere inside the reactor drawing to select all of its components, combined earlier as Group #1--Reactor.

2. Use <u>E</u>dit <u>C</u>opy to place a copy of the group on the Windows Clipboard.

3. Go to the Control Rods scene by clicking on the right-facing arrow on the scene name bar of the Control Panel. Action! displays a blank screen and the scene name bar changes to "Control Rods."

4. Use <u>E</u>dit <u>P</u>aste to copy the reactor group to the scene.

5. Advance the time bar on the Control Panel to 10 seconds to display the entire group of objects. The screen should look like the Reactor scene, but without the buttons.

6. Use <u>O</u>bject <u>U</u>ngroup to ungroup these objects so you can manipulate them individually. Action! ungroups the objects and selects them all. Notice that many handles appear, cluttering the screen.

7. Click anywhere in the scene outside the reactor graphic to deselect all of the reactor objects.

8. Press and hold the **Shift** key and use the mouse pointer to select all of the objects in the reactor drawing *except* the control rods. Simply click on each object in sequence until everything but the control rods is selected.

You can group these objects in another way: Drag the three control rods out of the reactor image, placing them temporarily at one side of the presentation screen. Draw a selection box around the remaining reactor components, then use the Object Group command. Now you can move the control rods back to their previous location.

9. Use <u>O</u>bject <u>G</u>roup to combine these objects into a group.

10. Double click on this group to display the group's Edit Object dialog.

11. Change the group name to Group #2--Reactor.

12. Pull down the Transition: menu and choose Reveal, Bits.

This causes Action! to draw the image as a series of dotted lines until the picture is complete. This technique helps the viewer focus on individual components of the reactor, and keeps some action on the screen for a relatively long period. By building the reactor in pieces, we also emphasize the relationship among various reactor components.

13. Use the slider bar to change the duration to 15 seconds.
14. Click on OK to accept the changes.

The next step is to add some motion to the control rods to help emphasize them. Here's how:

1. Double click on the left-most control rod to display its Edit Object dialog.
2. Change the name to Control Rod 1.
3. Pull down the menu beside the Motion: field and select From Upper Left.
4. Use the slider bar to change the duration to 5 seconds.
5. Click on OK to accept the changes.
6. Repeat steps 1 through 5 for control rods 2 and 3, providing separate motion instructions for each.

The next step is to create a text box to describe the Control Rods. Here's how to do that:

1. Click anywhere on the presentation screen outside the Reactor graphic to deselect the group.
2. Use Object New Objects to display the new object menu.
3. Choose Text object. Action! displays a small rectangle ready to accept text data.
4. Type **Control Rods** in this box.
5. Click on the pointer tool on the Tool Palette to end text entry.
6. Use Text Size to change the size of the text to 16 points.
7. Grab a corner handle of the text box and shrink it to force "Control" on the first line and "Rods" on the second line. The text box should be just the size of the text.
8. Drag the text object so that it rests on top of the control rods inside the reactor graphic. The scene should look like Figure 5.19.

Figure 5.19
Control Rods
Scene with First
Text Box

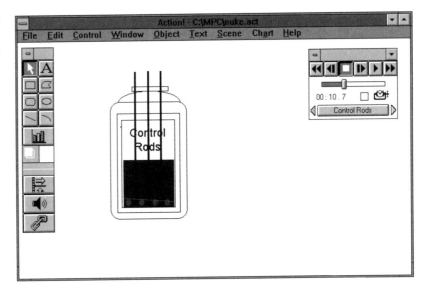

9. Double click on the Control Rods text object to display its Edit Object Dialog.

10. Choose From Upper Left in the Motion: field pulldown menu.

11. Move the slider bar to 5 seconds.

12. Click on OK to accept the changes.

Let's check our work on the Control Rods scene and use the Timeline to fine-tune positioning of the objects to this point:

1. Use Window Timeline to display the Timeline for this scene.

2. The Timeline should show five objects and look similar to the one in Figure 5.20.

Notice that all of the control rods and the group object start building at time zero. Depending on where the pointer was when you added the Control Rods text box, this box may start at zero or it may start at a later time. Whatever the Timeline shows at this point, you want to make sure it shows these characteristics:

Control Rod 1 starts at zero and runs to 0:30

Control Rod 2 starts at 0:05 and runs to 0:30

Control Rod 3 starts at 0:10 and runs to 0:30

The group object starts at zero and runs to 0:30

The text object starts at 0:10 and runs to 0:30

Figure 5.20
Timeline with
Five Objects—
Control Rod
Scene

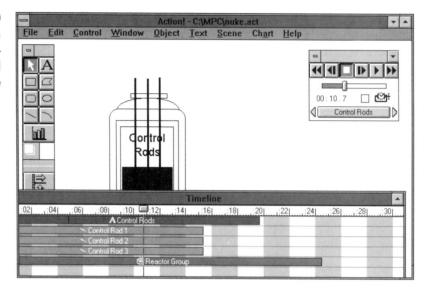

If the objects are not on the Timeline at these locations, simply grab the bar that represents the object you want to move and drag it to the new location. You can lengthen or shorten a bar as needed by grabbing one end and dragging it to the length you want.

The final object to be created for this scene is another text box that describes control rod function. You could also create a sound object and add narration to this scene, if you wish.

First we'll create a colored box to hold the text, then create the text:

1. Select the pattern color chip from the Tool Palette and choose a pattern from the pop-up window.
2. Select the background pattern square and choose one from the choice within the range of colors you chose in Step 1.
3. Select the square box tool and draw a rectangle in the lower-right corner of the screen. Fill the area between the reactor and the right and bottom edges of the presentation window. The screen should look similar to the one in Figure 5.21.
4. Double click on the newly created color box to display its Edit Object dialog.
5. Change the name to "Control Rod Text."

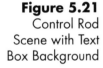

Figure 5.21
Control Rod
Scene with Text
Box Background

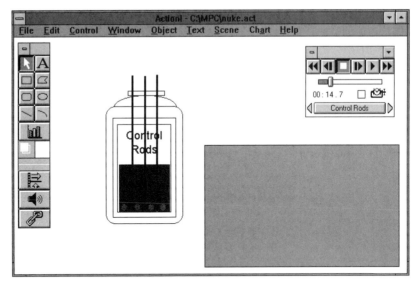

6. Specify "Reveal Down-Right" in the Transition: field for the Enter condition.

7. Use the slider bar to set duration to 15 seconds.

8. Use Object New Object to display the pulldown object menu.

9. Choose Text. Action! opens a small text dialog.

10. Type the following text in this new text object:

    Control Rods: Control rods are long cylinders of graphite that prevent a nuclear reaction from occurring by absorbing the neutrons given off by the fuel rods. The farther the control rods are drawn out of the reactor and away from the fuel rods, the faster the nuclear reaction occurs.

11. Use Text Size to set the size of the title (Control Rods) to 16 points and the size of the body text to 12 points.

12. Click anywhere outside the text area to deselect it and end text entry.

13. Select the text box and move it on top of the colored background box created earlier.

    Oops! The text probably went away and it doesn't fit the background box anyway. Here's how to correct the problems:

14. Use Object Bring to Front to make the text visible.

    You may have to change the color of the text to make it readable, depending on the default color of the text and the color of the background you chose. If this is necessary, do this:

15. With the text box selected, click on the object color chip on the Tool Palette. Select a color from the pop-up list that is readable through the background box color. Experiment until you achieve a color combination that works.

 Some color combinations are hard to read. You can use Text Style and choose Bold to make text stronger against the chosen background color, if necessary.

16. Now size the text box to make it fit as nearly as possible over the background color box. Adjust the size of the color box as well, if necessary.

17. Use Window Timeline to display the Timeline. If necessary, adjust the timing of various objects, especially the text box. You want it to appear early in the scene and stay throughout.

Experiment with timing until the text appears at a logical time with the appearance of other objects. Try about five seconds into the scene for text appearance and make it last for the full 30 seconds in the scene. (It should take about 10 seconds to read the text about Control Rods.)

That completes the programming for the Control Rods scene. The entire scene is built in about 20 seconds; it will pause another 10 seconds, then return automatically to the Reactor scene (Scene #3).

You can program this scene further, of course. For example, we have not specified any music to accompany the Control Rods information. Refer to the music steps in the previous scenes and, if you wish, add music to this scene as well.

Obviously, you also could include an interactive button so the user could select Continue, or provide some additional "direct access" buttons to let the user jump anywhere in the presentation. For now, though, let's return to the Reactor screen and discuss some of the options that remain there.

At this point, you have programmed only one of the interactive scenes: the Control Rods scene. Still left to build are the Fuel Rods and Reactor Info scenes, which we inserted earlier, but which don't have any data associated with them. In the next section, we'll give you a quick run-through for designing these scenes, but we'll leave the majority of the design of these scenes up to you. You can use the concepts and steps developed in the Control Rods scene to complete the remaining work on your own.

Fuel Rods

We've already programmed the Fuel Rods button to go to the Fuel Rods scene if the user clicks on this button. Now, all we have to do is design a scene with some motion and information to accompany it.

As you've seen so far, the way you design a scene, the elements you include, and how you present the information are all subjective ideas. You can use Action!'s features in a variety of ways to get the same information to the user. We won't tell you step by step how to program the Fuel Rods scene, but we'll offer some suggestions on things you might do, and we'll show you a finished screen that represents our design.

Take this information—and what you've learned in previous sections of this chapter—to build your own Fuel Rods scene.

The first step in programming the Fuel Rods scene is to make another copy of the Reactor group and move it to the Fuel Rods scene:

1. Select the reactor, then use Edit Copy to place a copy of the group of objects on the Clipboard.

If the reactor is not displayed, you can use the slider bar or the single-step button on the Control Panel to advance the display until all of the reactor is displayed.

2. Pull down the scene list from the scene name button on the Control Panel.

3. Click on Fuel Rods on this list. Action! displays a new, blank screen. The name of the scene is shown on the Scene Name button on the Control Panel.

4. Press **Shift+Ins** to copy the Clipboard object to the scene.

Oops! Nothing appeared on the screen? That's because when you copied the group, you also copied the offset from the beginning of the scene. Use the slider bar to advance the scene time to about 15 seconds and you'll see the group you just copied. For now leave it there; later you may want to use the Timeline to move this group earlier in the current scene.

Now you have an image that can provide the basis for a moving, descriptive screen for the Fuel Rods. You could (probably should) pattern this screen after the Control Rods screen discussed earlier. Although it doesn't have to match this design precisely, remember that the various elements of a presentation should fit together well and should offer no surprises to the user.

Here's a block of descriptive text you can use in this scene:

Fuel Rods: Long cylinders made of zirconium alloy with pellets of uranium oxide inside. Uranium is radioactive, which means it is constantly emitting neutrons and alpha, beta, and gamma waves. The escaping neutrons bounce around, striking other pellets of uranium, causing them to give off more neutrons in a process called nuclear reaction. The heat generated from these neutrons boils the water.

You should place this text somewhere on the screen, perhaps under a colored rectangle as we did in the Control Rods scene.

Remember, if you want to manipulate the Fuel Rod images independently from the rest of the Reactor image, you should do the following:

1. Select the reactor group.

2. Ungroup the images with the Object Ungroup command.

3. Drag each of the Fuel Rod images outside of the reactor.

4. Regroup the remaining reactor components with the Object Group command sequence.

Now you have the main reactor that you can manipulate as a unit and the fuel rod images that you can control individually. Use the Edit Object dialog for each of the Fuel rods and give them some motion. You could have them enter at the upper-left of the screen like we did the Control Rods earlier, add a title, then place the descriptive text above them.

The image in Figure 5.22 shows how this screen might look about half way through the scene.

Figure 5.22
Fuel Rods Scene about Half Way Through

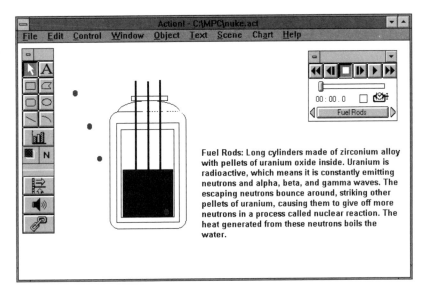

Remember to use Scene Edit Scene to specify what will happen when this scene is finished. In the Control Rods scene, we told Action! to return to the Reactor scene after all of the data is displayed and the completed images have been static on the screen for several seconds. That's probably a good choice for this scene as well.

Reactor Info

The final scene that results from this first round of interactive buttons is the Reactor Info scene. This scene describes the over-all operation of the reactor.

As with the Control Rods and Fuel Rods scenes, you'll want to copy the reactor from the Reactor scene to the Reactor Info scene.

Use Edit Copy to place a copy of the Reactor object on the Clipboard, then paste it onto the Reactor Info scene.

Here's the text we used in this scene:

> **Reactor:** The reactor is surrounded by the 12-foot-thick concrete walls of the containment building. Inside the reactor, fuel and control rods immersed in water interact to produce a nuclear reaction that boils the water, sending steam to the turbine. Care must be taken that the reactor does not become too hot, because then a nuclear meltdown can occur in which all the radioactive material melts the containment walls and escapes into the surrounding land.

You could pattern this scene after the previous two, or you could design this one differently. For example, you could design, say, three text boxes and have them appear with the different components of the reactor.

Have the containment building appear and present the first sentence. Then draw the internal boxes, the water, the control rods and the fuel rods in sequence as the text that describes these items is displayed.

Here's an idea: Use the Edit Object dialog to specify a "Shrink to Center" transition for the Exit phase. Then increase the Duration to eight seconds or so, and the reactor appears to melt toward the center as the scene ends.

And remember to use Scene Edit Scene to tell Action! to return to the Reactor scene when this one is over. Be sure to make the scene long enough for the user to read all of the text you have included, and to absorb the drawings.

Adding To The Reactor Scene

We've now completed the first interactive screens for this presentation, and we're ready to draw the next phase of the nuclear power plant image. This includes supply and return pipes, a turbine, and a heat exchanger.

These components are a little more difficult to draw, but you can do it if you follow the instructions we offer here, and if you're willing to experiment. Put your hands on the drawing tools, and don't be afraid to make mistakes. And, of course, save your work frequently so you don't run the risk of losing data.

To draw the heat exchanger, supply pipes, and turbine:

1. Select the rounded corner rectangle tool.
2. Click on the fill color chip and choose a deep blue color from the options displayed.
3. Build a vertical, blue rectangle toward the right side of the screen and in line with the reactor chamber to represent the Heat Exchanger module.
4. Use Object Send to Back to make the new rectangle a background object.
5. Click on the fill color chip and choose white (or the color of your presentation screen background if you have changed the default).
6. Select the square rectangle tool.
7. Draw a long, thin rectangle that starts in the upper part of the reactor chamber and extends horizontally almost to the far right side of the blue Heat Exchanger module you just completed. This is the outlet pipe (that carries steam from the reactor to the Heat Exchanger). At this point your drawing should look like the one in Figure 5.23.
8. Select the square rectangle tool and draw another long, thin rectangle that starts in the lower part of the reactor chamber (where the water and fuel rods are) and extends horizontally nearly to the right side of the Heat Exchanger rectangle. This is the inlet pipe (that carries water from the heat exchanger to the reactor).
9. Select the rounded corner rectangle tool and use it to draw a rectangle on top of the inlet and outlet pipes you just drew in the previous steps.

The top horizontal edge of this rectangle should overlay the top horizontal edge of the outlet pipe (the top pipe); the lower horizontal edge of this rounded corner rectangle should overlay the lower horizontal edge of the inlet (bottom) pipe. The new

Figure 5.23
Heat Exchanger
with Outlet Pipe
Drawn

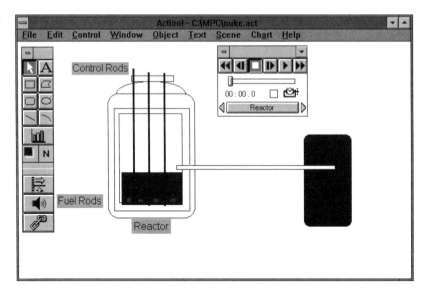

rectangle will be the object on top, obscuring a portion of the inlet and outlet pipes.

Next, we'll draw three thin rectangles with blue fill to cut away portions of the rounded corner rectangle that we just completed.

When we're finished, it will look as if the inlet and outlet pipes are one pipe connected by a coil of pipe viewed from the side:

1. Select the rounded corner rectangle tool.
2. Click on the fill color chip and choose the same dark blue you used for the heat exchanger fill.
3. Draw a thin, blue rectangle at the upper edge of the larger rectangle.

This rectangle should extend from the left edge of the white rectangle on the left, almost to the right edge of the white rectangle. The topmost horizontal edge of the blue rectangle should line up with the bottom horizontal edge of the outlet pipe previously drawn.

The idea is to erase a portion of the large, white rectangle to create a coil of pipe that connects the inlet and outlet pipes.

To erase a portion of the rectangle:

1. Draw another thin blue rectangle that starts on the right edge at about the middle of the large white rectangle. This object will extend toward the left, but won't touch the left edge of the larger rectangle.

2. Draw a third thin blue rectangle at the bottom of the larger white rectangle. Its origin should be at the left, with the lower horizontal edge lined up with the upper horizontal edge of the inlet pipe.

As you draw these objects, try to make them all the same size and shape. The figure at this point should look like Figure 5.24.

Figure 5.24
Heat Exchanger
with Coil
Finished

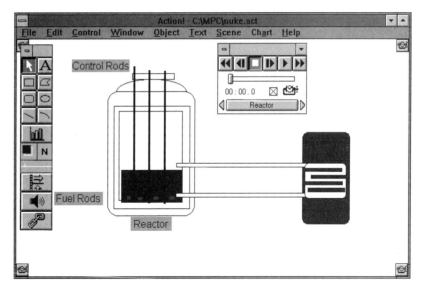

 When drawing a series of repeated objects like this, draw one object of the proper size and shape, then select it and use Edit Copy to place a copy of it on the Clipboard. Now you can use Edit Paste to place several instances of the same object on the presentation screen, dragging each one to its proper location.

Now we're going to add some finishing touches.

First, we'll build a couple of small rectangles that represent pumps for the inlet and outlet pipes:

1. Select the square corner rectangle tool.
2. Click on the fill color chip and choose white (or your background color) from the color squares.
3. Draw a small rectangle (almost a square) with the longer side along the horizontal plane. This figure should be just slightly wider than the inlet and outlet pipes you drew earlier.
4. Copy the rectangle and paste a copy of it on the inlet pipe, next to the heat exchanger.
5. Drag the original rectangle over the outlet pipe, next to the reactor. Your drawing should look like the one in Figure 5.25.

Figure 5.25
Reactor, Heat Exchanger, and Pipes

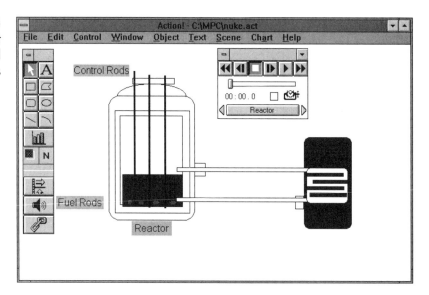

Next, we'll draw the turbine.

This is a simple drawing that consists only of a circle with a dot in its center:

1. Select the circle drawing tool from the Tool Palette.
2. Click on the fill color chip and choose white (or your background color) from the pop-up choices.

3. Draw a small circle on top of the outlet pipe, close to the heat exchanger. You can adjust the size of the circle that represents the turbine after it's drawn by selecting the circle and using one or more handles to drag the circle into a larger or smaller size.

4. Select black fill from the color fill chip.

5. Select the circle drawing tool and draw a small hub circle at the center of the turbine circle.

You can now use the line drawing tool to construct two small arrows to indicate the flow of steam and water through the system, as shown in Figure 5.26.

Figure 5.26
Completed Turbine with Arrows on Inlet and Outlet Lines

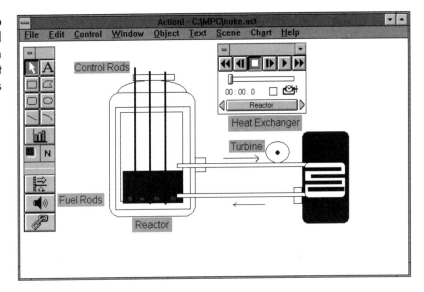

To draw the arrows:

1. Select the line drawing tool from the Tool Palette.

2. Draw a short horizontal line parallel to the outlet pipe, positioned close to the reactor.

3. Use the line drawing tool again to build a point for the small arrow on the right end of the line.

4. Repeat the arrow-building process for the inlet pipe, facing the arrow in the opposite direction.

Now we'll add two more light touches, just to fine-tune the drawing and to show you another drawing and editing technique with Action!:

1. Click on the line drawing color chip, and choose white (or the current background color).
2. Select the line drawing tool, then draw a short vertical line at the reactor end of the outlet pipe. Cover up the line that closes this pipe inside the reactor. When you're finished, you should have what appears to be an open pipe entering the reactor chamber.
3. Repeat this process on the inlet pipe, opening the end of the rectangle inside the reactor chamber.
4. Set the drawing color to black, then select the line drawing tool.
5. Create two short lines that run obliquely from the open end of the inlet pipe out to the left, closing up the inlet pipe to a nozzle that remains open.

Note that attention to drawing detail and refinement enhances your presentations and offers a subtle message about quality and believability of your material.

While we're at it, let's draw the cooling lake that is at the right side of the power plant image. This is a simple process, as you can see:

1. Click on the fill color chip and choose dark blue from the options presented. This should be the same blue you used as the background for the heat exchanger.
2. Select the circle drawing tool and draw a long, vertical oval to the right of the heat exchanger.
3. Select the round corner rectangle tool and draw a short thin rectangle at the top of the heat exchanger. This is the outlet pipe from the heat exchanger, which carries hot water to the lake.
4. Add another thin rectangle at a right angle to the first. This "pipe" should extend all the way to the top of the lake.
5. Repeat the process at the bottom of the heat exchanger to construct an inlet pipe, carrying cool water from the lake to the heat exchanger.

The nuclear power plant should look like the one in Figure 5.27.

Figure 5.27
Nearly
Completed
Nuclear Plant

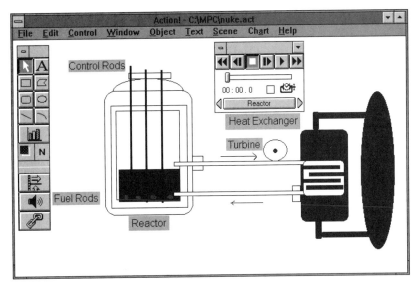

Now we'll add four more labels, construct links for them to four new scenes, and build the new scenes. First, the scenes:

1. Use Scene New Scene to add another scene at the end of this presentation.
2. Use Scene Edit Scene to display the Edit Scene dialog.
3. Change the scene name to "Turbine."
4. Pull down the menu at the end of the At End of Scene: field and choose "Go to Scene."
5. Pull down the menu at the right of the Scene: field and choose "Reactor" from the list.
6. Click on OK to accept these changes.

Now, repeat the previous six steps to add three more scenes: Heat Exchanger, Lake, and Summary. Make the same changes to the At End of Scene: and Scene: fields.

Next, we'll create buttons, name them, size them, and create links between each button and the scene created earlier for each button:

1. Use Object New Object Button to place a large rectangle labeled "Button" on the screen.
2. Double click on this new button to display the Edit Object dialog.

3. Name the button "Turbine."

4. Pull down the menu at the end of the Action: field, located just below the Link: field on this dialog.

5. Select Go to Link from this list.

6. Pull down the menu to the right of the Scene: field and select Turbine from the list.

7. Click on Highlight to tell Action! to highlight this button when it's depressed.

8. Click on OK to accept these button changes.

9. Grab a corner handle and size the bottom so that it's just the size of the word "Turbine."

10. Drag the button to a position on top of the turbine image.

11. Repeat the button creation process for buttons labeled "Heat Exchanger," "Lake," and "Summary."

You now have created all of the interactive buttons for this scene. All that remains is to build the scenes you have specified as the links with each of these buttons. The process is the same as we have used for previous scenes. We'll point you in the right direction here, offering some suggestions for scene design.

Turbine

First, let's build the Turbine scene. This scene could be as complex or as simple as you wish. The basic operation of a turbine is relatively simple, and since we've kept the descriptions of other power plant components simple, this is the best choice for this scene as well.

First the text. Somewhere on this scene you'll include a description of the turbine's operation. We used this text:

> **Turbine:** Pressurized steam from the reactor turns a huge turbine that is connected to a generator which, in turn, creates electricity.

As with the other linked scenes, this scene design can start with a copy (from the Reactor scene) of the major components under discussion:

1. Draw a selection box around the objects you want to include.

2. Use <u>E</u>dit <u>C</u>opy to place a copy of the objects on the Clipboard.

3. Select the Turbine scene from the pulldown list on the scene name bar of the Control Panel.

4. Press **Shift+Ins** to copy the objects into the new scene.

Now you can edit or enhance the images as you wish, to build the scene. One thing you might do with the Turbine scene is enhance the turbine drawing to include more detail.

Here's one possibility: Copy the heat exchanger, the turbine, and the inlet/outlet pipes from the Reactor scene to the Turbine scene. This gives you the main components that have to do with the Turbine discussion, including the Turbine and Heat Exchanger buttons, as shown in Figure 5.28.

Figure 5.28
Turbine Scene
with First Copies
of Components

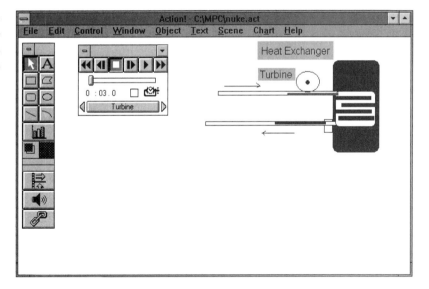

We'll leave these buttons as labels, and retain the link between the Heat Exchanger button and the Heat Exchanger scene so that the user can jump directly to the Heat Exchanger information from the Turbine scene if desired.

But on this scene, the Turbine is what we are interested in promoting and describing. First let's put the general descriptive text about the Turbine on the screen with a background screen, as we've done with previous scenes. One possibility is shown in Figure 5.29.

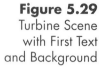

Figure 5.29
Turbine Scene
with First Text
and Background

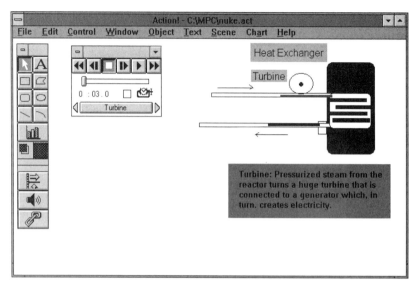

Now, after the text is presented, or during the time the text is being displayed, we can "grow" the turbine and provide more details about its operation. **Here's how to create that module:**

1. Make a copy of the turbine symbol and move it to the lower-middle area of the screen at time zero. It should be placed beneath the inlet and outlet pipes and to the left of the heat exchanger.

2. Double click on this copy to display the Edit Object dialog.

3. Pull down the Motion menu and choose Start/end.

4. Drag the Duration slider bar to about the five-second mark and click on OK. Action! displays a Done button along with two copies of the turbine with a directional arrow showing the movement from the original location to the new location. Fine-tune the positioning if necessary, and click on Done.

5. Use the Control Panel to rewind the scene and click on Play to see how the turbine image moves from its original location atop the outlet pipe to its new location in the lower-middle area of the screen.

Now we can create another turbine image to overlay the mid-screen copy.

By carefully adjusting the timing and positioning of this new image, we can make it appear as if the copy of the turbine image moves to the new location, then grows to magnify details:

1. Advance the scene timing with the Control Panel slider until the mid-screen copy of the turbine appears (about five seconds).

2. Click on the line draw color chip, choose black, then specify a white (or background color) background.

3. Select the circle drawing tool and use it to draw a much larger version of the turbine over the existing copy in the middle of the screen. Since this is a later object, it automatically achieves front status, covering up the original.

4. Click on the fill color tool and select black.

5. Select the circle drawing tool and add a center hub, or core, to the large turbine image. Your screen should now look something like the one in Figure 5.30.

Figure 5.30
New, Larger
Turbine Image

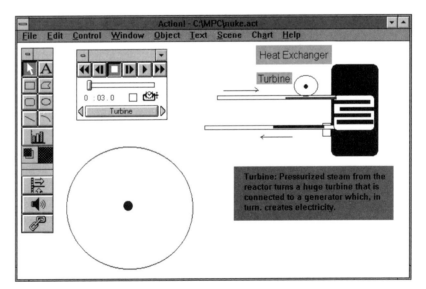

6. Select the polygon drawing tool. Use it to draw a turbine blade from the center hub to the outer rim of the Turbine. (Okay, this is a simplistic, "conceptual" drawing, not an engineering endeavor.) Our version looks like the one in Figure 5.31.

Figure 5.31
Large Turbine
with Single
Blade

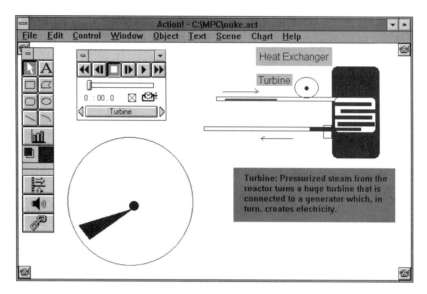

Draw this blade by starting in the hub and drawing a straight line to a position just shy of the outer rim. Then, draw a short horizontal line to the right and complete the polygon by drawing a line from this new point to the center hub.

Next, add several more blades around the turbine to show the internal structure of the device.

We suggest you use the arc drawing tool to add some arrows showing the direction of motion:

1. Select the black line color chip.
2. Select the arc drawing tool and position the pointer between any two blades.
3. Draw a short arc with the outside approximately parallel to the outside of the turbine circle.

 You can use two short arcs positioned end to end to produce a smooth curve.

4. Use the line drawing tool to add an arrow point to the arc, with the point indicating a counter-clockwise rotation. (Remember,

the steam from the reactor in our drawing is coming from the left and moving to the right, and the steam is entering from the bottom of the turbine housing, This would produce a counter-clockwise rotation.)

5. Add another arc-arrow to the inside of the turbine about 180 degrees to the right of the first arc.

Now add an inlet and outlet pipe for the turbine. This is really a "section" of the original outlet pipe from the reactor in the main drawing. **This pipe carries steam from the reactor to spin the turbines.**

1. Select the square rectangle drawing tool. Use it to draw a "pipe" at the lower-left side of the turbine. Use a background-color fill so the new pipe is covering the edge of the turbine.

2. Repeat Step 1 to draw an outlet pipe (the other end of the reactor outlet pipe) on the lower-right side of the turbine. Your drawing should look something like Figure 5.32.

Figure 5.32
Large Turbine with Inlet/Outlet Pipes and Directional Arrows

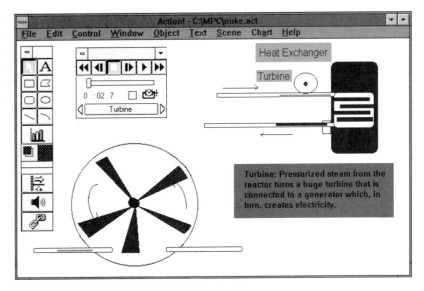

Now let's add some motion to show the flow of steam through the turbine:

1. Select the red line color and the red fill color from the pop-up boxes on the color chips.

2. Draw a small, thin red rectangle that fits inside the inlet pipe going into the turbine. Position it to the left of the pipe.

3. Double click on the new rectangle to display its Edit Object dialog.

4. Pull down the Motion menu and select Path Editor. Action! grays out other objects and replaces the Control Panel with a Done button and time slider.

5. Move the time slider to about 5 seconds.

6. Grab the red rectangle you just created and drag it to a position almost out of the outlet pipe on the right side of the drawing. When you drop it, Action! displays an arrow that indicates motion from the original position to the new position.

7. Click on Done to close the path editor. Now when the scene runs, the red line will move from the left to the right, through the turbine.

Now we'll suggest motion inside the turbine, again using the path editor:

1. Select one of the components of one of the arrows you drew previously inside the turbine.

2. Hold down the **Shift** key and select the remaining components of the arrow. This may be two arcs and two lines that form the point.

3. Use Object Group to group these objects.

4. Double click on this group to display its Edit Object dialog. Choose the Path Editor from the Motion menu.

5. Move the time slider bar to about 5 seconds.

6. Move the arrow object to a position about 90 degrees around the turbine pointing in the same direction the turbine spins.

7. Click on Done to return to the Edit Object dialog.

8. Click on OK in the Edit Object dialog to complete the operation.

9. Repeat Steps 1 through 8 to create an arrow on the other side of the turbine.

Finally, we want this scene to continue playing, showing the movement of fluid through the turbine. In Action!, you can do this with a loop.

To set a loop for this scene:

1. Play the scene and note what portion of it you want to repeat in a loop. You'll need to know the beginning and ending time of the loop.
2. Use <u>C</u>ontrol Set <u>L</u>oop to display the Set Loop dialog.
3. Enter the Start Time and End Time in the appropriate fields and click on OK.

Now when the scene plays, the arrows will move to their new positions, indicating rotation of the turbine blades, and this part of the scene will continue until the scene is canceled or the user clicks on an interactive button.

You can let the simple text shown earlier carry the scene, or you can display additional text that describes steam flow and turbine operation. Also, we have shown only the turbine. Remember that the turbine is only one part of this area of the nuclear power plant. You must have a generator connected in some way to the turbine to actually generate any electricity. An excellent enhancement for this module would be to add a shaft to the center of the turbine and draw a generator, add some power lines, and show the movement of electricity down the lines to homes and businesses.

Such an enhancement would require a lot more work and the addition of one or two modules, but it would help the user of your application relate the information being presented to some real-life situations. Such "relations" are excellent additions to your presentations. Remember, the idea is to make the information being presented as clear and visually interesting as possible, so anything you can do to achieve these goals, the better the presentation.

Be sure to use <u>S</u>cene Edit <u>S</u>cene to tell Action! what to do at the end of the scene. You'll want to specify Go To Scene and choose Reactor from the Scene: pulldown menu.

Heat Exchanger

By now you should have considerable experience using the Action! tools. Designing a screen to explain the operation of the heat exchanger should be a piece of cake.

First, return to the Reactor scene and advance the time until all of the components in this scene are displayed. Use object grouping or draw a selection box around the objects you want to include in the Heat Exchanger scene.

Jump to the Heat Exchanger screen and copy the group from the Clipboard. Now you're ready to go to work on this next scene.

Again, with programs such as Action!, you have a broad range of options in how you design a given scene. Use what you have learned to this point and your own imagination to create a scene that describes the heat exchanger.

You likely will want to include a block of text somewhere during this scene. Here's what we used:

> **Heat Exchanger:** Water from a nearby lake is pumped into the heat exchanger. Pipes immersed in the lake water carry steam into the heat exchanger where the much cooler lake water converts the steam back to water. This water is then pumped back to the reactor. The radioactive steam and water inside the pipes never come in contact with the lake water.

This is one module where very little happens, at least not obviously. However, we can come up with some ideas for action objects to enhance this basic screen. We designed a scene that used some of the same techniques applied in the Turbine scene, namely moving a colored rectangle along the inlet and outlet pipes. We also designed some small arrows to represent the heat being pulled out of the coil and into the cooling water. The composite screen looks like the one in Figure 5.33.

Remember that steam and very hot water that leaves the turbine on the top pipe enters the heat exchanger at the top, flows through the coil inside the cooling water and out the bottom of the coil relatively cool.

We'll show this by moving a red rectangle along the pipe into the heat exchanger, and show a blue rectangle moving out of the heat exchanger along the output pipe back toward the reactor:

Figure 5.33
Composite Heat
Exchanger
Screen

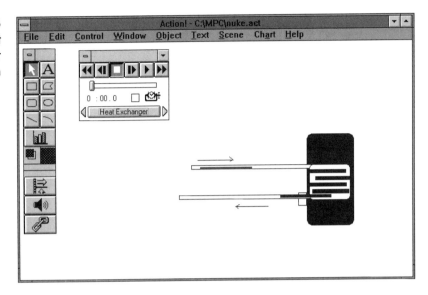

1. Select red from the border color chip on the Tool Palette.

2. Select red from the fill color chip on the Tool Palette.

3. Choose the rounded corner rectangle tool from the Tool Palette.

4. Create a thin, red rectangle that fits inside the top pipe going into the heat exchanger. Position this rectangle at the left end of the pipe, away from the heat exchanger.

5. Select blue from the border color chip on the Tool Palette.

6. Select blue from the fill color chip on the Tool Palette.

7. Choose the rounded corner rectangle tool from the Tool Palette.

8. Create a thin, blue rectangle that fits inside the bottom pipe coming out of the heat exchanger. Position this rectangle at the right end of the pipe, partially into the heat exchanger.

Let's enhance the drawing with a couple of arrows that show the direction of water flow. We can see this as the red and blue boxes move along the pipes, but arrows that emphasize this won't hurt:

1. Select the black outline color chip from the Tool Palette.

2. Choose the line drawing tool and use it to draw a short horizontal line above the top pipe going into the heat exchanger and at about the mid-point of this pipe.

3. Draw another horizontal line below the bottom pipe at about the same left-right position as the previous one.

4. Use the line drawing tool to build arrow points on each of these lines, a right-facing point on the top line and a left-facing point on the bottom line.

Now we'll add some motion to these objects to show movement of the hot and cold fluid through the system:

1. Double click on the red rectangle to display its Edit Object dialog.

2. Drag the duration bar to about 10 seconds.

3. Select Path Editor from the pulldown Motion menu.

4. Drag the red rectangle along the inlet pipe and into the heat exchanger.

5. Click on Done.

6. Click on OK in the Edit Object dialog.

7. Repeat Steps 1 through 6 with the blue rectangle on the outlet pipe.

As with any Action! scene, you can add music or other sound to any of these objects, as well as narration or additional text to the scene. The key to successful presentations is to use your imagination to fit your audience, the topic, and the facilities you have at your disposal.

Lake

For the Lake scene, we used one of the simple but useful features of Action! to add some motion to this basically static scene. As before, use the grouping technique to copy the lake and its supply and outlet pipes (and perhaps the heat exchanger) from the Reactor scene to the Lake scene. How much of the original scene you copy depends on your ultimate scene design.

Here's the text we used for this scene:

Lake: A nearby lake provides water to cool the steam and convert it back into water. In emergencies, lake water can be pumped directly into the reactor to help cool it and prevent a meltdown.

To show some form of motion while the reader views the descriptive text (or listens to the narration, if any), we'll specify a shimmer action for each of the components in the heat exchanger-to-lake loop.

We copied the heat exchanger and the lake, then erased all of the coil and pipe components inside the heat exchanger. All that remains is the rectangular blue outline of the heat exchanger and the large oval of the lake connected by a top and bottom supply pipe, as shown in Figure 5.34.

Figure 5.34
Lake Scene
with Basic
Components

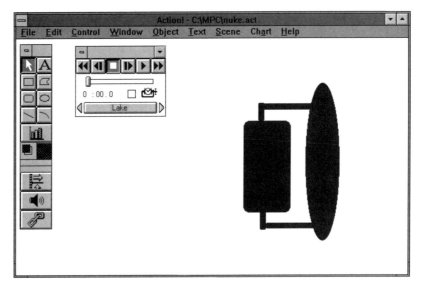

Now, let's add some motion:

1. Double click on the vertical pipe at the top of the heat exchanger to display the Edit Object dialog. (The heat exchanger-to-lake loop consists of six components: a vertical pipe at the top of the heat exchanger, a horizontal pipe at the top of the heat exchanger, the lake, a horizontal pipe at the bottom of the lake, and a vertical pipe at the bottom of the heat exchanger.)

2. Choose Hold from the pulldown menu in the phase field of this dialog.

3. Pull down the Light Effect menu and choose Shimmer Up.

4. Click on OK.

Although the Action! manual implies that you can specify a color for the Shimmer motion, and although the Action! Help file says you can, and although a color chip appears on the Edit Object dialog when you select Shimmer, you can't do it. You just can't do it. The color specification does work, however, for the Sparkle selections on this dialog.

5. Repeat this process with each of the pipes in the loop. For the top horizontal pipe, specify Shimmer Right in the Hold phase; choose Shimmer Left for the lower horizontal pipe and choose Shimmer Up for the lower vertical pipe.

Now, save the file and run this scene. The lake and its associated components appear and the blue water appears to move out of the heat exchanger at the top, through the lake, and back into the heat exchanger at the bottom.

Notice that we don't need to specify a loop for this action because we specified action in the Hold phase of the scene. If you want the "shimmer phase" of this scene to last longer, specify a longer duration time in the Edit Object dialog for each object in the scene.

Don't forget to provide the user a way out of this scene. Use Object New Object Button to create an interactive button to jump back to the Reactor scene.

Summary

What will you do with the Summary scene? Again, the final decision is up to you, but we'll offer one possibility in this section.

Let's start with this summary text:

Summary: Modern nuclear reactors are really steam engines that use uranium as fuel. Inside the reactor, the close proximity of the enormous amounts of uranium in the fuel rods causes a nuclear reaction. The nuclear reaction (and resulting heat) is regulated by control rods. When the control rods are fully inserted, they absorb the neutrons given off by the uranium fuel rods, preventing any nuclear reaction. As the control rods are drawn out of the reactor, neutrons from one uranium pellet are free to strike other uranium pellets, causing more neutrons to be released. This escalating effect is called a nuclear reaction.

The nuclear reaction generates heat and turns the reactor water into steam. The steam shoots out of the reactor and turns a turbine connected to a generator to create electricity. The steam then is carried through pipes into the heat exchanger where the cooler lake water surrounding the pipes causes the steam to condense and convert back to water. The water is pumped back into the reactor to become steam again.

This summary text has several identifiable sections that you can use to build a scene that touches on the major issues you've already presented in other scenes. We're not going to show you every step required to do this, but we will point you in the right direction.

First, let's break down the text so you can see how we're thinking about designing this summary:

General: Modern nuclear reactors are really steam engines that use uranium as fuel.

Reactor: Inside the reactor, the close proximity of the enormous amounts of uranium in the fuel rods causes a nuclear reaction. The nuclear reaction (and resulting heat) is regulated by control rods.

Control: When the control rods are fully inserted, they absorb the neutrons given off by the uranium fuel rods, preventing any nuclear reaction. As the control rods are drawn out of the reactor, neutrons from one uranium pellet are free to strike other uranium pellets, causing more neutrons to be released. This escalating effect is called a nuclear reaction.

Turbine: The nuclear reaction generates heat and turns the reactor water into steam. The steam shoots out of the reactor and turns a turbine connected to a generator to create electricity.

Heat Xcgr: The steam then is carried through pipes into the heat exchanger where lake water surrounding the pipes causes the steam to condense and convert back to water. The water is pumped back into the reactor to become steam again.

So, here's one scene scenario you might consider:

1. Place a text box at the top of the screen with the general information.

2. Draw the reactor and pop up the Reactor text next to it. Cause the fuel rods to appear as the text discusses the heat of the reaction.

3. Drop in the control rods, then draw them out as the text discusses how they control the rate of the nuclear reaction.

4. Add the turbine and its associated pipes, and display the Turbine text.

5. Add the heat exchanger and its pipes, dropping in the text to describe it.

6. Draw the lake and show the flow of cooling water through the heat exchanger as the appropriate text is displayed.

How do you do this? We've demonstrated all of these techniques in previous sections, but in general, here is the process:

1. Create individual text objects (Object New Object Text) for each of the text sections. Place a colored box behind this text if you wish.

2. Use the master power plant drawing in the Reactor scene to copy individual components: the reactor, the control rods, the turbine, the heat exchanger, and the lake. Insert these components in the Summary scene by placing them on the screen where you want them to appear and adjusting the timing on the Timeline.

3. Use the Edit Object dialog to specify motion, sound, and other attributes for each object.

4. Create a button to let the user exit this summary scene.

There are some other things you might design into this scene for enhancement. For example, you could create a link between each object on the screen and a few lines of additional text, so the user could view the summary screen, then pop up some additional information or jump to another scene. You could create a link between the turbine and the turbine scene, for instance.

And, of course, you could add narration to this or any other scene. Audio is an excellent way to enhance the attention-getting aspects of your scenes and to help the user retain more of the information in your scenes.

In addition, video is a powerful tool for presentations like this one. In the following sections, we'll discuss briefly how to add narration and video to your Action! presentations.

Adding Audio

Action! provides fairly strong support for audio in your presentations, but you have to use other products to produce the sounds, music, or narration you want to use with Action!. How you create these audio files in the first place depends on what type of sound card and other multimedia facilities you have available.

And, you have to capture or convert the sound into a format that Action! can use, such as:

- MIDI (*.MID) Files
- WAVE (*.WAV) Files
- CD Audio Input

Once you have the source audio you want to use, you can attach audio to an Action! object, or you can import sound that appears alone on the Timeline so you can place it anywhere in a scene, perhaps to use as background music.

Suppose you are using a Creative Labs SoundBlaster card—one of the main sound cards that Ultimedia Tools Series CD-ROM is designed to use.

Here's the process for capturing narration sound and getting it ready for importing into an Action! presentation:

1. Attach a microphone to the SoundBlaster microphone input connector on the back of your computer.
2. At the DOS prompt, enter the command **VREC**, then the filename.

Make sure you have specified a PATH that points to this utility in your SBPRO subdirectory, or that you have set this directory as the current directory before issuing this command. The filename specification can also include a path.

The result is a file in the directory you specified that is stored in the SoundBlaster *.VOC format. The VREC command automatically adds the .VOC extension and uses the Voice sound format.

However, you can't import SoundBlaster voice files into Action!. To do this, you need to convert the *.VOC file to a WAVE (*.WAV) file. To do so, use the following command at the DOS prompt:

VOC2WAV sourcefile targetfile

The **sourcefile** specification is the file in Voice format and the **targetfile** specification is the file and path you want to use for the WAVE file. Now you have a file in WAVE format that Action! can use.

To use a WAVE file with an Action! scene:

1. Make the scene you want to use the WAVE file with the current scene.
2. Click on the audio icon on the Tool Palette.
3. To attach the sound to an object, click on that object; to make the sound file a "floating" part of the scene, click anywhere on the presentation window that does not contain an object. The Import dialog shown in Figure 5.35 is displayed.

Figure 5.35
Import Audio
Dialog

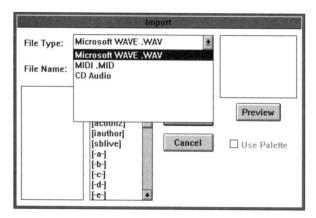

4. Select the directory that contains the WAVE file you want to import into Action!.
5. Choose the filename from the list at the left of the dialog.
6. Click on Preview to listen to the sound before importing it.
7. Click on Import to bring the sound into Action!, attaching it to the scene or to a specific object in the scene if you specified one.

Now you can use the Timeline to adjust sound placement to coordinate the sound file with other objects in the scene. If the sound file is attached to a specific object, then the sound output coincides with the appearance and placement of the object.

Adding Video

You can use video to enhance presentations with Action! (if you're using version 2.5 or later) in the same way you use audio. Again, the video clip you want to use with Action! must have been generated through another application and saved to disk. Then you can use Action! facilities to manipulate the video files.

Like the audio files we described earlier, video information is imported into Action! with the Import dialog. Action! supports video files from:

• QuickTime for Windows
• Microsoft Video for Windows
• Autodesk Animator

as well as other products that can save in *.AVI or other compatible formats.

Treat imported video like any other object that can be moved along the Timeline.

Other Features and Facilities

There are a few other features supported by Action! that we haven't talked about. One is support for MacroMind Director files imported from the Macintosh environment. Director files have to be converted to PC format, then you can use the Import dialog to use these *.MMM files as Action! presentation objects.

Director files are animation files, a number of which are included with the retail version of Action!. For example, you get a spinning globe, a moving alarm clock, moving telephones, printers, gears, and more. These objects can easily be included in Action! scenes.

There also is a CONVERT program that can help you convert among graphics formats, and you can import existing presentations from other software packages, including:

- Lotus Freelance
- Harvard Graphics
- Aldus Persuasion
- Microsoft PowerPoint

Action! is a capable, though potentially complicated product. It won't do everything some other products can, but it is easier to use than most.

With that said, we urge you to be imaginative as you work with Action! (or any other presentation product). Even when the way to do what you want isn't obvious, you can probably do it, if you consider the problem from all sides. And, Action! has enough power and enough tools to handle a wide variety of development situations.

Building Multimedia Presentations with IconAuthor

THE BASICS

IconAuthor is an unusual product, one that may be the forerunner of the way all custom computer applications will work before long. This program is a developmental tool in much the same way that Borland's dBase or Paradox databases are tools. With IconAuthor, you "program" applications by specifying the built-in application components you want to use and the order you want to use them by selecting screen components, importing graphics, adding sound and narration, and so on. So far, IconAuthor sounds kind of like a database application, right?

But there the similarity ends. IconAuthor is an *object-oriented* tool that lets you create complex program applications by using objects you select from a programming library. Many of these objects have built-in instructions that tell them what functions to perform. Your job is to customize object behavior, create objects of your own as necessary, and to arrange the objects in the proper order.

The result is a complex program that includes branching, input from the user, data storage, and support for graphics, sound, and motion video. And you do all this "programming" by using Windows-like dialog boxes and dragging objects to different parts of the screen.

In this chapter, we'll introduce you to the concept of *object authoring*, and show you how to use the specific object-oriented tools contained in IconAuthor.

Understanding IconAuthor

IconAuthor falls into the *authoring* software category, and is designed to help you build interactive multimedia applications. At its basic level, IconAuthor is a programming language, which you use to build a series of complex instructions that tell the computer, among other things:

- What to display on the screen
- Where and how to display it
- To accept input from the user and how to handle it
- How to play sound and video files
- How to display graphics files
- How to store information from the user or computed by the program

Although you use IconAuthor to "program" applications, you don't really need to know how to program in a conventional programming language, such as C or COBOL. While some programming experience will help you to understand some of the IconAuthor concepts—such as branching, input, variables, and data storage—the icon-based design makes it relatively easy for even inexperienced users to design and build complex applications.

When you load IconAuthor, the screen shown in Figure 6.1 is displayed—a typical Windows-based application with tools and symbols that you access with a mouse.

Figure 6.1
Opening
IconAuthor
Screen

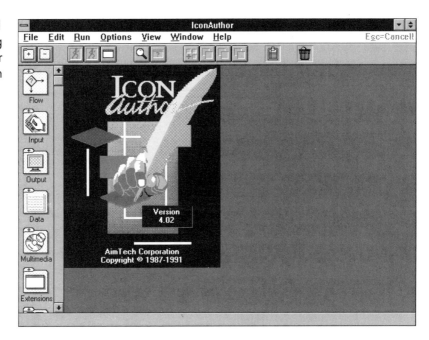

Instead of entering conventional program code that controls program flow, you use a series of objects that contain built-in instructions. The short program sample in Figure 6.2 shows how a typical database program might look. Figure 6.3 shows a sample screen from IconAuthor.

Notice that with the conventional database, the programmer must tell the program every step, and every possible event must be considered and written into the code. With IconAuthor's object programming, however, you use objects that already contain these program modules.

So, for example, instead of writing a long series of statements to tell the computer to display some menu items, you simply select the menu icon from the library and drag it into the position where you want it to appear.

Figure 6.2
Conventional
Database
Program
Fragment

```
* Set display characteristics - depends on hardware
IF ISCOLOR()
  c_normal = "W+/B,GR+/R,B"
  c_pop   = "B/W,GR+/R,W+/R"
  red    = "R/W"
  blue   = "B/W"
  lt_blue = "W/BG"
ELSE
  STORE "W+/N,N/W" TO c_normal, c_pop
  STORE "W"  TO red, blue
  STORE "N/W" TO lt_blue
ENDIF

* Define popup
DO Main_def

* Display menu and loop for choices
**mstrloop = .T.
DO WHILE BAR() <> 13
  SET COLOR TO &c_normal.
  CLEAR
  DO Title
  SET COLOR TO &c_pop.
```

Figure 6.3
Sample
IconAuthor
Application
Screen

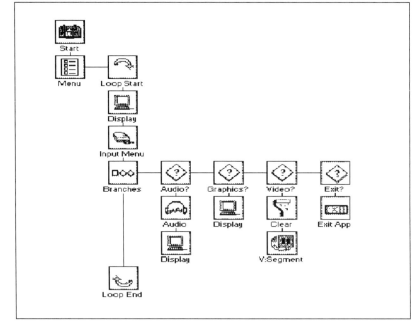

In addition to the authoring component, IconAuthor includes additional utilities to help you build and present your applications, including:

- A Presentation System to run the applications you create with the authoring system
- A Smart Object editor to change or enhance the objects you use as part of an IconAuthor application
- A debugging utility (IAScope) to help you find and fix program problems
- A graphics editor (Graphics Editor) that you can use to design and create still or motion images to use within your presentations
- An animation editor (IconAnimate) that you use to write scripts to animate graphics images
- A video editor (Video Editor) that you use to preview analog or digital video clips for use in your presentations
- RezSolution, a graphics utility that changes the resolution of bitmap graphics so they can run on almost any target system

Each of these utilities appears within the IconAuthor application window once you have installed the package in Windows. Figure 6.4 shows a typical Windows installation of IconAuthor.

Figure 6.4
Windows
Screen Showing
IconAuthor
Application
Window and
Tools

In the next section, we'll show you what each of the IconAuthor tools is and how to use them to build your own applications. Then in Chapter 7, we'll show you how to design and build a sample application step by step with IconAuthor.

Using IconAuthor

If you want to try some hands-on work with IconAuthor without having to learn each program component, turn now to the tutorial in Chapter 7. Use the information in this chapter as a reference during the tutorial process.

To help you follow this discussion, use your Ultimedia Tools Series CD-ROM disk and load the Working Module for IconAuthor. You can then view the screens and tools as they're discussed here.

To load IconAuthor from your Ultimedia Tools Series CD-ROM disk, do the following:

1. From the DOS prompt, make the drive that is your CD-ROM reader the default by typing the drive letter, a colon, and pressing **Enter**.
2. Type **UTSDOS**, then press **Enter**.
3. Click on the Produce Selector button.
4. Click on the Down Arrow at the bottom of the scroll bar to display the IconAuthor button.
5. Select the IconAuthor button, then click on Working Model.
6. Press **Y** when the program asks if you want to copy files to the hard disk. After a few moments, the opening screen, shown in Figure 6.1, should be displayed.

In Figure 6.5, we've labeled the various components so you can refer to the names for screen areas, components, and tools throughout the rest of this discussion.

To get a quick look at what a typical IconAuthor application looks like under development:

1. Click on <u>F</u>ile and select Open from the main IconAuthor menu.
2. Click the Down Arrow on the scroll bar to the right of the Files window until TUTORIAL.IW is displayed.

Figure 6.5
IconAuthor
Opening Screen
with Labels

Title Bar

Menu Bar

Ribbon

Icon Library

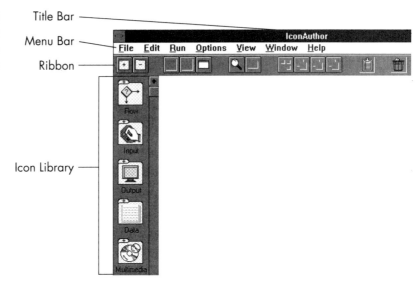

3. Select TUTORIAL.IW and click on OK, or double click on the filename TUTORIAL.IW.

4. Ignore the ominous error message about TUTORIAL.PTH file not found. This simply means that IconAuthor is using the default path to files, not that anything is wrong.

5. Click on OK to clear the IconAuthor Evaluation dialog with the error message. A *structure* screen like the one in Figure 6.6 is displayed. This screen is called the structure screen or the structure window.

To get an idea of how IconAuthor uses objects to build an application, use the scroll bars on the structure screen to view some of the icons in this presentation. Notice that each icon contains a name and a picture representing what it does. And, while you can't tell it from a cursory look at these objects, each one also contains some program code that forms a module within the finished application.

To get some more information about what one of these icons contains, move the *writing hand* cursor over the Display icon to the right and beneath it. You should see the following text displayed on the IconAuthor status line at the bottom of the main screen:

2,3: Display,bitmap,MM_MENU.BMP,0,0,squareiris,out,medium

Figure 6.6
IconAuthor
TUTORIAL.IW
Structure
Display

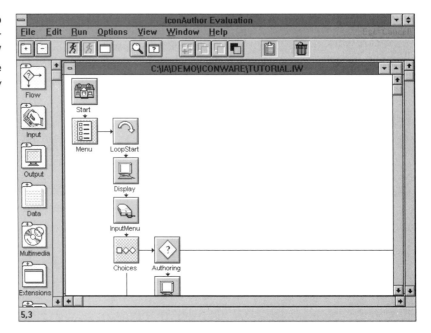

The Display icon is typical of a reusable tool that establishes some user-definable parameters. When placed in the flow chart in this way, the Display icon tells the computer what information to display and where to display it. Table 6.1 shows the interpretation of the status display associated with the Display icon in the Tutorial application.

Table 6.1 The Status Display Messages Associated with the Display Icon

Statement	Meaning
2,3:	Icon Number and Position
Display	Icon Name
bitmap	Type of data being displayed
MM_MENU.BMP	Name of file to be displayed
0	Horizontal display position
0	Vertical display position
squareiris	Effect to use in presenting data
out	Direction of effect (out or in)
medium	Effect speed (slow, medium, fast)

The information in this display is called the *content* of the icon. This is variable information that you can change to affect what information is displayed and the way information called for in the icon is presented. You make these changes to icon objects through the Content Editor.

Pull up the Content Editor for the Display icon by double clicking on the icon. The dialog box shown in Figure 6.7 is displayed.

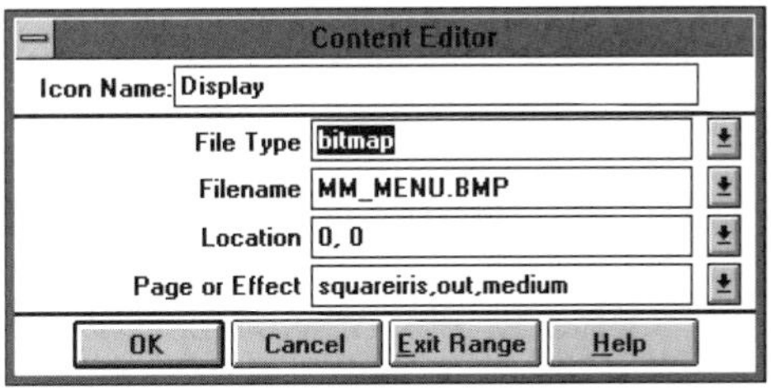

Figure 6.7
Content Editor
Dialog for
Display Icon

Now you can see readily where the information on the status display for this icon comes from. It's presented on the status line in the same order as it appears in the Content Editor dialog.

Notice that each field of this dialog (except the Icon Name field) includes a Down Arrow attached to the right of the field. This arrow indicates that more information is available for you to select.

For example, click on the Down Arrow to the right of the File Type: field to see the display shown in Figure 6.8.

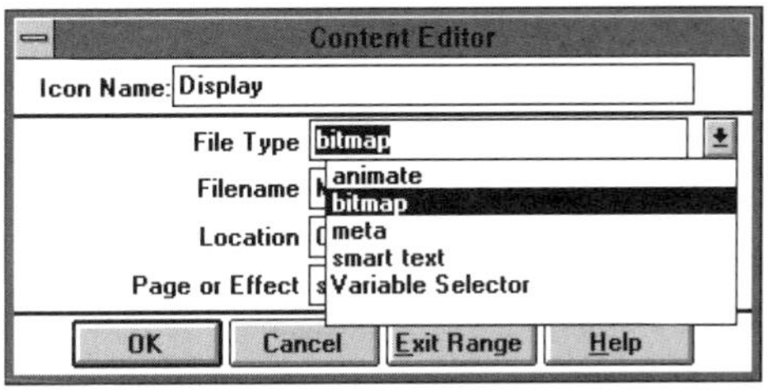

Figure 6.8
File Type
Pulldown list
from Content
Editor

The bitmap type is highlighted because that's what already is in this display icon. Don't worry about the other formats. We'll discuss some of these later.

Where do the icons used to build applications come from? They're stored in the Icon Library, displayed at the left of the screen, as you saw in Figure 6.5. Notice that all of these icons are shown as yellow file folders. Each folder tab contains a plus sign (+), indicating that there is more information inside the folder.

For example, click on the Output icon to display the 14 icons contained in this folder. Use the scroll bars to display all of them; one of these is the Display icon.

To see how simple it is to add information to the structure window:

1. Grab the display icon and drag it into the structure window. Position it so that it overlaps one of the existing icons, then drop it. The new display icon is inserted into the flow chart at this location and it's automatically selected, which is indicated by it turning blue.

2. Move the cursor anywhere inside the structure box and click once to deselect the icon. It should turn yellow, indicating that this icon requires some content, but that none has been specified.

In fact, notice that the icons in the structure window are different colors. These colors are used to denote the type of icon and its state, as shown in Table 6.2.

Table 6.2 Icon Color Codes	
Icon Color	**Meaning**
Green	Composite icon with multiple components
Gray	Single icon or icon that requires and has had content added
Blue	Icon is selected in structure window
Yellow	Icon requires content

As you saw earlier, you add content to an icon by double clicking on it to access the Content Editor. Each icon that requires content has an associated Content Editor. The information included in the Editor dialog depends on the type of icon you're editing.

So, for example, the Display icon has the Content Editor screen shown in Figure 6.7, while the Input icon has a Content Editor dialog like the one shown in Figure 6.9.

Figure 6.9
Input Icon
Content Editor
Dialog

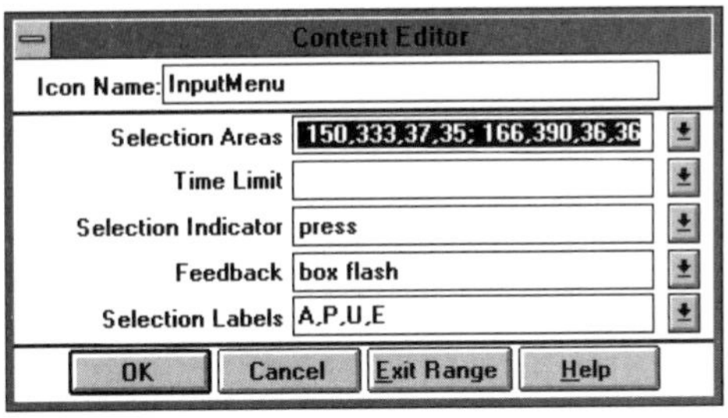

This is a more complicated dialog than the one for the Display icon, but you don't have to worry about the specifics of it because you use more icons and prompt screens to build the information contained in this dialog. (We'll show you how to do that in Chapter 7.)

Using Commands and Menus

You've already learned quite a bit about the IconAuthor user interface by moving icons into the structure window and using the Content Editor. These operations are typical of everything you do within IconAuthor, even when you're performing complex tasks.

Let's look again at the main IconAuthor screen with labels, shown in Figure 6.10.

Notice that there are six major areas of the IconAuthor screen:

- Title Bar
- Menu Bar
- Ribbon
- Icon Library
- Status Line (visible at the bottom of Figure 6.10 but without data, since no application is loaded)
- Structure Window

In this section, we'll provide a reference to each of these major sections.

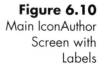

Figure 6.10
Main IconAuthor
Screen with
Labels

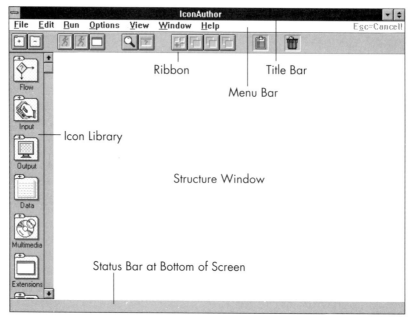

Title Bar

The Title Bar serves the same function in most Windows applications: to display the path and filename of the item currently loaded when the structure window is displayed full screen. If you reduce the structure window (IconAuthor default), then the Title Bar shows only the following:

IconAuthor Evaluation

If you click on the Up Arrow at the upper-right corner of a structure window to enlarge the window, however, then the full path and filename information is displayed on the Title Bar. When you load and select the TUTORIAL.IW application, for example, the Title Bar shows something like this:

IconAuthor Evaluation-
C:\TOOLSHOP\DEMO\ICONWARE\TUTORIAL.IW)

Notice that each time you load a new application, IconAuthor defaults to a reduced structure window, which automatically removes the path and filename information from the Title Bar.

Menu Bar

The Menu Bar is a typical Windows-compatible menu that offers seven main commands:

- File
- Edit
- Run
- Options
- View
- Window
- Help

Each of these commands contains subcommands, which we'll describe in the next section.

File

The File command contains many subcommands familiar to Windows users, as well as some commands unique to IconAuthor. The File menu subcommands are shown in Table 6.3.

Table 6.3 The File Menu Subcommands	
Menu Selection	**Description**
New	Start a new file
Open	Open an existing file
Save (Ctrl+S)	Save current file under current name
Save As	Save current file under new name
Application	Additional commands for applications
Auto Save	Saves applications at specified interval
Copy	Copy application for distribution to other users
Install	Install application after copy
Library	Additional commands for library files
Open	Load a different library file
Save	Save a library file
Save As	Save library file to another name
Delete	Delete an application or other object
	continued

Table 6.3 The File Menu Subcommands (*Continued*)	
Menu Selection	**Description**
Page Setup	Format a page
Print	Print an application or other object
Printer Setup	Set printer parameters
Exit	Exit IconAuthor

Edit

With the exception of the last three items in Table 6.4, the Edit menu is Microsoft Windows all the way.

Table 6.4 The Edit Menu Commands	
Menu Selection	**Description**
Undo (Alt+Backspace)	Reverse the last operation
Cut (Shift+Del)	Remove selection to the Clipboard
Copy (Ctrl+Ins)	Copy selection to the Clipboard
Paste (Shift+Ins)	Insert the Clipboard data at cursor
Clear (Del)	Delete selection
Select All	Select all text or icons
Copy To	Copy selection to new application
Paste From	Insert data from another application
Find (Ctrl+F)	Locate an icon in current structure
Find Next (F3)	Locate next occurrence of an icon
Application	Additional commands for applications
Compress Composite (Ctrl+C)	Hide all of the icons in a composite icon, displaying only the lead icon
Make Composite (Ctrl+O)	Convert a selected range of icons into a composite icon
Add Composite to Library	Add a composite icon to the Custom folder of the icon library
Disable Selection (Ctrl+D)	Disable selected range of icons; disabled icons do not execute in an application
Enable Selection (Ctrl+E)	Reverse the Disable command to make a range of icons executable

continued

Table 6.4 The Edit Menu Commands (*Continued*)

Menu Selection	Description
Enable All	Enable all icons within a structure; reverses the Disable command for the entire structure
Add Content (Ctrl+A)	Open the Content Editor for a selected icon
Clear Application Variables	Clear any application variables generated during a previous run
Library	Additional commands for library files
Expand Categories	Open all library folders
Compress Categories	Closes all library folders
Add Content	Open Content Editor of a selected icon in the library
Build	Attach the selected Library icon to the cursor so you can move the icon into the structure for placement within the application
Remove Icon	Remove the selected icon from the library
Variables	
Clear Application Variables	Remove any data from application variables
Set Path From File	Establish custom path (*.PTH file)

Run

The Run command executes the current application from the beginning or from the location of the cursor, establishes default setup, and loads several utilities (Table 6.5).

Table 6.5 The Options for the Run Command

Menu Selection	Description
Application from Top (Ctrl+R)	Run the current application from the Start icon
Application from Selected	Run the current application, starting at the selected icon instead of the Start icon
Default Window Setup	Establish the default window configuration for an application; use this selection to run an application in a resizable window, for example, or full screen

continued

Table 6.5 The Options for the Run Command (*Continued*)

Menu Selection	Description
Editors	Display editor selection list
Animation	Create, edit, and save animation files
Graphics	Create, edit, and save graphics files
RezSolution	Alter the resolution of graphics images
SmartText	Create smart text files
Video	View video files from laser disk or video tape
1 Calculator	Run Windows Calculator application
2 Clipboard	Display contents of Windows Clipboard
3 Notepad	Run the Windows Notepad text editor

Options

The Options pulldown menu offers nine additional features unique to IconAuthor (Table 6.6).

Table 6.6 The Options Menu Commands

Menu Selection	Description
Structure Setup	Display the Structure Setup dialog shown in Figure 6.11 to customize icon characteristics when they are displayed in the structure window
Library Setup	Display the Library Setup dialog shown in Figure 6.12, which lets you specify how icons are stored in the library
Color Scheme	Display the Color Scheme dialog shown in Figure 6.13 to let you customize the colors used to show the current state of icons
Video Setup	Display the Video Setup dialog shown in Figure 6.14 to let you configure IconAuthor for a specific video player
Overlay Setup	Display the Setup Overlay dialog shown in Figure 6.15, which is used to specify a particular video overlay card
Audio Setup	Display the Setup Audio dialog shown in Figure 6.16, which is used to specify a particular audio (sound) card for use with IconAuthor

continued

Table 6.6 The Options Menu Commands (*Continued*)	
Menu Selection	**Description**
Add Content On Build	A toggle that causes the Content Editor to open automatically each time an icon is added to the structure; when enabled, a check mark is displayed beside this menu choice
Backup Structure On Save	A toggle that causes IconAuthor to create a backup application file when the selected application is saved; when enabled, a check mark appears beside this menu choice
Confirm Clear	A toggle that tells IconAuthor to ask you to confirm anytime you use the Clear command from the Edit menu or if you drag an icon to the Trashcan. The Trashcan icon is used to "throw away" or delete objects

Figure 6.11
Structure Setup
Dialog

Figure 6.12
Library Setup
Dialog

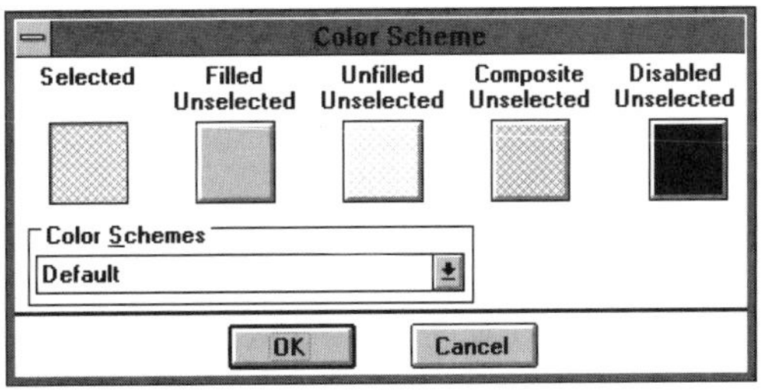

Figure 6.13
Color Scheme
Dialog

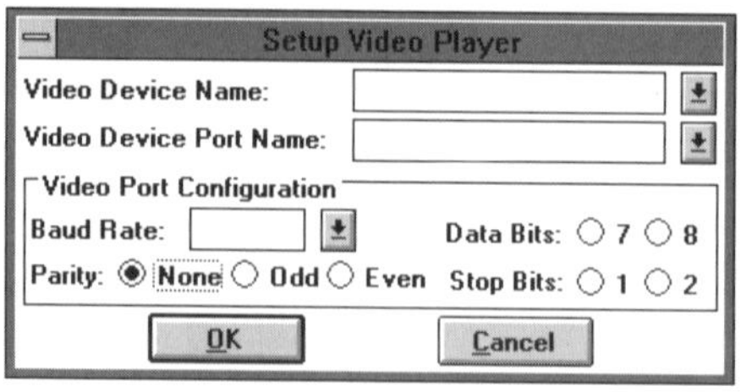

Figure 6.14
Video Setup
Dialog

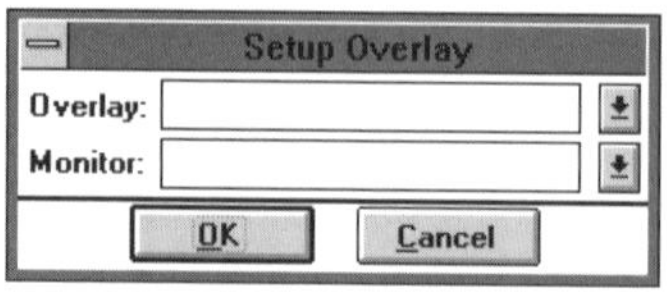

Figure 6.15
Setup Overlay
Dialog

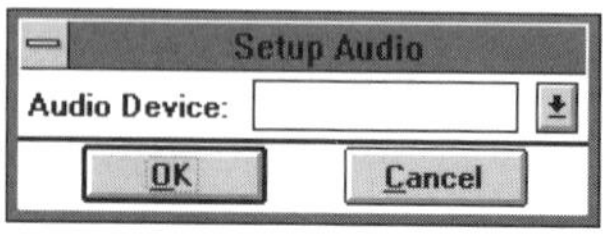

Figure 6.16
Setup Audio
Dialog

View

The View menu determines how IconAuthor will display certain features on the screen (Table 6.7).

Menu Selection	Description
Library	A toggle that determines whether IconAuthor will display the library icons at the left of the main screen; when enabled, a check mark is displayed beside this menu item
Ribbon	A toggle that determines whether IconAuthor will display the ribbon under the Menu Bar; when enabled, a check mark is displayed beside this menu item
Status	A toggle that determines whether IconAuthor will display object information on the status line at the bottom of the IconAuthor screen; when enabled, a check mark is displayed beside this menu item
Zoom	Determine the relative size of the icons displayed in the structure window; reducing the icon size enables you to view more of the application flow chart at a time
Window Contents	Determine what information will be displayed in the current window; the choices are Structure (the default), User Variables, System Variables, and Path Variables

Table 6.7 The View Menu Commands

Window

The Window menu is typical of a Windows application, with a couple of additions (Table 6.8).

Table 6.8 The Window Menu Commands	
Menu Selection	**Description**
Tile (Shift+F4)	Display open structure windows side by side so that each window is completely visible
Cascade (Shift+F5)	Display open structure windows in an overlapping format, similar to a deck of cards
Close All	Close all open document windows; if unsaved changes are contained in any file, you'll be asked to confirm the close or to save the file
Duplicate	Create a duplicate of the active document window
Show File Path	A toggle that causes IconAuthor to display the entire path as well as filenames in the Title Bars of applications

Help

Help is a Windows-compatible application that offers additional information on most aspects of IconAuthor. Simply click on Help and then select the desired topic.

Ribbon

The Ribbon displays 15 icons (13 in sampler) that represent tools you can use to manipulate other IconAuthor features (see Table 6.9).

Table 6.9 The Tools Available in the Ribbon		
Icon	**Name**	**Function**
	Open Library Folders	Show all folders
	Close Library Folders	Show only title folders

continued

Icon	Name	Function
	Table 6.9 The Tools Available in the Ribbon	
	Run from Top	Run from Start icon
	Run from Selected	Run from current icon
*	Stop Points	Set/clear program stops
	Editors	Edit text, animation, and graphics
	Zoom Window	Size window 25%-100%
	Window Contents	Change window display
*	Variables	Clear and manage variables
	Expand/Compress	Change composite display
	Disable Selected	Disable selected icons
	Enable Selected	Enable selected icons
	Enable All	Enable all icons
	Clipboard	Cut, copy, and paste icons
	Trashcan	Icon eraser (Delete icon)

*Not available in Sampler version of IconAuthor

In the next section, we'll provide you with an expanded description of each of these choices.

Open Library Folders

By default, icon library folders are stored under a general icon that describes the type of utilities it contains. The first icon in the library, for example, the Flow folder, is displayed as shown in Figure 6.17.

Figure 6.17
Flow Folder Icon
Closed

When you select Open Library Folders from the Ribbon, or click on the plus sign (+) at the top of the folder, all of the icons contained in the Flow Folder are displayed beneath it, as shown in Figure 6.18.

Figure 6.18
Flow Folder Icon
Open

Note that when you click on the plus sign (+) at the top of a single folder, only the icons in that folder are displayed. When you click on the Open Library Folders icon on the Ribbon, all of the folders in the library are opened.

Close Library Folders

Clicking on the Close Library Folders icon on the Ribbon does the reverse of clicking on the Open icon. When the library folders are expanded to show available icons, you can close the display by clicking on the Close Library Folders icon on the Ribbon.

Note that you can close a single folder instead of closing all library folders by clicking on the minus sign (–) at the top of any single folder. Clicking on the Close Library Folders icon on the Ribbon closes all of the open folders in the library.

Run from Top

Applications displayed as icons in the structure window are "run" to step through the command sequence and put on the screen the items called for in the program. When you click on the Run from Top icon on the Ribbon, the application is run from the Start icon, regardless of where the cursor is within the program.

Run from Selected

During checkout and debugging, it may be useful to execute (run) only a portion of an IconAuthor application. In this instance, select a portion of the program and click on the Run from Selected icon on the Ribbon. The program begins at the beginning of the selected portion instead of from the top.

Stop Points

Stop points can be used in a script during debugging to help you determine where problems are occurring. To set a stop point, position the cursor at the beginning of the segment where you want program execution to cease, click on the Stop Points icon and choose Set Stop Points from the pulldown menu.

Clear a stop point or all stop points by choosing Clear Stop Point or Clear All Stop Points from the Stop Points pulldown menu.

> This option is also available under the Debug menu from inside Run on the main menu with the production version of IconAuthor. These commands are not available with the sampler.

Editors

In addition to the IconAuthor screen, IconAuthor contains a number of additional utilities to help you build a presentation. To access one of these additional utilities, click on the Editors icon on the Ribbon and choose an editor from the pulldown list. Figure 6.19 shows the options in this menu.

Figure 6.19
Editors Pulldown
List from Ribbon

Each of these selections opens its own editor, which you can use to edit or create objects for use in IconAuthor presentations. The Animation editor screen is shown in Figure 6.20.

Figure 6.20
Animation
Editor Screen

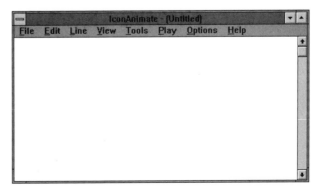

IconAuthor animations are stored as *.ANI files. To get a sample of the type of animation you can do with this utility, use the File Open command to display the list of available animation files shown in Figure 6.21.

Figure 6.21
Animation File
Open Pulldown
File List

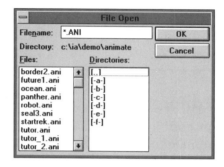

Select the STARTREK.ANI file from the list to present the screen shown in Figure 6.22.

Figure 6.22
STARTREK.ANI
File Displayed
in IconAnimate

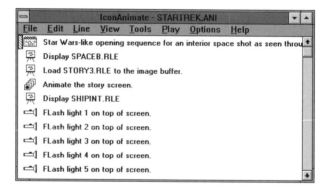

This screen shows the various animation elements that make up this file. For a look at what it does, click on Play and choose Run Script (or press **Ctrl+R** from the keyboard).

Use the Graphics Editor, shown in Figure 6.23, to create and edit graphics images for use in IconAuthor scripts.

You can create or edit *.BMP, *.RLE, or *.PCX files with the editor. To view a file included with the sampler disk, use File Open to display the list shown in Figure 6.24.

View a file by selecting one of the names from the list.

Figure 6.23
IconAuthor
Graphics Editor
Screen

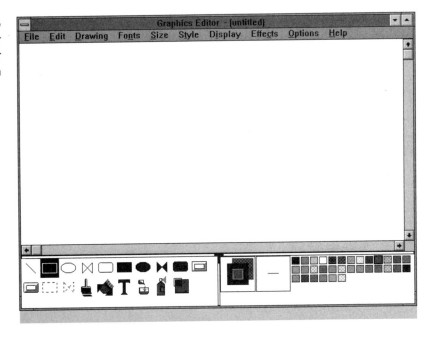

Figure 6.24
Graphics Editor
File Open List

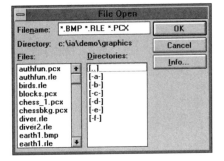

You can load and edit one of these files with the sampler software, then save the changed image to another file on your hard disk. Obviously you can't save the edited version of the file back to the CD-ROM disk.

Use the RezSolution editor to alter the resolution of graphics images. You may wish to do this to enable a variety of users with different hardware platforms to access and view graphics images. The RezSolution editor screen is shown in Figure 6.25.

This editor contains a number of useful features, including the ability to let you capture a window or screen image, to resize

Figure 6.25
RezSolution
Editor Main
Screen

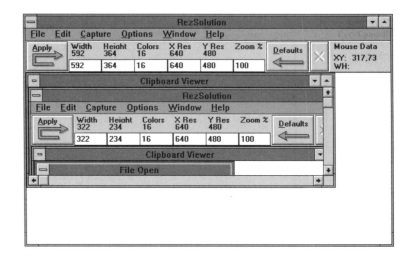

the images, and to specifically set the resolution and color display for each image.

The Smart Text editor looks very much like other Windows editors, as you can see from Figure 6.26.

Figure 6.26
IconAuthor
Smart Text
Editor Screen

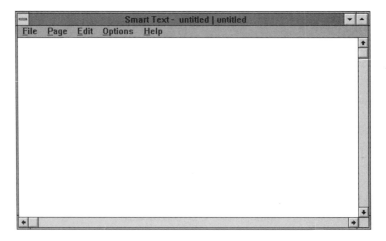

Load a file from the CD Sampler in the same way as you would within other Windows programs (File Open). Smart Text files are stored with the *.SMT suffix.

The commercial version of IconAuthor includes more extensive editing features under this menu choice. The menu entry is Smart Object instead of Smart Text. The Smart Text editor is one component of the Smart Object editor in the commercial version of IconAuthor.

You can't access the Video editor (the last entry in the Editors pulldown menu) from within the Sampler, but with the commercial version of IconAuthor you can use this selection to capture, view, and edit video information.

The basic Video Editor screen is shown in Figure 6.27.

Figure 6.27
IconAuthor
Video Editor
Screen

Zoom Window

When you click on the Zoom Window icon, IconAuthor displays a list of four possible zooming choices, as shown in Figure 6.28.

Figure 6.28
Zoom Window
Pulldown Menu
in IconAuthor

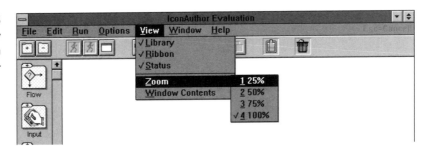

As the list implies, you can display the current window at 100 percent of its normal size, or at different sizes less than 100 percent, down to as small as 25 percent. You can easily see how this works by loading a file into the structure window, choosing the Zoom Window icon, then selecting 25%. The current window is reduced in size by 75 percent of its original.

Window Contents

The Window Contents icon contains four pulldown choices, as shown in Figure 6.29.

Figure 6.29
Window
Contents
Pulldown List

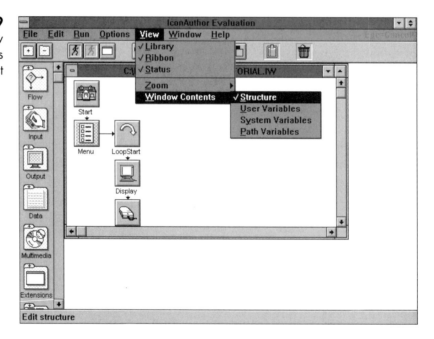

The most common view is Structure, which shows the icons contained in the presentation in flow chart format.

If you select one of the variable choices (User Variables, System Variables, or Path Variables), IconAuthor displays any available information. The values displayed in any of these windows depends on the application currently loaded.

There may be no information associated with user variables if you haven't used any in the design of the current application.

By default, IconAuthor uses the current program path with default subdirectories for various program components. If you haven't specified custom directories for any program components, the defaults will be shown in the Path Variables display.

@ Variables

The Variables icon (not available in the IconAuthor sampler included with this book) displays a two-line menu, shown in Figure 6.30.

Figure 6.30
Variables Icon
(@) Pulldown
Menu

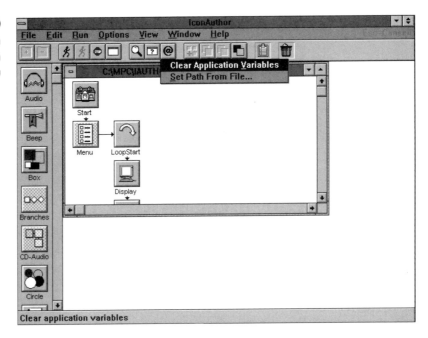

Choose the Clear Application Variables selection when you want to reset all application variables after a previous run. This sometimes is helpful during program development and debugging so you can start a new application run and be sure what information each variable contains.

The second choice—Set Path From File—lets you establish a custom .PTH file for any application. The entries in this path file tell IconAuthor where to find various application components. Establishing a file with this menu choice will do away with the annoying "File Not Found" error message when you load a new application. Figure 6.31 shows a typical .PTH file loaded into the path editor.

Figure 6.31
Typical .PTH File
in Path Editor

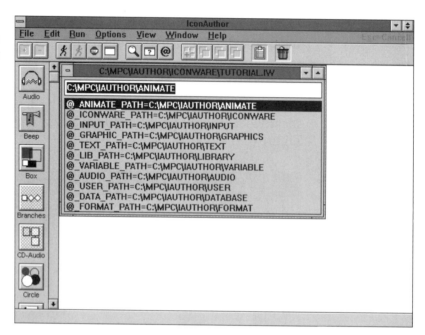

Expand/Compress

The Expand/Compress icon does just what the name implies: It compresses a structure icon display or expands it again. This is a toggle icon that works differently depending on the current state of the selected composite icon. (Remember, a composite icon is one that contains more than one icon function.) You can display composite icons compressed (only the lead icon showing) or expanded (all icons contained within the lead displayed).

Figure 6.32 shows a composite icon displayed in expanded mode with its components visible.

The sample in Figure 6.33 shows how this same icon looks after you've clicked on the Expand/Compress icon on the Ribbon.

Notice also that the Expand/Compress icon itself changes, depending on whether a selected composite is compressed or expanded. When you select an expanded icon, the Ribbon icon shows a minus sign (-), indicating that the selected composite can be compressed. When a selected composite already is compressed, however, the Expand/Compress icon on the Ribbon displays a plus sign (+), indicating that you can expand the selected icon.

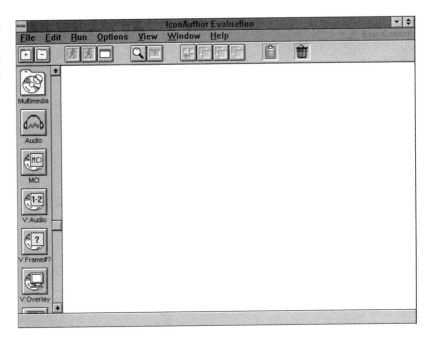

Figure 6.32
Composite Icon
Displayed
Expanded

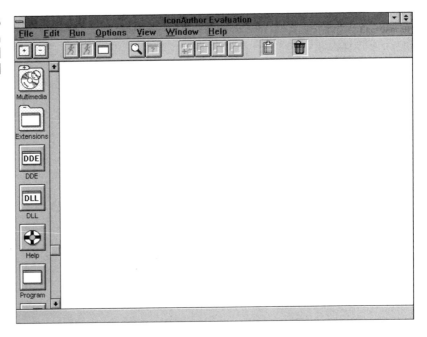

Figure 6.33
Composite Icon
Displayed
Compressed

Disable Selected

Sometimes during debugging or application design, you may want to disable certain icons already installed in the structures window. To do this, simply select the icon you want to disable, so when the application is run, this icon and any of its features will be ignored.

When you disable a selected icon, the color changes to black, indicating that it will not execute with the rest of the application.

It may be helpful to compress composite icons (see the Expand/Compress icon section above) before disabling them. This simplifies your structures display, removing from the window any features that aren't being executed.

Enable Selected

You can re-enable a disabled icon by selecting it, then clicking on the Enable Selected icon.

This icon is not accessible (grayed out) until an icon is selected in the structures window.

Enable All

The Enable All icon re-enables all disabled icons within the selected structure window. This is useful when you have been debugging an application, perhaps disabling several icons along the way. Now you want to restore the application to full functionality. Use the Enable All icon and you won't forget to enable a crucial icon.

Clipboard

The Clipboard icon works like the Windows Clipboard to hold temporary information while you cut and copy data. To use this feature, simply drag an icon onto the Clipboard. Now a copy of it exists on the Clipboard, but it has been removed from within the structure in which you are working.

To insert this copy elsewhere within the current structure, or another structure, simply drag a copy of the Clipboard icon to the location within the window where you want it to appear, then drop it there. Now you have two copies of the icon—one in the Clipboard and another at the new location within the structure.

To copy an icon to the Clipboard without deleting it from its present location, use Edit Copy from the main IconAuthor menu.

If you want to copy an icon (leave one copy in its original location and place another copy somewhere else), then the second step in this process is to drag a copy of the Clipboard icon over the original location. Drop a copy there to restore the structure to its original form. Now move the cursor to the new location and drag another copy of the Clipboard (and the icon it contains) over this location and drop it. You can repeat this drag-and-drop procedure as often as you like. The icon you dropped into the Clipboard stays there until you replace it with another icon.

Trashcan

When you want to remove an icon from a structure—and you don't want to copy it back to another location—drag the icon onto the Trashcan icon.

Icon Library

The Icon Library consists of a series of pre-programmed objects that you can use to design and build your own IconAuthor applications. The basic library is contained in seven library folders:

Flow	Directs program execution, including branches and exits
Input	Accepts and controls data input during application execution
Output	Directs and controls data output during an application execution
Data	Manipulates data storage and structures
Multimedia	Plays and controls music and other audio, plus video and still images

| Extensions | Manipulates subroutines and provides "utility" functions, such as *snapshot* |
| Custom | Contains CD-Audio, MIDI, and Wave Audio icons to let you include your own audio files within an IconAuthor application. |

As mentioned earlier, each of these folders contains multiple icons that can serve specific purposes within an IconAuthor flow chart design. To view the content of any one folder, click on the plus sign (+) in the upper-right corner of the folder.

Status Line

The status line actually serves as an easy-to-use, continuous Help line. Anytime you want to know a little about some screen object, simply place the cursor over it and read all about it on the status line.

For example, move the cursor over an icon within a structure window, and the status display shows you the location of the cursor relative to the Start icon, and also offers a brief description, including any "content" it may contain.

Or, move the cursor over one of the icons on the Ribbon and you'll see a brief description of its function on the status line.

Structure Window

The structure window is where an application's flow chart of icons is displayed. There may be no structure windows if you have not yet opened or created an application, or there may be several structure windows displayed in tile or cascade format if you have one or more applications open. Figure 6.34 shows an IconAuthor screen with multiple structure windows in cascade format.

By default, any structure window is displayed as a small window, reduced in size from the size of the entire IconAuthor application window. You can grow the current structure to full screen size simply by clicking on the Up Arrow on top of the scroll bar at the right of any structure window.

When you open a new structure window, however, the full-sized window is reduced to match the size of the new application.

Figure 6.34
Multiple
Structure
Windows in
Cascade Format

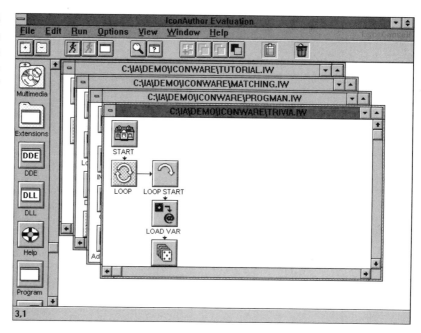

Creating Multimedia Applications with IconAuthor

HANDS ON

You learned the basics of IconAuthor in Chapter 6. In this chapter we'll show you step by step how to build useful presentations with IconAuthor. You'll learn how to create interactive menu systems based on graphics images and how to link intrinsic IconAuthor intelligent icons into a unified structure.

With the procedures in this chapter as a basis, you can branch out, using what you already know about IconAuthor, to build presentations with your own designs. Of course, you can use the material we show you how to construct here as a beginning point for your own work as well.

The material in this chapter assumes you will be following along with IconAuthor on your system as we step you through the process of designing and building a presentation. You don't have to do this, of course, but the material will be a lot easier to follow and to understand if you do. And, remember, whenever you have questions about a particular procedure, use the built-in IconAuthor Help facility, and the information in Chapter 6 to get you back on track.

Let's do some work with IconAuthor.

IconAuthor Summary

Here's a quick re-cap of IconAuthor in case you skipped here without studying Chapter 6. IconAuthor is an authoring program that comes with the following major components:

- An Authoring System used to author an application
- A Presentation System used to run the applications that you create with the Authoring System
- A Smart Text Editor for all of your object-oriented, text-editing needs
- A Graphics Editor that lets you create colorful graphics to be used as still images or images in motion
- An Animation Editor that allows you to build scripts to display your graphics in motion
- RezSolution, a graphics utility that lets you change the resolution of your bitmap graphics to accommodate different systems where your applications may be used

IconAuthor's graphical interface helps make authoring easier because you use icons that represent the building blocks of the structure of an application.

You create an application with IconAuthor in two basic steps:

- Using icons to build the structure of the application
- Using dialog boxes to "add content" or define how each icon in the structure performs at runtime

This design separates the logical structure from the content, so you can use logic sequences repeatedly. Since virtually any content item (graphics, text, etc.) can be identified as a variable, the logic structure can be very efficient. This also allows design teams to divide development tasks among team members based on experience and expertise.

This evaluation software incorporates all the current features of the retail version of IconAuthor, except that the number of icons you can save has been limited to 80. In addition, you can only save presentations under the file name EVAL.IW. Even with these limitations, you can develop full-featured, multimedia applications.

Designing the IconAuthor Application

Creating an IconAuthor application involves at least four general steps:

1. Planning
2. Building
3. Adding content
4. Editing

For fairly simple applications, you can combine some of these steps, and for complex applications you may have to expand them, but in general these are the steps you'll take to design and prepare an IconAuthor application. (See additional information on planning and designing applications in Chapter 3.)

Planning

When you plan an application, you should answer these questions:

- What do you want your application to do?
- How will the application do what you want it to do?
- How will the effectiveness of the application be measured?

In addition, consider which parts of your application you will use more than once. You can plan graphic backgrounds, for example, that you can then use in many different presentations.

Building

Building is the process of creating the structure of your application by selecting icons from the Icon Library and placing them in the structure. When you build icons into the structure, they're placed in the logical order that you want them executed.

Adding Content

After you build the structure, you add content to each of its icons. Through a series of dialogs, called *Content Editors*, you determine what the application will do when it's executed. Every icon has its own Content Editor. For example, there is a Box icon Content Editor, a Pause icon Content Editor, and so on.

Editing

As you build your application structure and add content to it, you can run it and check it at any time. As you check your application, you can edit either the structure, the content, or both.

When you edit the structure, you perform tasks such as copying, inserting, and deleting icons from the structure. To edit the content of the application, you reopen an icon's Content Editor and change the values. You can change only the values in the dialog, or the underlying graphic, animation, or text files that the Content Editor invokes.

We've done the planning for this sample application for you. Hopefully, you'll see components of this planning and design process as you work through the steps to create your own application.

Follow the steps in this chapter to get started quickly with IconAuthor. In it you'll learn the fundamentals of using IconAuthor by creating a small application called EVAL.IW.

When you finish creating the application, you'll have an interactive IconAuthor screen like the one shown in Figure 7.1.

Figure 7.1
Finished Sampler
Interactive
Screen

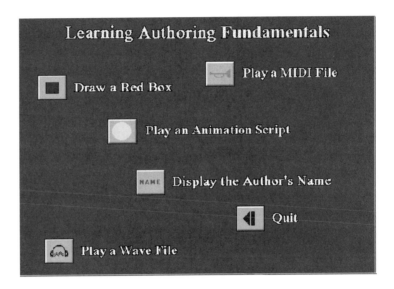

Each button to the left of an option on this screen will be selectable. When you finish building the entire application, you'll be able to click on these buttons to view a small sampling of IconAuthor's multimedia capabilities.

By the time you've entered all of the components for this apparently simple screen, you will have experienced much of the power of IconAuthor, and you will have learned how to use some of its most important features. After you've built this screen with its interactive components, we'll show you how to design and create another screen that can serve as the "front end" for this module and others, which, taken together, can provide a full-featured, interactive demonstration of IconAuthor utilities.

You can experiment with a completed version of the application we show you in this chapter by using File Open from the IconAuthor main menu to load the file TUTORIAL.IW from the Ultimedia Tools Series CD-ROM. Run the application and click on "Authoring Fundamentals" to interact with the module you'll build in this chapter.

Building the Application

As we told you in Chapter 6, IconAuthor applications are built around a flow chart format that uses intelligent icons to direct program functions and features. Each icon represents a function that can be performed by your computer. When combined into a logical sequence, the icons form a flow chart called the *structure* of your application. Figure 7.2 shows an example of a structure created with IconAuthor.

Figure 7.2
Sample Structure
from IconAuthor
Application

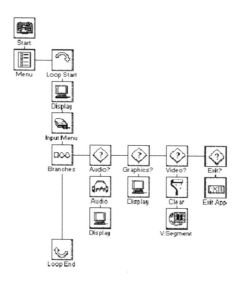

The Start icon, shown as the first symbol in the flow chart, is automatically built into every structure and marks the beginning of the application.

The icons that you use to build a flow chart are found in the Icon Library, a scrollable region on the left side of the screen. Each icon in the library causes your application to perform a specific action. For example, the Box icon causes your application to draw a box on the screen.

In addition, you can edit these pre-programmed icons to meet your particular needs. For example, each time you use the Box icon, you indicate the kind of box that is created, and define its characteristics, such as its size and location. You can then save the edited version of the icon and use it repeatedly.

To build our sample application, we'll use screens supplied with your CD-ROM sampler disk. As you work through the instructions, you'll likely see areas where your own drawing or text files could be used. Hopefully, this will help you see how to generate your own unique applications in IconAuthor.

To begin building your sample application, start IconAuthor, then do the following:

1. Make the logical drive that represents your CD-ROM reader the current drive (for example, type **E:**, then press **Enter** if your CD-ROM is on the E: drive).

2. Type **UTSDOS** at the DOS prompt.

3. Choose Product Selector from the main Ultimedia Tools menu.

4. Use the scroll bars at the right of the Product Selector screen to locate the IconAuthor button.

5. Click on the IconAuthor button to display the demo screen.

6. Click on Working Demonstration to display the opening IconAuthor screen shown in Figure 7.3.

Figure 7.3
Opening
IconAuthor
Sampler Screen

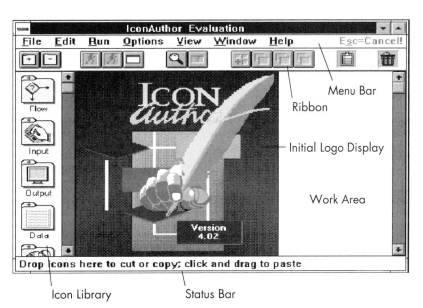

Notice that the second line of the display holds the IconAuthor menu bar; below that is the ribbon. You may need the menu items for some features, but in general you can perform most

IconAuthor functions with the tools on the ribbon, shown with function labels in Figure 7.4.

Figure 7.4
IconAuthor
Ribbon with
Labels

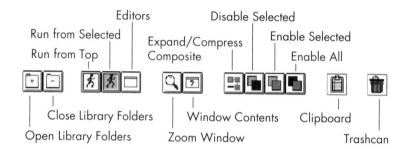

Here are the general steps we'll use to build this sample application:

1. Open a new application window.
2. Customize the Icon Library.
3. Place icons in the structure in the proper order.
4. Add content to the display icons.
5. Run, test, and debug the application.

These steps don't necessarily occur in neat, separate, sequential order, but we'll discuss each part of the process in the following pages.

Opening a New Application Window

The first time you begin work on an application you must open a new application window.

Here's how:

1. Use File New from the main menu to display the New dialog with the Application Window option selected.
2. Choose OK to open a blank, untitled application window.

Notice that the shape of the mouse pointer changes depending on its location on the IconAuthor screen. When the mouse pointer is within the application window, for example, it appears as a hand holding a pen. At other locations on the screen and when you are performing different tasks, the mouse pointer has different shapes.

We'll refer to this pointer as the *cursor* or the *pointer*, regardless of its shape at the time. You'll learn more about the various pointer shapes as you build the sample application.

Customizing the Icon Library

The Icon Library (usually called, simply, the *library*) is the scrollable vertical box to the left of the work area, as shown in Figure 7.5. Each of the folders displayed in the library contains one or more icons you can use within the structure of your application. (Refer to the library discussion in Chapter 6 for more information on this feature, if necessary.)

Figure 7.5
Icon Library in
IconAuthor

To open library folders and make icons available for use as you work:

1. Use Options Library Setup from the main menu to display the Library Setup dialog shown in Figure 7.6.
2. Click on the Show Icon Categories option to deselect it, then choose OK to close the dialog and convert the library into a scrollable list of usable icons arranged in alphabetical order, as shown in Figure 7.7.

Figure 7.6
Options Library
Setup Dialog

Figure 7.7
Expanded Icon
Library in
Alphabetical
Order

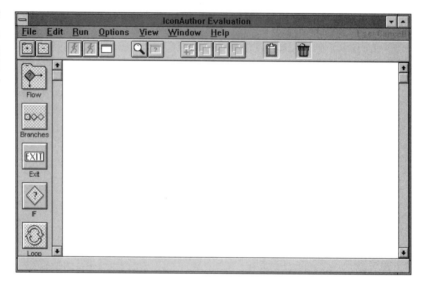

Placing Icons in the Structure in the Proper Order

Placing icons to build a flow chart structure is the heart of building an application in IconAuthor. We'll place a number of icons to build this relatively simple structure, so it's important for you to be able to find the proper icons.

> When you add an icon from the Icon Library to a structure, you actually use a *copy* of that icon. The original icon remains unchanged and available for use in the Icon Library.

The first icon you'll place in your structure is the Menu icon.

Here's how to find the Menu icon in the library:

1. Click on any one of the icons within the library.
2. Type **M**.

Your view of the icons in the library changes as the first icon that begins with M (the MCI icon) appears, as shown in Figure 7.8.

Figure 7.8
Icon Library
with MCI Icon
Displayed

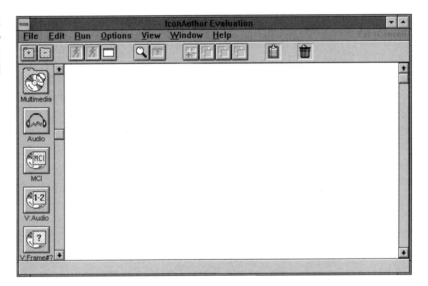

Different icons in the library appear in different colors. This color scheme identifies composite icons, which icons are selected, and which icons require content. For more information on icon color codes, refer to Chapter 6.

You move icons from the library into a structure by *dragging and dropping*. It's called drag and drop because you use the mouse to select an icon in the library, drag a copy of that icon to a position in the structure, and drop the icon into place.

To add the first icon to the blank structure:

1. Position the pointer over the Menu icon in the library.
2. Press and hold the left mouse button with the pointer over the icon. The icon is selected and appears indented as though it's a button that has been pushed in.

3. Drag the icon toward the application window.

> Unless you position the icon you are dragging so that it touches the Start icon already on the structure screen, the icon appears as a red circle with a diagonal bar through it (A "Not" or "NO" symbol). This symbol indicates that the icon is in an invalid position and you can't drop it there.

4. Position the Menu icon (probably displayed as the "NOT" icon) just below the Start icon (slightly overlapping it). The cursor again takes the shape of the Menu icon because it's now in a valid drop position.

5. Drop the icon into the structure by releasing the mouse button.

The Menu composite is built into your structure. Note that such a composite icon contains multiple icons within it. When the icon is on the library bar, it's displayed as a single icon; when you drop it into the structure window, the icon automatically expands, displaying all of its components. Figure 7.9 shows how the Menu icon automatically expands when you drop it under the Start icon on the new structure screen.

Figure 7.9
Menu Icon
Expanded on
Structure Screen

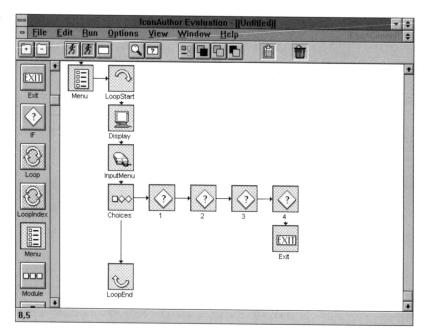

The first icon in any composite (set of multiple icons) is called the *lead icon*.

The Menu composite consists of the following pre-programmed components:

- A LoopStart icon
- A Display icon
- An Input menu
- A Choices (or branching) menu
- Four If icons
- An Exit icon
- A LoopEnd icon

We'll add more information to some of these icons in the next section.

First, now that you've added something to the structure, you should save your work. Saving the structure at this point serves two purposes:

- It stores the structure to reduce the chance of losing any information.
- It provides a name for the new application so you can save it easily with the File Save command from the main menu.

To save the new application for the first time, use File Save from the main IconAuthor menu. The word "Untitled" on the Title Bar of the new application changes to EVAL.IW. Now as you make changes to the structure of this sample application, use File Save (or press **Ctrl+S**) to save the changes frequently.

With the sampler version of IconAuthor, you cannot use the File Save As command. The name EVAL.IW is chosen for you automatically. The file is saved in the temporary TOOLSHOP directory created by the Ultimedia Tools software. (C:\TOOLSHOP \DEMO\ICONWARE is the directory used if your system was set up with Ultimedia defaults.)

Adding Content to the Display Icons

You must add content to many IconAuthor pre-defined icons. This content is entered with a Content Editor, linked to each icon type. This icon content determines how the icon will perform when you run the application.

We'll add content first to the Display icon, one of the sub icons under the Menu composite. You'll use the Display icon to display the previously created graphics file AUTHFUN.PCX that serves as the background menu for your application. This file was created using IconAuthor's integral graphics editor. You can create custom drawings in this editor, or import files from other applications to use as backgrounds for menus or lists.

You can get a preview look at this menu screen by using IconAuthor's Graphics Editor. Use Run Editors Graphics to load the Graphics Editor. Then issue the File Open command from the Graphics Editor menu. Choose the file AUTHFUN.PCX from the Files: list on this dialog.

To add content to this Display icon:

1. Double click on the Display icon to display its Content Editor, as shown in Figure 7.10.

Figure 7.10
Display Icon
Content Editor
Dialog

Content Editor
Icon Name: Display
File Type bitmap
Filename AUTHFUN.PCX
Location 0, 0
Page or Effect zoom,horzout,medium
OK   Cancel   Exit Range   Help

2. Accept the default Icon Name: field, File Type field, and Location field values. (Don't change these fields.)
3. Click in the Filename field and type **AUTHFUN.PCX**.
4. Click on the Down Arrow to the right of the Page or Effect text box to display a list of frequently used effects, as shown in Figure 7.11.

Figure 7.11
Page or Effect
Pulldown List

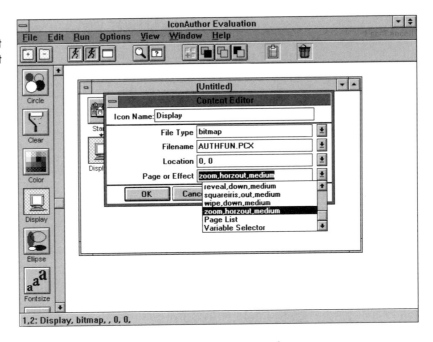

5. Use the scroll bar to locate the zoom,horzout,medium listing, then click on that item. The Content Editor should appear as it does in Figure 7.12. (For more information on what this effect means, refer to Chapter 6.)

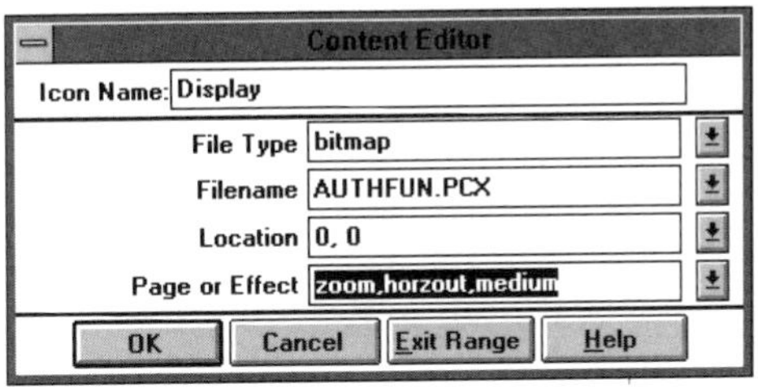

Figure 7.12
Finished Content
Editor

6. Click on OK to close the Display icon Content Editor.

Next, you need to add content to the Input Menu icon. The procedure is generally the same as with the Display icon, but because this icon has characteristics different from the Display icon, the Content Editor is different as well.

Whereas you used the Display icon Content Editor to specify the name of a file for the icon to display, when you add content to the Input icon you'll identify each of the six on-screen menu options as a "hot spot" on the main display. These hot spots are used to provide the user with a place to click to select various menu items.

First you'll provide a value for Selection Areas. This is where you specify the size and location of each rectangular hot spot that marks an option in your menu.

For each rectangular area, you'll indicate the x,y coordinates of the upper-left corner, as well as the width and height. For example, a value of 100,200,50,50 specifies a hot spot that starts at 100 pixels over (the x coordinate), 200 pixels down (the y coordinate), is 50 pixels wide, and 50 pixels tall.

Fortunately, you don't have to get out your pencil, paper, and calculator to figure out the hot spot locations. IconAuthor's Input Template Editor will do that for you.

To add hot spot content to the Input icon (immediately beneath the display icon in the structure window):

1. Double click on the Input Menu icon to display its Content Editor.
2. Click on the Down Arrow to the right of the Selection Areas text box.
3. Double click on Input Template Editor. The screen clears (temporarily) and the Input Template Editor is displayed, as shown in Figure 7.13.

Figure 7.13
Input Template
Editor Display

The Input Template Editor lets you draw the hot spots on the screen. When you exit the editor, the data that describes those hot spots will be automatically returned to the Selection Areas text box.

Before you can specify hot spots, you must display the image that will serve as your background display.

Here's how:

1. Use Show Graphics File to display a File Open dialog.
2. Double click on AUTHFUN.PCX to display this graphics file behind the Input Template Editor dialog.

Now you'll draw the selectable areas (hot spots) on this graphic so IconAuthor can find the screen coordinates for you. The first selectable area will be the square button to the left of the Draw a Red Box option. Then you'll specify hot spots for each of the on-screen buttons that comprise the menu for this screen.

Here's how:

1. Choose New.
2. Position the pointer on the upper-left corner of the Draw a Red Box button.
3. Drag the pointer to the lower-right corner of the button, defining a colored box around the button. Don't worry if the box doesn't surround the button precisely. You can grab any of the handles on the box edges to reshape the box so that it very closely surrounds the existing button.

Notice that coordinates of the selection area appear next to the Coordinates: field and the number of the selection area appears next to the Template Area: field in the editor. Each selection area will be assigned a unique number in the order in which it is created, starting with 1. The number of the selection area plays an important role in how you add content to other icons in the Menu composite. Therefore, it's important that you're systematic when you create selection areas. For example, in general, try to work from the top to the bottom of a menu, and from the right to the left.

If you make a mistake while drawing a selection area, you can always delete, move, or resize the rectangle:

• To delete an area, choose Delete and click anywhere inside the unwanted area.

• To move an area, click anywhere inside the area and drag the rectangle to a new location.

• To resize an area, click within the area so that eight sizer blocks (handles) appear around the border of the area. Position the cursor over one of the sizer blocks (the cursor appears as a double-headed arrow indicating the directions in which you can resize the area), then drag it in the desired direction.

Now you should repeat the previous instructions for each of the five remaining menu labels to draw boxes around each one and generate a coordinates list. You should define these areas in the following order:

1. Play a MIDI File
2. Play an Animation Script
3. Display the Author's Name
4. Play a Wave File
5. Quit

> You can drag the Input Template Editor out of your way as necessary to access the areas you want to mark. (To drag the window, move the pointer into the dialog's title bar, hold the left button, drag the dialog to a new location, and release the left button.)

When all of the hot spots have been marked, click on OK to close the Input Template Editor. The coordinates for each area are returned to the Selection Areas text box in the Input Menu icon Content Editor.

The next text box is labeled Feedback. Use this text box to control how a selectable area appears when a user selects it.

To change the content for this field:

1. Pull down the Feedback text box.
2. Select the box flash item.

The Selection Labels text box lets you specify the names of keys on the keyboard that a user can press instead of using the mouse. We'll leave this field blank for this application.

At this point, the Content Editor should appear as it does in Figure 7.14.

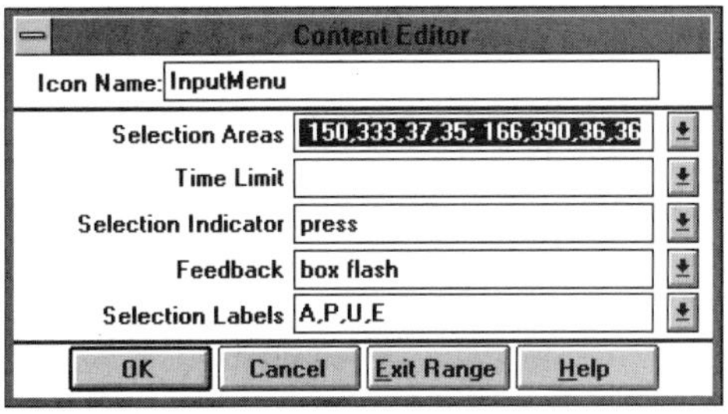

Figure 7.14
Input Icon
Content Editor
Dialog after
Editing

Click on OK to accept the content of this box and return to the main IconAuthor screen.

Expanding the basic Menu icon provides much of the structure of the application we're building. However, we need to modify the basic structure. This process is covered below.

Notice that there is a composite within the Menu composite. The Choices composite contains a lead icon labeled Choices, four icons labeled 1 through 4, and an Exit icon. The numbered icons are called *If* icons. Each numbered icon in the Choices composite should correspond to a choice in the menu, but by default the Choices composite contains just four choices. You need to add two more If icons to the composite to provide one icon for each of the hot spot areas you defined in the previous steps.

You're going to copy two of the If icons and paste them to the left of the fourth If icon. Then you'll have the correct number of branches (one for each option button on the menu).

If you wanted to select just one icon, you'd click on it. However, you're going to select two icons, or a *range*.

Here's how to select a range of icons:

1. Click anywhere in the work area (not on an icon) to deselect the icons in the Menu composite.
2. Click on the If icon labeled 3, the first icon in the range you are selecting.
3. While holding down the **Shift** key, click on the If icon labeled 4, the last icon in the range.
4. Release the Shift key.

The selected icons become blue. Notice that the Exit icon below the 4 If icon is also selected. That's normal. Whenever you select an If icon, all the icons contained in the path below it are also selected.

Copying icons and moving icons are somewhat similar procedures.

To move a selected range of icons within the structure:

1. Select the icons.
2. Click on any one icon in the range, holding down the left button.
3. Drag the icons to the new location..

Note that when the cursor is in a valid drop position, it looks like the one in Figure 7.15.

Figure 7.15
Valid Drop
Position Cursor

The image on the face of the selected icons indicates whether you're performing a copy or move. If the image disappears from the original icons as you drag, you're performing a move. If the pictures remain on the face of the selected icons, you're performing a copy.

To copy a range of icons (keeping the original icons intact), press and hold the **Ctrl** key as you drag them to the new location.

To copy the additional If icons you need for this application:

1. Press and hold the **Ctrl** key.
2. Press and hold the left mouse button on any of the selected icons in the range.
3. Drag the selected icons to the right of the 4 If icon.
4. Release the mouse button and Ctrl key.

The Choices composite for your menu now contains six If icons, as shown in Figure 7.16.

Figure 7.16
Six If Icons
in Tutorial
Application

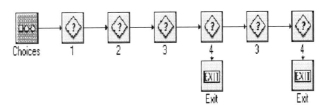

The icon numbers will not be in the proper order. You've copied the icon names as well as the icons themselves. The names are actually numbers. Also, there is an extra Exit icon as a result of the copy operation. We'll correct these problems in the next steps.

Remember, the If icons are really the menu choices you'll have in the finished application. So let's edit the content of some of these icons so that they have more meaningful labels. You'll name the first If icon "Box" because later this branch will execute icons that draw a red box. Rename the second If icon "MIDI," and so on.

To rename the If icons:

1. Double click on the 1 If icon to open the Content Editor.
2. Double click in the Icon Name text box.
3. Type **Box**.

4. Choose OK.

5. Use the same technique to rename the second If icon "MIDI." Rename the third icon "Animate," the fourth icon "Show Name," the fifth icon "Wave Audio," and the sixth icon "Quit."

When you've completed these steps, the If icon section of your growing application should look like the one in Figure 7.17.

Figure 7.17
Six Icons with
New Names

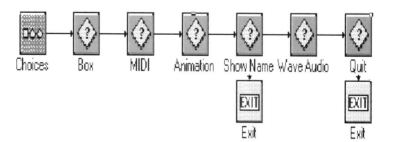

You also have to change additional content of the Wave Audio and Quit icons. For now, don't be concerned about what the different fields and default values mean. They'll be explained shortly.

To change the content of the Wave Audio and Quit icons:

1. Open the Wave Audio icon Content Editor by double clicking on the icon.

2. Click in the Condition 2 text box to select the current value.

3. Type **5**.

4. Choose OK.

5. Open the Quit icon Content Editor, then change the Condition 2 value to 6.

> Notice that the Condition 2 values correspond to the position of the icon. This value is used to help make the If comparison.

Finally, you need to remove the extra Exit icon that is below the "Show Name" icon.

Here's how to remove the extra Exit icon:

1. Press and hold the mouse button on the Exit icon below the Show Name icon.

2. Drag the Exit icon to the Trashcan in the function ribbon, then release the mouse button. The message box in Figure 7.18 appears.

Figure 7.18
Clear Selected
Icons Warning
Dialog

3. Choose Yes to verify that you want to delete the icons, and the Exit icon is removed.

You've made some significant changes to the application. To avoid losing any of your work, save what you've done up to this point. Simply press **Ctrl+S** or use the File Save command.

Running, Testing, and Debugging the Application

With the application safely stored on disk, you can try running it. We aren't finished developing the application, of course, but you can run what you've created at this point, just to make sure everything is working as it should.

To conduct a test run of the application so far, simply click on the Run-From-Top button in the ribbon to display the main menu screen from the new application.

You'll be able to click on any of the six selectable buttons you created earlier. Because the structure is only partially built at this point, not much happens when you select most of the buttons. The only button that is fully active at this point is the Quit button, which ends execution of the application. Another way to quit the application is to press the **Esc** key.

Notice as you click on one of these buttons, the button appears to depress, and a border around the button flashes briefly. This is the feature you set when you added content to the Input icon by setting the Feedback field to box flash. It's good design practice to give the user some form of feedback any time there is input from the keyboard or mouse. You can use a flashing technique such as this, you can change colors on selected components, you can play a short sound file, and so on.

If you fail to give the user immediate feedback, and it requires a second or two for a program to execute, users tend to keep clicking buttons or pressing keys until something happens. The type ahead buffer in your computer will load up with several instructions and the application will seem to run away, or incorrect information will be entered.

Before we continue building this application, let's look at the work we've done at this point and try to understand how the program works.

Learning How the Application Works

Remember that IconAuthor applications are built with a series of intelligent icons arranged in a particular order. These flow charts are, in reality, object-oriented programs that control your application.

Execution flow is the order in which icons are executed in your application. Sometimes execution flow is simple. For example, first the Display icon is executed, then the Input Menu icon. At other times, execution flow is a little more complicated. In fact, there are icons whose sole job is to control where execution flows next.

To relate this to the menu you've been creating, if a user runs EVAL.IW and selects Draw a Red Box, you want execution to flow to the icons in the application that display a red box. If the user selects another option, execution should flow to a different part of the application structure.

To get a look at the contents of one such control icon:

1. Double click on the Choices icon in your EVAL.IW application. The dialog in Figure 7.19 is displayed.

Figure 7.19
Choices Icon
Content Editor

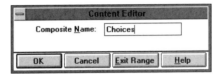

Note that this Content Editor has only one text box: Composite Name. The value "Choices" causes the label "Choices" to appear below the icon in the structure. Like any composite, the real purpose of the lead icon is to identify the beginning of the composite. The other icons within the composite can be defined to create different effects.

We don't want to change this name, so:

2. Click on OK. The Choices icon Content Editor is removed and the next composite in the range is automatically opened. This is the first If icon in the composite range, the one you labeled Box earlier. The Content Editor for this icon should look like the one in Figure 7.20.

Figure 7.20
Box If Icon
Content Editor
Dialog

An If icon determines where execution flows next. When an If icon is executed, it asks whether a condition is true and, depending on the result, it causes execution to flow down or to the right.

To understand the purpose of the If icon, take a moment to consider the Input Menu icon. Each time a user makes a selection from a menu, IconAuthor is working behind the scenes recording the number of the chosen hot spot. For example, when a user selects the first selection area, the value 1 is assigned to a *system variable* called @_SELECTION. (You can see this variable assignment in the Condition 1 field of the Content Editor in Figure 7.20.)

Don't panic. A system variable isn't as unfriendly as it sounds. A variable is like a labeled, empty container where you can store different values on different occasions. For example, if the user had selected the second selection area, the value 2 would be stored in @_SELECTION. A system variable is just a holding place for a number that will be important later on to the If icon. Don't worry about the details of variables right now.

To review, the Input Menu icon lets the user click on an option, and the number of the selection area the user picked is stored in @_SELECTION. Let's say that the user picked selection area 2, which is the button labeled Play a MIDI File. Behind the scenes, IconAuthor stores the value 2 in @_SELECTION. Next, execution flows to the Choices icon, which is simply a marker, and execution is directed to the right, to the first If icon.

This Content Editor is predefined to ask if @_SELECTION is equal to the value 1. In our scenario, the user chose selection area 2 so we know this is false. Therefore execution flows to the right, to the second If icon.

3. Choose OK in the Content Editor of the If icon labeled Box to display the Content Editor for the second If icon. The dialog in Figure 7.21 is displayed.

Figure 7.21
MIDI Icon
Content Editor

This Content Editor is predefined to ask if @_SELECTION is equal to the value 2. Since the user chose selection area 2, we know this is true. Therefore execution flows down, not to the right as before.

Refer to Figure 7.22 to review the structure at this point so you can better visualize the logic flow just described.

Figure 7.22
Menu Composite
Display Expanded
with All Submenu
Icons

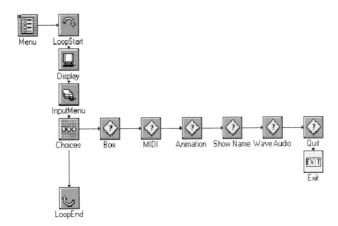

At this point, your structure has no icons below the first five If icons, so execution flows back out to the lead icon in the composite (the Choices icon) and drops down to the LoopEnd icon.

4. Choose Exit Range in the Content Editor of the If icon labeled Wave Audio to close the Content Editor.

The description above mentioned the logic flow through the LoopEnd icon. This is the bottom or closing icon in a loop pair. The beginning icon in the pair is the LoopStart icon.

The LoopStart and LoopEnd icons are two more important icons in your structure that were placed there automatically as part of the Menu composite. They're unusual because they don't have Content Editors. They always perform the same function and cannot be edited. Like the If icons, the purpose of these icons is to control execution flow by forming a loop in your structure. All of the icons within the loop execute repeatedly until an exit occurs.

Try running the application again and think about what is happening behind the scenes each time you make a selection.

1. Choose Save from the File menu.
2. Click on the Run-From-Top button. The Display icon presents the main menu screen with six possible choices.
3. Click on the third button labeled Play an Animation Script.

As you perform step 3, @_SELECTION is assigned the number 3 and the Choices composite begins to execute. It tests the first If icon, the second, and then the third, which it finds to be true. Execution flows down (nothing happens because there are no icons below the If icon yet), out to the LoopEnd icon, and up to the LoopStart icon. The main menu is displayed again.

You won't notice the redisplay of the main menu because the graphic is being displayed over itself. At most, you may notice the mouse cursor disappear briefly.

4. Click on the sixth button labeled Quit.

The same execution flow occurs, except that if the fourth If icon tests true, the application is exited. The authoring window then returns to view.

Take a look at the Exit icon Content Editor to see what it's doing.

5. Double click on the Exit icon below the "Quit" icon. The Exit icon Content Editor shown in Figure 7.23 is displayed.

Figure 7.23
Exit Icon
Content Editor
Dialog

The Exit icon is giving an instruction that causes execution to flow out of the current loop. Because a Menu composite is essentially a loop, this Exit icon is the way out of the application. If a user selects the sixth option button, execution flows out of the application.

6. Click OK to close the Exit icon Content Editor.

Creating Lower-Level Logic

Now you're going to add icons to the structure so that each button in the menu causes the appropriate actions to occur. For example, under the first If icon (labeled Box) you'll build icons that draw a red box.

Drawing a Red Box

The Box icon dynamically creates a graphic on the screen (as opposed to displaying a graphic from a file, as with the menu AUTHFUN.PCX).

Use a Box icon to draw a box on the screen:

1. Click on any icon in the library.
2. Type **B** on the keyboard until the Box icon is selected
3. Drag the Box icon to just below the If icon labeled Box.
4. Release the mouse button to drop the Box icon into place.
5. Double click on the new Box icon in the structure to open its Content Editor.

Now change the name of the icon so you don't confuse it with the If icon above it (which is also called Box).

To change the icon's name:

1. Double click in the Icon Name text box, then type **Draw Box**.

   Now you're going to indicate where you want the box to appear on the screen. You'll need to specify (in pixels) the coordinates of the upper-left and lower-right corners of the box. You'll use the *Area Editor* to do the calculating for you:

2. Pull down the Upper Left Corner text box.
3. Select Area Editor.

   The Area Editor is displayed with the AUTHFUN.PCX graphic in the background. Use the Area Editor to draw the outline of a small box on the screen where you'd like it to appear when EVAL.IW is run:

4. Position the pointer at the location where you want the upper-left corner of the box.
5. Press and hold the left mouse button.
6. Drag the mouse to the lower-right corner of the box area.
7. Release the mouse cursor to freeze the box coordinates in the Area Editor dialog. Your screen should now look like Figure 7.24.

Figure 7.24
Menu Display
with Box Drawn
on Screen

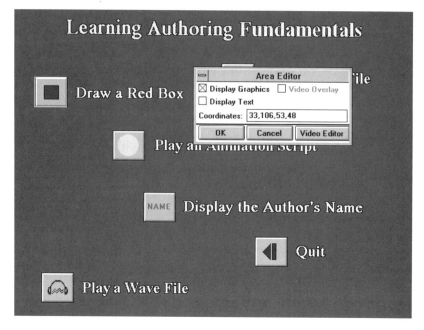

The coordinates of the box appear next to Coordinates: in the editor. The first two numbers are the x,y coordinates of the upper-left corner. The second two numbers are the x,y coordinates of the lower-right corner. If you make a mistake while drawing the box, you can try again. As soon as you begin drawing a new box, the old box disappears. When you finish, exit the editor:

8. Choose OK.

The Content Editor will contain the coordinates for your box, as shown in Figure 7.25.

Figure 7.25
Area Editor Icon
Content Editor
with Box
Coordinates

The coordinates for the upper-left corner are automatically returned to the Upper Left Corner text box of the Content Editor.

The coordinates for the lower-right corner are returned to the Lower Right Offset text box. If you want to change the coordinates, you can re-access the Area Editor and redraw the box, or you can type a different value into one of the text boxes.

Use the Line Width text box to indicate how wide you want the border of the box to be.

To create a box with an outline border that is two pixels wide:

1. Change the Line Width value to 2.
2. Pull down the Filled or Outline text box.
3. Select filled to force the box to be filled rather than empty.
4. Choose OK to close the Draw Box icon Content Editor.

    Now put the Pause icon below the Draw Box icon so that the box will stay on the screen for a few seconds when you run the application. Otherwise, the menu will redisplay so quickly the box will just flash on and off the screen:

5. Find the Pause icon in the library.
6. Drag the Pause icon below the Draw Box icon.
7. Double click on the Pause icon Content Editor to open it.
8. Change the Number of Seconds field to 3.
9. Click on OK to close the Content Editor.

By default, the box will be white filled with a black border. You need to use one more icon, the Color icon, to change the default. You'll build this icon into the structure above the Draw Box icon so that the new color settings will already be in effect when you execute the Draw Box icon:

1. Find the Color icon in the library.
2. Drag and drop the Color icon between the Box icon and the Draw Box icon.
3. Double click on the Color icon.
4. Pull down the Outline Color text box.
5. Select white.
6. Pull down the Fill Color text box.
7. Select red.

8. Choose OK. The branch of icons that draw a red box should appear as they do in Figure 7.26.

Now would be a good time to test this portion of your program.

To test your program:

1. Choose Save from the File menu.
2. Click on the Run-From-Top button on the tool ribbon.
3. Click on the Draw a Red Box button.

   IconAuthor draws a red box with a white two-pixel border. Shortly after the red box is drawn, it appears to be quickly wiped from the screen. At first glance, you would think you'd included an icon in your structure to specifically remove just the red box. However, what's really happening is that after the Draw Box icon finishes, execution flows back out to the beginning of the loop, and the Display icon displays the menu again.

4. Press **Esc** to quickly exit EVAL.IW and return to the structure window.

Playing an Animation Script

The third branch of the menu is executed when the user selects "Play an Animation Script." When the appropriate icon is executed, a brief animation routine plays. The animation that plays is stored in a file called TUTOR.ANI and was previously created using IconAuthor's animation editor, *IconAnimate*.

You've already used a Display icon (part of the Menu composite) to display a graphic file on the screen.

Now you're going to use another Display icon to play the animation file:

1. Find the Display icon in the library.
2. Drag the Display icon into the structure just below the If icon labeled Animate. The branch should appear as it does in Figure 7.27.

Figure 7.27
Animation Script
Icon Branch

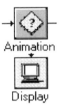

Animation

Display

3. Open the Display icon Content Editor.
4. Change the icon name to "Play Script."
5. Choose animate from the drop-down list of the File Type box.
6. Type **TUTOR.ANI** in the Filename text box. The Display icon Content Editor should now appear like the sample in Figure 7.28.

Figure 7.28
Play Script Icon
Content Editor

Content Editor
Icon Name: Play Script
File Type: animate
Filename: TUTOR.ANI
Location: 0, 0
Page or Effect:
OK   Cancel   Exit Range   Help

7. Choose File Save from the main menu.
8. Run the application by clicking on the Run-From-Top button on the tool ribbon.
9. Choose Play an Animation from the EVAL application screen.
10. Choose Quit to return to the structure screen.

Displaying the Author's Name

The fourth branch of the menu is executed when the user selects Display the Author's Name. When the appropriate icon is executed, your name is displayed on the screen.

Use a Write icon to display text on the screen. The color of text displayed with the Write icon is determined by the current fill and outline color settings.

Now let's put a Color icon before the Write icon to ensure that your name is displayed in yellow:

1. Find the Color icon in the library, then drag it to below the Show Name icon.

2. Find the Write icon in the library, then drag it to below the Color icon.

   Complete the branch with another three-second Pause icon so that your name will be displayed for an adequate period of time. To make it simple, copy the existing icon in the Box branch:

3. While pressing and holding the **Ctrl** key, drag the Pause icon from the bottom of the Box branch to the bottom of the Show Name branch. The branch appears as shown in Figure 7.29.

Figure 7.29
The Show Name
Program Branch
in EVAL.IW

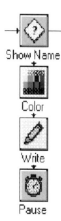

Show Name

Color

Write

Pause

4. Open the Color icon.

5. Pull down the Outline Color text box and select yellow.

6. Pull down the Fill Color text box and select TRANSPARENT.

7. Choose OK.

   The Write icon dynamically displays the text you specify just as the Box (renamed Box Draw) icon dynamically displays the box.

8. Double click on the Write icon, then click on the Text To Display text box.

9. Type **Authored by:** followed by your full name.

   Now you're going to use the Location Editor to pick the point on the screen where you want to display your name.

10. Pull down the Location text box and select Location Editor. At this point, the menu "Learning Authoring Fundamentals" should be showing within the Location Editor.

11. Click on the screen where you want the first character of the text to display. (Specifically, this point will be the starting location for the upper-left corner of the first character displayed.)

A good starting point would be near the right side of the screen, below the Quit option.

A small block appears at the point at which you clicked. The coordinates of the point you selected are displayed in the Coordinates: box in the Location Editor dialog, as shown in Figure 7.30.

Figure 7.30
Location Editor
Dialog with
Coordinates

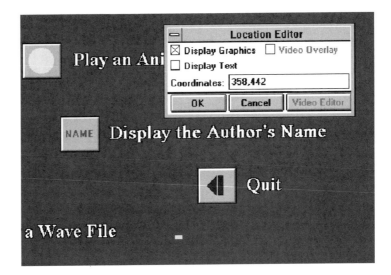

12. In the Location Editor, choose OK.

The coordinates of the point you selected are returned to the Location text box. The Write icon Content Editor should appear similar to the one in Figure 7.31.

Figure 7.31
Write Icon
Content Editor

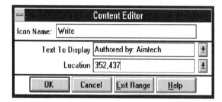

13. Choose OK in the Write icon Content Editor.
14. Save and run the application.
15. Choose the Display the Author's Name option.
16. Choose Quit to return to the structure screen.

Playing the MIDI File

The second branch of the menu is executed when the user selects Play a MIDI File. MIDI (Musical Instrument Digital Interface) files are audio files made up of musical instrument instructions. The MIDI file that your application will play was created previously and will play back using a "palette" of available sounds.

You use a MIDI composite to play a MIDI file. Three MCI (Media Control Interface) icons form the backbone of the composite. MCI is part of the Microsoft Multimedia Extensions for Windows. MCI allows an application to access and manipulate several different kinds of devices *if* those devices are designed to support Multimedia Extensions.

Although you must be familiar with the MCI command syntax to fully take advantage of the MCI feature, the MIDI composite already contains some values (that require minimal editing) so that you can quickly include a MIDI file as part of your IconAuthor application.

Here's how to start building the MIDI branch of this application:

1. Find the MIDI composite in the library.
2. Drag it below the MIDI branch in your structure. The MIDI composite appears as shown in Figure 7.32.

Figure 7.32
MIDI Composite
Icon Branch

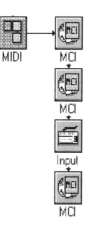

By default, the MIDI composite is made up of a lead icon, three MCI icons, and an Input icon. **For the purposes of this application, you do not need the Input icon:**

1. Click anywhere in the work area (not on an icon) to deselect the icons in the MIDI composite.
2. Select the Input icon and drag it to the Trashcan.
3. Choose Yes to confirm the Clear action.
4. Open the lead icon in the MIDI composite, labeled MIDI.
5. Rename it "Play MIDI."
6. Choose OK.

The Content Editor of the first MCI icon opens automatically, as shown in Figure 7.33.

Figure 7.33
Content Editor
of First MCI Icon

Content Editor
Icon Name: MCI
MCI Command: mid type sequencer alias sound
MCI Result:
MCI Error Number: @error_number
MCI Error Message: @error_message
OK   Cancel   Exit Range   Help

Each MCI icon that makes up the MIDI composite is designed to specify a different MCI command. As you saw in Figure 7.33, the first text box, MCI Command, contains a default command. Although the entire command is not immediately visible, by default it's as follows:

open c:\iauthor\audio\filename.mid type sequencer alias sound

The basic purpose of this command string is to initialize the MIDI sequencer software and identify the path and filename you want to play. It also takes the path, filename, and *type sequencer* identifier and assigns that information to one word, *sound*. By specifying this "alias," the remaining MCI icons only need to use the word "sound" when they want to reference this information.

> The choice of the word "sound" is arbitrary. You could use any alias you want as long as you continue to reference the alias as necessary in subsequent commands.

You only have to make one change to the default command string for this application. You need to change the generic, default filename.mid to the name of the specific file you're going to play for this application. The new filename is tutor.mid, and because you're using a sampler application, you need to change the path that points to the location of this file.

The new command string should be as follows:

1. open c:\toolshop\demo\audio\tutor.mid type sequencer alias sound.

> If you're using a drive other than the Ultimedia Tools default, you'll have to change the C: drive designation in this command to the proper drive.

2. Edit the command string in the MCI command text box so that the filename is tutor.mid (instead of filename.mid).
3. Change the path to this file to C:\ToolShop\Demo\Audio.
4. Change the icon name to Open.
5. Choose OK.

The Content Editor of the second MCI icon opens automatically. The default MCI command string in this icon is "play sound."

This command string causes the file (represented by the word "sound") to play. The only change you need to make to this command string is to add the keyword "wait." This will cause IconAuthor to wait until the entire MIDI file finishes playing before it executes the next icon.

When you edit the command string, it will appear as follows:

1. play sound wait.
2. Edit the command string in the MCI command text box by adding the keyword "wait" to the end.
3. Change the icon name to "Play."
4. Choose OK.

The Content Editor of the third MCI icon opens automatically. The default MCI command string in this icon is as follows:

close sound

This command suspends playback and relinquishes access to the MIDI device. **You don't need to make any changes to this command string:**

1. Change the name of the icon to "Close."
2. Choose OK.

   The icons in the branch that plays a MIDI file are now complete and should appear as shown in Figure 7.34.

Figure 7.34
MIDI File Icon
Branch

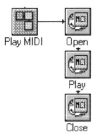

Play MIDI   Open

Play

Close

3. Save and run the application.
4. Choose the Play a MIDI File option.
5. Choose Quit.

Playing the Wave File

The fifth branch of the menu is executed when the user selects Play a Wave File. A Wave file is a digital audio file. The specific file that will be part of your application is TUTOR.WAV and was created previously.

You use a WaveAudio composite to create this branch of the application. The WaveAudio composite is similar to the MIDI composite because it also has three MCI icons as its backbone.

Like the MIDI composite, the WaveAudio composite already contains some values (that require minimal editing) so that you can quickly include a Wave file as part of your IconAuthor application:

1. Find the WaveAudio composite in the library.
2. Drag it to a position below the Wave branch in your structure. The WaveAudio composite appears as shown in Figure 7.35.

Figure 7.35
WaveAudio
Composite
Branch

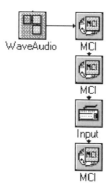

By default, this composite is made up of a lead icon, three MCI icons, and an Input icon. **For the purposes of this application, you do not need the Input icon:**

1. Click anywhere in the work area (not on an icon) to deselect the icons in the MIDI composite.
2. Click on the Input icon and drag it to the Trashcan.
3. Choose Yes to confirm the Clear action.
4. Open the lead icon in the WaveAudio composite, labeled WaveAudio.

5. Rename it "Play Wave."

6. Choose OK.

The Content Editor of the first MCI icon opens automatically, as shown in Figure 7.36.

Figure 7.36
Content Editor
for First Wave
Composite

Each MCI icon that makes up the WaveAudio composite is designed to specify a different MCI command. As shown in the previous figure, the first text box, "MCI Command," contains a default command. Although the entire command is not immediately visible, by default it is as follows:

open c:\iauthor\audio\filename.wav type waveaudio alias sound

The basic purpose of this command string is to initialize the wave audio software and identify the path and filename you want to play. It also takes the path, filename, and "type waveaudio" identifier and assigns that information to one word, "sound." As a result, the remaining MCI icons only need to use the word "sound" when they want to reference this information.

As in the MIDI composite, the use of the alias "sound" is arbitrary. Also, it doesn't matter that you're using the same alias for both Wave audio and MIDI because you're closing the device each time a file finishes playing.

You only have to make one change to the default command string for the purposes of this application. You need to change the generic, default filename.wav to the name of the specific file you're going to play for this application. The new filename is tutor.wav and, since the demonstration version of this software is not installed in the IAUTHOR subdirectory, you need to change the path.

The new command string should be as follows:

1. open c:\Toolshop\Demo\audio\tutor.wav type waveaudio alias sound

> If your Ultimedia Tools temporary files are stored on a drive other than drive C:, enter the proper drive letter in this path.

2. Edit the command string in the MCI command text box so that the filename is tutor.wav (instead of filename.wav).
3. Change the path to c:\Toolshop\Demo.
4. Change the icon name to "Open."
5. Choose OK.

The Content Editor of the second MCI icon opens automatically.

The default MCI command string in this icon is as follows:

play sound from 0

This command string causes the Wave file to play from the beginning. The only change you need to make to this command string is to add the keyword "wait." This will cause IconAuthor to wait until the entire Wave audio file finishes playing before it executes the next icon.

When you edit the command string, it will appear as follows:

play sound from 0 wait

To change the command string:

1. Edit the command string in the MCI command text box by adding the keyword "wait" to the end.
2. Change the icon name to "Play."
3. Choose OK.

   The Content Editor of the third MCI icon opens automatically. The default MCI command string in this icon is "close sound."

   This command suspends playback and relinquishes access to the Wave audio device.

You do not need to make any changes to this command string.

4. Change the name of the icon to "Close."

5. Choose OK.

   The icons in the branch that plays a Wave file are now complete and should appear as they do in Figure 7.37.

Figure 7.37
Wave File Icon
Branch

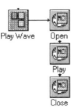

6. Save the application.

   At this point, you can choose any one of the six menu options. If any option doesn't work as it should, review the instructions in that part of the tutorial to make sure the icon is placed properly and contains the correct content.

   The screen in Figure 7.38 shows how the entire structure of EVAL.IW should appear when complete.

Figure 7.38
Completed
EVAL.IW Icon
Structure

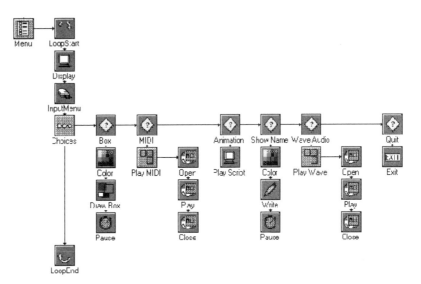

7. Run the application and try each option. When you're finished, choose Quit.

Learning More About IconAuthor

Using just a handful of icons in the Icon Library, you've created a colorful, menu-based, multimedia sampler program.

However, you used existing screens and sound files. In this section, we'll show you how to create another menu layer for this sample application, a layer that you can design from scratch. You'll use many of the techniques you learned in the previous section. Therefore, we'll present the steps to complete this additional menu in a somewhat shortened format. The finished menu will look like the sample in Figure 7.39.

Figure 7.39
Finished
"Understanding
Multimedia"
Menu

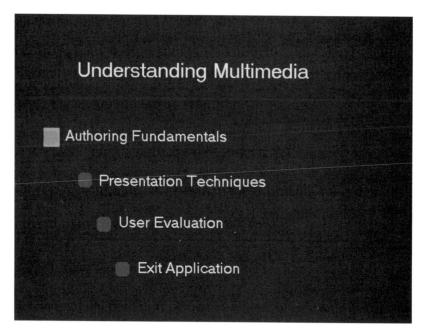

You'll design this screen using these general steps:

1. Open the Graphics Editor and create a dark blue background.
2. Select a font and font color.
3. Enter the title and individual menu choices.

4. Create boxes for buttons beside each menu item.

5. Save the graphics image.

Then, if you want, you can add another menu icon to the EVAL.IW presentation you created earlier. This menu and its associated display and input icons will present the new menu screen and let you select the authoring introduction created for EVAL.IW.

First, let's design the graphics image that you'll use as the menu.

Opening the Graphics Editor and Creating a Dark Blue Background

The IconAuthor Graphics Editor is just one of the tools supplied with the program to help you design your own objects for use in presentations.

Use the Graphics Editor to create the new menu screen:

1. Use Run Editors Graphics to load the graphics editor. The main Graphics Editor screen is shown in Figure 7.40.

Figure 7.40
Graphics Editor
Main Screen

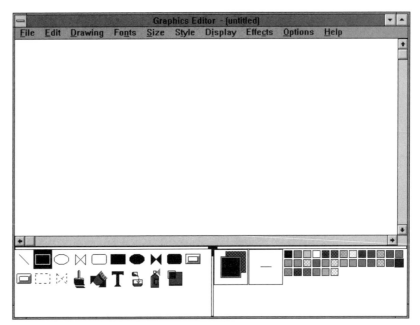

2. Use File New from the Graphics Editor menu to display the New dialog shown in Figure 7.41.

Figure 7.41
Graphics Editor
File New Dialog

3. Click on OK to accept the default image size of 640 pixels by 480 pixels.

4. Use Options FullScreen (**Ctrl+F**) to display the new image in full-screen mode. The menu and tool display are reduced in size, but you still can access all of the editor's features.

5. Click on the darkest blue color square in the color selection area of the tools display. The color display box changes to show a dark blue center and a black border.

6. Click on the black border of the color display square and click again on the darkest blue color square to change the border to dark blue as well.

7. Select the fill tool and move the pointer anywhere on the graphics image screen and click once to create a dark blue background.

8. Use File Save to create a name for the new menu file. We called it C:\Toolshop\Demo\Graphics\DEMOMENU.BMP.

Now you have created a plain blue background. In the next series of steps, we'll add text to the screen to create the basic menu.

Selecting a Font and Font Color

First we'll enter a title, then four menu choices:

1. Grab the Graphics Editor menu and tools display and drag it toward the bottom of the screen to make room to enter the title. A white area may be exposed.

2. Move the pointer to the white area (if any) and click to fill the area that was behind the menu box.

3. Select the text tool.

4. Select the darkest yellow color from the color squares and click on the border area of the color display box to set a yellow border color. Leave the center area dark blue.

5. Choose Fonts from the main menu and select MS Sans Serif.

6. Choose Size from the main menu and select 46/20 as the font size. The first number in this pair represents the character height; the second number is the character width.

7. Choose Display and select Mouse Position from the pulldown menu (or press **Ctrl+O**). This will open a window that shows you the current coordinates of the pointer.

Entering the Title and Individual Menu Choices

Now you can enter the text that makes up the title and the individual menu choices:

1. Move the pointer to approximately 70/50 (the precise position is not important) and click once. Simply place the pointer near the upper-left corner, but far enough away from the corner for pleasing positioning of the title.

If you don't see an x: y: cursor position display, use Display Mouse Position (Ctrl+O) to turn on the display.

2. Enter the title of this menu screen (**Understanding Multimedia)**, but DO NOT PRESS ENTER. The display will look like Figure 7.42.

   Notice that the text is surrounded by a lighter background that intrudes on the solid blue background we created earlier. To make the text blend into the original background, do the following:

3. Choose Drawing from the main menu and select Transparent. The text background becomes transparent to let the dark blue main screen background show through.

   Note that you're able to do this because you did not "set" the title by pressing Enter. At this point you can also experiment

Figure 7.42
First Line of
Understanding
Multimedia
Menu

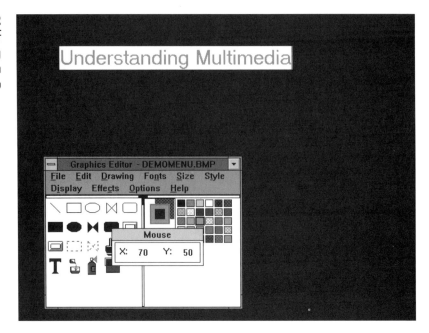

with different fonts and sizes. When you're satisfied with the title appearance, press **Enter** to set the text.

Now, enter the four menu choices, using a slightly smaller font:

You can drag the Graphics Editor menu and tools display around the screen as necessary to get it out of the way of your typing.

4. Choose Size and select 36/15 as the font size.
5. Position the pointer at approximately 90/175 and click once.
6. Type the first menu item, **Authoring Fundamentals**, then press **Enter**.
7. Position the pointer at approximately 130/230, enter the second menu item, **Presentation Techniques**, then press **Enter**.
8. Position the pointer at approximately 170/310, enter the third menu item, **User Evaluation**, then press **Enter**.
9. Position the pointer at approximately 200/380, enter the final menu item, **Exit Application**, then press **Enter**.
10. Use File Save to store the latest version of your menu screen, which should look like the one in Figure 7.43.

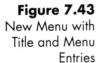

Figure 7.43
New Menu with
Title and Menu
Entries

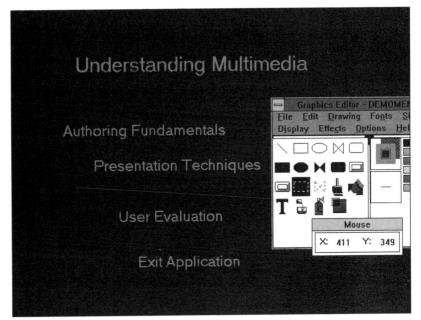

Creating Boxes for Buttons beside Each Menu Item

Next, you'll insert four red buttons, one beside each menu choice. These buttons will be set up as "hot spots" so you can use them to select a menu item.

To place the four buttons:

1. Click on the brightest red color square in the tools area. The border color, shown in the color display square in the color bar, should change from blue to red.

2. Click on the center area of the color display square and select the brightest red color square again to change the center of the square to red.

3. Select the rounded button tool, located just above the Text tool.

4. Position the pointer to the left of the first menu entry, at approximately 60/175. Click once to install a button at this location.

5. Insert a button beside all of the other menu entries. The screen should look like the one in Figure 7.44.

Figure 7.44
Finished Menu
Screen with
Buttons and
Titles

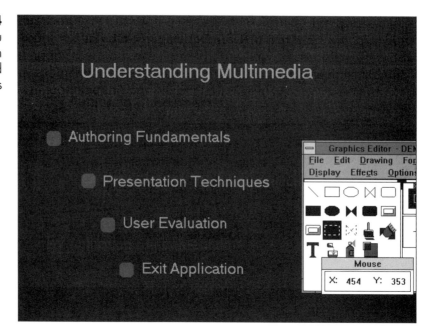

6. Use File Save to store the finished menu screen.
7. Use File Exit to return to the main structure screen.

This completes the design of the basic menu screen.

Inserting the Menu into the EVAL.IW Structure and Adding Content

The next step is for you to place a menu and display icon into the existing EVAL.IW display. We'll then specify the hot spots and the effects that go with them.

To place the newly created screen into the EVAL.IW structure:

1. Click on the Up Arrow at the upper-right corner of the EVAL.IW structure window to expand the display to full screen.
2. Locate the Menu icon in the library.

3. Drag the Menu icon to a position between the Start icon and the existing Menu icon in the EVAL.IW structure. The new Menu composite icon will expand into its individual icons and the display will appear like the one in Figure 7.45.

Figure 7.45
New Menu
Icon Added
to EVAL.IW
Structure

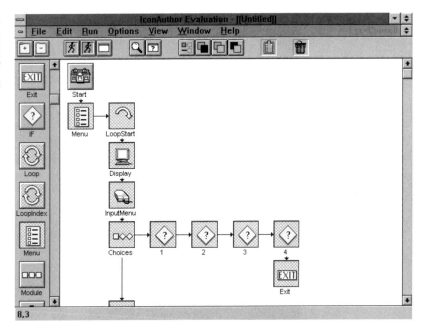

4. Double click on the new Menu icon to display its Content Editor.
5. Change the Composite Name to Main Menu and select OK. The Display icon part of this Menu composite will display automatically.
6. Click in the Filename field and enter the name of the menu screen you just created: **DEMOMENU.BMP**.
7. Select OK. The InputMenu icon Content Editor will be displayed automatically.

Now you'll set the Selection Areas coordinates, or hot spots, to establish the menu choice buttons that are part of the new menu screen.

We'll also specify the special effect that each button will use when it's selected:

1. Click on the Down Arrow to the right of the Selection Areas field in the InputMenu Content Area.

2. Select Input Template Editor from this pulldown list. The Input Template Editor is loaded with the new menu graphics screen displayed in the background, as shown in Figure 7.46.

Figure 7.46
Input Template
Editor over
DEMOMENU.BMP

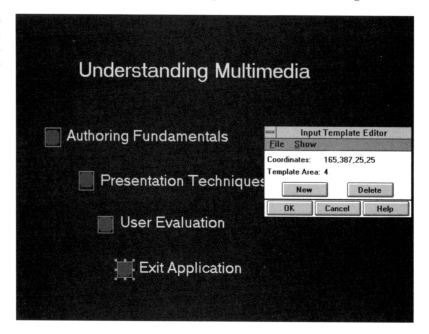

You'll use the Input Template Editor to establish hot spots around each of the four buttons beside the menu choices.

Here's how:

1. Click on New and position the pointer at the upper-left corner of the button beside the first menu item, Authoring Fundamentals.

2. Hold the left mouse button and draw a box tightly around this button. Release the mouse button and a yellow box with handles should appear around the box.

3. Repeat Step 2 three more times to draw boxes around each of the remaining buttons on the menu screen.

4. Click on OK to accept the coordinates and return to the InputMenu icon Content Editor. The coordinates for the boxes you just drew are displayed in the Selection Areas field of this dialog.

5. Click on the Down Arrow to the right of the Feedback field in this dialog to display the feedback pulldown menu.

6. Select "block flash" from this menu.

7. Select OK. The Choices icon Content Editor is displayed automatically.

8. Change the Choices composite name to Main Choices to differentiate this box from the one created earlier.

9. Click on OK. The Content Editor for the first If icon under this choices icon is displayed.

10. Change the Icon Name from 1 to Authoring and click on OK. The Content Editor for the second If icon is displayed.

11. Change the Icon Name in this dialog to Presentation and click on OK. The Content Editor for the third If icon is displayed.

12. Change the name of the third If icon to Evaluation and click on OK. The Content Editor for the fourth If icon is displayed.

13. Change the name on the final If icon in this branch to Exit Menu and click on OK. The Exit icon Content Editor is displayed.

14. Click on Exit Range to close this dialog series.

15. Use File Save to store the changed EVAL.IW file.

Next, you need to move the previously created menu series so that it branches off of the menu you just created instead of the main menu. This is a simple process.

To move the original menu branch:

1. Use the scroll bars to display the original menu branch and click on the lead icon to select the branch.

2. Press and hold the left mouse button and drag the menu branch to a position beneath and overlapping the Authoring If icon you just created.

3. Release the mouse button to drop the icon branch to its new location.

4. Use File Save to store the changed file.

Now try running the application again. If you select Run Application from Top you should see the new menu with its four choices. Only two of these choices are operational: the first one that selects the Authoring branch, and the Exit choice that ends the application and returns you to the structure screen. If you click on one of the other choices, the button will flash, execution will fall through the loop and the menu screen will be redisplayed.

5. Click on the first menu choice, Authoring Fundamentals. The original screen created in the first step of this tutorial should be displayed.

6. Click on Exit from this secondary screen and you should be returned to the main menu.

7. Click on Exit on this screen to return to the structures screen.

Saving the Graphics Image

You now have created a main menu structure and one branch off of that menu for a multimedia demonstration under IconAuthor. Again, you can view a slightly different version of this presentation by running the TUTORIAL.IW structure. In fact, you can load the TUTORIAL.IW file into a structure window and study the structure so you can complete the EVAL.IW structure you've started, or use this basic structure as a starting place for one of your own.

But first you need to save your new presentation. Right now it's stored in a temporary directory that will be erased when you exit the IconAuthor sampler.

To save your new presentation:

1. Click on the Down Arrow at the upper-right corner of the IconAuthor screen to shrink the application to an icon, revealing the Presentation Manager icon.

2. Open the Presentation Manager.

3. Find and open the Main application window.

4. Select MS-DOS from this application to enter the operating system window.

5. Type **MD MPC**, then press **Enter**. This command creates a new directory off of the root of the current hard drive.

6. Type **CD\Toolshop\Demo\Iconware**, then press **Enter** to change the default directory to the one that contains the new EVAL.IW structure.

7. Type **COPY EVAL.* \MPC**, then press **Enter** to copy all of the files associated with the EVAL presentation to the MPC subdirectory.

8. Type **EXIT**, then press **Enter**. The DOS window is closed and you are returned to the IconAuthor demo screen.

Finally, you should rename the EVAL.IW application stored in the \MPC directory so that you can conduct another session with IconAuthor, using the default structure name, and copy it to the MPC directory like you did for this one.

In summary, here are some of the skills you've learned with this chapter. Use them to design and create an IconAuthor application of your own:

- Opening the IconAuthor evaluation software
- Designing applications
- Expanding the icon library
- Selecting and placing icons within a structure
- Editing the content of various icons using the Content Editor
- Creating a graphics screen to use as a menu
- Specifying "hot spots" or selection areas on this screen
- Specifying feedback when a hot spot is selected
- Copying and moving structure icons and structure icon branches
- Saving a structure file
- Copying the default EVAL.IW file from the volatile demo directory to a permanent hard disk location

Special thanks: Portions of the IconAuthor and Ultimedia Tools sampler material in Chapter 7 have appeared in the AimTech documentation. The material is used here with permission of AimTech Corporation, 20 Trafalgar Square, Nashua, NH 03063-1973.

Multimedia Resources

A SELECTED DIRECTORY

> The Ultimedia Tools Series CD-ROM packaged with this book is a convenient source of information for over 50 multimedia products. See Appendix A for more information on using the CD.

There are a few companies who aren't on the CD that offer hardware and software products to enhance your multimedia PC platform. In this chapter, we'll familiarize you with some of these companies, and provide you with telephone numbers and addresses so you can get more information, if desired.

Hardware

In Chapter 1, we discussed the basic hardware you need for a multimedia platform. The companies and products in this section provide those basic needs, or offer you enhancements that go beyond the basics.

345

Video

We've mentioned the value of motion video in several sections of this book. With the cost of video interface cards and software declining, you might want to consider some form of video for your multimedia platform. (See Appendix D for more information on using full motion video with your multimedia PC.)

SnapPlus
Video and VGA interface card for PCs
Cardinal Technologies, Inc.
1827 Freedom Road
Lancaster, PA 17601
717-293-3000
800-233-0187

VideoBlaster
Full motion video capture
Creative Labs, Inc.
1901 McCarthy Boulevard
Milpitas, CA 95035
408-428-6600
800-647-9933

Video Machine for PCs
PC-based video editing platform
Fast Electronics U.S., Inc.
5 Commonwealth Road
Natick, MA 01760
508-655-3278
Fax: 508-655-0447

ActionMedia II
Video capture with sound and video output
IBM Corporation
4111 Northside Parkway
Atlanta, GA 30327
404-238-1282
800-426-9402

Olivia
Video capture, video editing, and scan conversion interface card
Jovian Logic Corporation

47929 Fremont Boulevard
Fremont, CA 94538
510-651-4823

TV Link
VGA-NTSC interface
KDI Precision Products, Inc.
3975 McMann Road
Cincinnati, OH 45245
513-943-2000
800-377-3334

Video capture hardware and software
NewMedia Graphics Corporation
780 Boston Road
Billerica, MA 01821-5925
508-663-0666
800-288-2207

Video Toaster
PC-based video production studio
Newtek, Inc.
215 SE Eighth Street
Topeka, KS 66603
913-354-1146
800-765-3406

Truevision
Video capture and output
Truevision
7340 Shadeland Station
Indianapolis, IN 46256
317-841-0332
800-344-8783

Mediator
PC graphics to video converter hardware
VideoLogic, Inc.
245 First Street
Cambridge, MA 02142
617-494-0530

CD-ROM

CDX-431-Series
CD-ROM Reader
Chinon America, Inc.
615 Hawaii Avenue
Torrance, CA 90503
310-533-0274

CDR-74, CDR-84
Multispin (high speed) CD-ROM readers
NEC Technologies, Inc.
1255 Michael Drive
Wood Dale, IL 60191-1094
708-860-9500
800-632-4636

For now, most of the work you do with digital data read off of CD-ROM disks likely will be done at your desk with a full-sized computer. A few companies already are offering CD-ROM readers installed in laptop computers to put CD-ROM power on the road. And now, Philips, for one, is offering a dedicated CD-ROM reader that is positioned and marketed more as an electronic book than as a computer. The Philips CDI 360 Portable shown in Figure 8.1 is a hand-held CD-I (Compact Disc-Interactive) delivery system with a six-inch active matrix color LCD screen. The screen displays 756 pixels by 556 pixels, and shows both NTSC and PAL images. The 360 includes a built-in pointing device, stereo speakers, and multiple video and audio connections to allow the unit to attach to a TV, monitor, or a video projector. You can use AC or battery power with the 360.

Philips Consumer Electronics Company
One Philips Drive
P.O. Box 14810
Knoxville, TN 37914-1810
615-521-4316

Some 600Mb of data on a single disk may sound like a lot of data at your fingertips, but once you start using multimedia products, including music, sound, motion video, and high resolution graphics with animation, you'll quickly see how little

Figure 8.1
Philips CDI 360
Portable

storage that really is. For several years now, users of mini- and mainframe computers have used WORM jukeboxes as backup and online archiving devices. Now, you can add a jukebox for CD-ROM to your PC with the Pioneer DRM-604X Minichanger. This drive holds six CD-ROM disks, which it switches in and out as you need them. In addition, the access time and transfer rates on this machine go well beyond minimum MPC requirements.

Pioneer Communications of America, Inc.
Optical Memory Systems Division
3255-I Scott Boulevard
Suite 103
Santa Clara, CA 95054
408-988-1702
800-527-3766

Texel Corporation produces high-quality, high-speed CD-ROM players for internal or external mounting. The external units are slightly larger than those of some competitors, but they're ruggedly built and offer excellent reliability.

DM-3024 (internal)
DM-5024 (external)
CD-ROM player
Texel Corporation
1605 Wyatt Drive
Santa Clara, CA 95054
408-980-1838

XM-3401 Series, double-speed drives (see Figure 8.2)
CD-ROM player
Toshiba America Information Systems, Inc.
Disk Products Division
9740 Irvine Boulevard
Irvine, CA 92718
714-583-3000

Figure 8.2
Toshiba
XM-3401 Series
CD-ROM
Reader

Presentation Aids

If your audience is more than five or ten people, it becomes difficult
for everyone to be able to see your computer monitor during a
presentation. One answer is to place a string of large-screen
monitors around the presentation room, a technique used successfully by many multimedia presenters. Large-screen monitors

provide the best quality imaging, but even one such monitor is a burden to transport, store, and set up.

Another solution is a computer projector, a device that you attach directly to the computer monitor and projects the screen image on the wall. The quality of this projected image is not quite as good as the on-screen image, but it's adequate in most cases, and it can be large enough to make your presentation visible to a large audience. The products listed here are just some examples of the projection hardware available. Check with your local audio-visual or computer dealer for details on these and other projection devices.

Boxlight
PC screen projector
Boxlight Corporation
17771 Fjord Drive, NE
Poulsbo, WA 98370
206-779-7901
800-762-5757

The Visual Presenter series (several models are offered) works like a 35mm camera to capture still images.

Visual Presenters
Still-image digitizer
Elmo Co., Ltd.
70 New Hyde Park Road
New Hyde Park, NY 11040-9980
516-775-3200

Touch monitors and software for Windows (see Figure 8.3)
Elographics, Inc.
105 Randolph Road
Oak Ridge, TN 37830
615-482-4100

VideoShow is a unique combination of hardware that can make your presentation proceed in a professional manner. VideoShow uses graphics images created on the PC, adds audio, motion video, graphics, and more to build a comprehensive multimedia show. The VideoShow ARC (Advanced Remote Control) puts control of the entire show in your hand with a hand-held

Figure 8.3
Elographics
TouchScreen
Monitor

video screen and control buttons so you can select scenes, advance the program, preview slides, and more.

VideoShow with Advanced Remote Control (ARC) (see Figure 8.4)
Presentation hardware and controller
General Parametrics Corporation
1250 Ninth Street
Berkeley, CA 94710
510-524-3950
800-223-0999

TVT-6000
Data and video projector
Infocus Systems, Inc.
7770 SW Mohawk Street
Tualatin, OR 97062
503-692-4968

Touchscreen technology can be an excellent enhancement to interactive multimedia presentations, especially those intended for a non-technical audience. By removing the keyboard from the presentation, people who don't type (and don't want to learn) can interact easily with the computer by responding to on-screen prompts. Generally, you must purchase a special monitor designed for a touch interface, but there are products, such as QuickPoint, that let you turn any monitor into a touchscreen device.

Figure 8.4
VideoShow
with ARC

QuickPoint
Snap-on PC touchscreen
MicroTouch Systems, Inc.
300 Griffin Park
Methuen, MA 01844-9867
508-659-9000

Multimedia is the newest presentation technology, and it takes advantage of the powerful computer, graphics, sound, and motion video technology available. Still, there are times when what you've produced with the latest high-tech tool on your PC would best be displayed through conventional means, such as 35mm slides. Several companies supply video film recorders to handle this task for you.

The premier supplier in this field is Polaroid. The company offers slide printers that attach to your computer and use desktop processed Polaroid slide film, or conventional slide stock that you send off for processing. In addition, Polaroid offers the CI7000 color film printer that produces quality Polaroid color prints from your computer in just over half a minute. These items aren't cheap by computer standards: the slide printers range from $4,500 to $6,000 and the CI7000 is about $2,000. Still, there's no substitute for having these capabilities right on your desktop.

CI-3000, CI-5000 (see Figure 8.5)
Polaroid or conventional film recorders with computer interface
Polaroid Corporation
575 Technology Square
Cambridge, MA 02139
617-577-2000

Figure 8.5
Polaroid
CI-3000 and
CI-5000 Slide
Printers

Figure 8.6
Polaroid
CI-7000
Polaroid
Computer
Printer

In addition to screen projectors, Proxima offers an interesting device for multimedia presenters: the Cyclops pointer and remote control wand. With the Cyclops and one of the Proxima LCD projectors, you can control the PC from the projected image, pull down a menu, launch an application, and save a file. Cyclops actually functions like a cordless mouse, while giving you the features of an electronic pointer at the same time.

Ovation and Ovation SX
PC screen projector
Proxima Corporation
6610 Nancy Ridge Drive
San Diego, CA 92121-3297
619-457-5500

LCD XG-2000
Front or rear projection portable LCD projector
SharpVision
Sharp Electronics Corporation
Industrial LCD Products
Sharp Plaza
Mahwah, NJ 07430-2135
201-529-8731

ProVision
PC screen projector
Spectrel International
1308 Bayshore Highway 100
Burlingame, CA 94010
415-343-5987

Audio/Sound Hardware

Some form of audio interface is an important part of your multimedia system. You need to be able to play standard-format sound files and you need a way to output the sound provided by many games and other multimedia applications. In addition, as your applications become increasingly complex, you'll want to be able to record your own sound from CD players, a microphone, or an external mixer and amplifier.

Fortunately, the decision on what to purchase isn't too difficult, because by far the majority of sound interface cards being offered today support these features. (For more information on multi-media PC configurations and hardware requirements, refer to Chapter 1.)

And, as this book is written, most of the available sound card add-ins are based on FM synthesis. However, most—of the companies listed here already—or soon will—provide wave table MIDI devices, as well. If you're interested in MIDI applications, contact these companies for more details.

Ad Lib Gold 1000
PC sound card
Ad Lib, Inc.
50 Staniford Street
Suite 800
Boston, MA 02144
800-463-2686

AudioMaster
PC sound card
Advanced Strategies Corp. (ASC)
60 Cutter Mill Road
Great Neck, NY 11021
516-482-0088

Cyber Audio
PC sound card
Alpha Systems Lab
2361 McGaw Avenue
Irvine, CA 92714
714-252-0117

Model 21
PC sound card
Antex Electronics
16100 South Figueroa St.
Gardena, CA 90248
310-532-3092

Stereo CD and stereo FX PC sound cards
ATI Technologies, Inc.
3761 Victoria Park Avenue
Scarborough, Ontario, Canada M1W 3S2
416-756-0718

Sound Galaxy NX Pro
PC sound card
Aztech Labs, Inc.
46707 Fremont Boulevard
Fremont, CA 94538
510-623-8988

CompuAdd Spectrum
PC sound card
CompuAdd Computer
12303 Technology Boulevard
Austin, TX 78727
512-250-2530
800-627-1967

Gallant SC 4000 & 5000
PC sound card
Compumedia Technology, Inc.
465600 Fremont Boulevard
Fremont, CA 94538
510-656-9811

Maestro Pro & 16 & 16VR
PC sound card
Computer Peripherals
667 Rancho Conejo
Newberry Park, CA 91320
805-499-5751
800-854-7600

Sound Master II
PC sound card
Covox, Inc.
675 Conger
Eugene, OR 97402
503-342-1271

MIDI wave table sound
Sound Blaster; Sound Blaster Pro; Sound Blaster 16, expansion
bus sound card
Creative Labs, Inc.
1901 McCarthy Boulevard
Milpitas, CA 95035
408-428-6600
800-647-9933

MIDI wave table sound
BSR Media Master sound card
DAK Industries, Inc.
8200 Remmet Avenue
Canoga Park, CA 91304
818-888-8220

Sonic Sound & Pro
PC sound card
Diamond Computer
1130 East Aerques Avenue
Sunnyvale, CA 94086
408-736-2000

Port-Able Sound
PC sound card
Digispeech, Inc.
550 Main Street, Suite J
Placerville, CA 95667
916-621-1787

2the Max Soundmedia
PC sound card
Focus Information Systems
4046 Clipper Street
Fremont, CA 94538
510-657-2845

AudioBahn
PC sound card
Genoa Systems
75 East Trimble Road
San Jose, CA 95131
408-432-9090

MIDI wave table sound
Kurzweil Music Systems
Young Chaing Research and Development Institute
1432 Main Street
Waltham, MA 02154
617-890-2929

MEDIA Concept Pro
PC sound card

Laser Digital, Inc.
1030 Duane Avenue
Suite 8 McHenry East
Sunnyvale, CA 94086
408-737-2666

HiSonic A
PC sound card
Logicode Technology, Inc.
1380 Flynn Road
Camarillo, CA 93012
805-388-9000

MSC-01
PC sound card
Media Resources
640 Puente Street
Brea, CA 92621
714-256-5048

Sound Commander Pro
PC sound card
Media Sonic, Inc.
96726 Fremont Boulevard
Fremont, CA 94538
510-438-9996

Pro Audio Spectrum Plus & 16
PC sound card
Media Vision
3185 Laurel View Court
Fremont, CA 94538
510-770-8600

Microsoft Windows Sound System
PC sound card
Microsoft Corporation
One Microsoft Way
Redmond, WA 98052-6322
206-882-8080

MIDI wave table sound
Okey Dokey & Pro Gold PC sound card
MIDI Land, Inc.

398 Lemon Creek Drive, Suite L
Walnut, CA 91789
909-595-0708

MIDI wave table sound
AudioMaster PC sound card
Omnilabs/RTM
13177 Ramona Boulevard
Erwindale, CA 91706
818-813-2630

TOPiX
Desktop CD recording system
Optical Media International
180 Knowles Drive
Los Gatos, CA 95030
408-376-3511
Fax: 408-376-3519

MIDI wave table sound
Roland Corp. USA
7200 Dominion
Los Angeles, CA 90040
213-685-5141

WinStorm
PC sound card
Sigma Designs
47900 Bayside Parkway
Fremont, CA 94538
510-770-0100

Golden Sound
PC sound card
Toptek Technology
14140 LiveOak Avenue, Number C
Baldwin Park, CA 91706
818-960-9211

ProSound
PC sound card
Tecmar
6225 Cochran Road
Solon, OH 44139
216-349-0600

MIDI wave table sound
MultiSound PC sound card
Turtle Beach Systems
P.O. Box 5074
York, PA 17405
717-843-6916

MIDI wave table sound
Yamaha of America
6600 Orangethorpe
Buena Park, CA 90620
714-522-9240

TeSS
PC sound card
Zoltrix
47517 Seabride Drive
Fremont, CA 94538
510-657-1188

Libraries

It's great that so many of the popular multimedia software packages let you incorporate motion video and CD-quality sound in your presentations. However, just where do you get quality video and sound bites to use? Sure, you can record your own, but that means you must have or buy recording equipment to do the job. And what if you need access to specific information, sounds, or video?

Not always possible.

So, when the time comes to put together that ultimate presentation, it makes sense to turn to resource libraries. You can order image, music, sound effects, and video subscriptions—sort of a "resource of the month" club. Or, you can order "one time only" CD's, slides, or computer disks with just the data you need.

You can get generic clip art that covers topics such as parties, the office, business, farming, students, computers, outdoors, and much more. Such clip art ranges from simple, silhouette drawings, to complex, color workstation graphics.

You can also purchase animation sequences constructed on a computer, and you can buy familiar songs and sound effects, as well as clips from familiar movies. Prices vary, but if you're into multimedia presentations, the cost is very reasonable.

Purchasing your effects from a library not only gives you professional results for a reasonable price, it saves you the time and effort of finding and recording these sequences yourself. In addition, purchased video and audio clips are cleared for public use, eliminating your responsibility for securing model releases or permission to use individual or company likenesses for public presentations.

Most companies offer a variety of packages, so begin your research by calling each company listed here and asking for a complete list of their libraries. Once you find a company you're satisfied with, try using them exclusively. Frequently, these companies offer discounts for subscription services or for multiple purchases.

Video

Cliptime is a collection of about 250 professionally produced color QuickTime movie clips. A wide variety of subjects are covered, including animals, medical, sports, aerial shots, business, education, industry, people, and transportation.

Alpha Technologies Group, Inc.
6921 Cable Drive
Marriottsville, MD 21104
410-781-4200

Stock Footage Library
Video clips
Archive Films
530 West 25th Street
New York, NY 10001
212-620-3955
Fax: 212-645-2137

Resource Library contains about 550 24-bit color images and some 60 color QuickTime movies, most of which include sound.

Included with Volume I of this series is nearly 200Mb of NASA material in movie and still format. Also available is a series of plant images and over 9Mb of cave still images.

Resource Library
Bliss Interactive Technologies
6034 West Courtyard Drive
Austin, TX 78730
512-338-2458

TV-ROM is a 500Mb disk with more than 400 color QuickTime movies and about 100 still images. The material is in the public domain, which means you are free to use it however you want to.

BMUG, Inc.
1442a Walnut Street, Box #62
Berkeley, CA 94709
510-549-2684

The Jasmine Six Pack
Stock video and music on CD for DVI (Digital Video Interface)
Jasmine Multimedia Publishing, Inc.
1888 Century Park East
Suite 300
Los Angeles, CA 90067
310-277-7523
800-798-7535

AdClips
Video clips
Mediacom
P.O. Box 36173
Richmond, VA 23235
804-794-0700
Fax: 804-794-0799

Video clips
Video Tape Library, Ltd.
1509 North Crescent Heights Boulevard
Suite 2
Los Angeles, CA 90046
213-656-4330
Fax: 213-656-8746

Media-Pedia
Video clips
Video Clips, Inc.
22 Fisher Avenue
Wellesley, MA 02181
617-235-5617

Video clips can come from nearly anywhere. Some companies supply computer-generated graphics, some produce custom clips, others offer excerpts from movies. The WPA Film Library (Figure 8.7) offers an interesting grouping of clips from a broad variety of sources, including classic advertising, documentaries, silent movies, and news footage. The company offers an interesting catalog that evokes memories and will provide you with stimulating ideas.

The WPA Film Library
Video clips
WPA Film Library
5525 West 159th Street
Oak Forest, IL 60452
708-535-1540
800-777-2223

Figure 8.7
From the WPA
Film Library

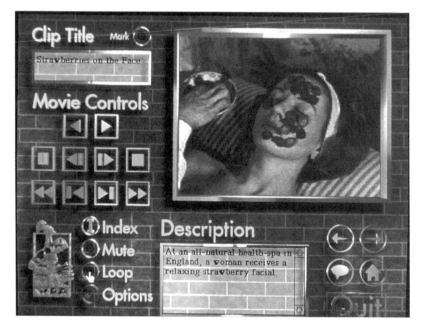

Graphics and Art

Designer's Club
Monthly PC graphics service
Dynamic Graphics, Inc.
6000 North Forest Park Drive
P.O. Box 1901
Peoria, IL 61656-9841
800-255-8800

The Multimedia Graphic Network specializes in a variety of graphics images you can use in your multimedia presentations or desktop publications applications. You can purchase these images as collections of related art, such as the Classic Art I series. Categories range from artistic to business.

This art can be supplied in 35mm slides, or as 24-bit .TIF images so you can use it directly from your PC. You can use these images like clip art, reproducing and distributing them as often as you wish, except that you can't reproduce the images and sell them as an art service.

Classic Art
Graphics images—classic art and other series
Multimedia Graphic Network
225 West Plaza Street
Encinitas, CA 92075
619-793-4121

Sound and Music

Max Trax
Four-CD package of short music clips. Other packages are also available, including sound effects.
Creative Support Services
1950 Riverside Drive
Los Angeles, CA 90039
213-666-7968
800-468-6874

Killer Tracks
Three-CD collection of production music

Killer Tracks
6534 Sunset Boulevard
Hollywood, CA 90028
213-957-4455
800-877-0078

Audio
Multimedia Arts, Inc.
3900 West Alameda Avenue
Suite 1700
Burbank, CA 90068
818-972-2625
800-468-9008

The Music Bakery
Monthly music subscription service
The Music Bakery
660 Preston Forest Center
Suite 300
Dallas, TX 75230
800-229-0313/warehouse only

Fresh Music Library
Library of 14 CDs for individual or multiple purchases
The Music Library
80 South Main Street
Hanover, NH 03755
603-643-1388
800-545-0688

Sound effects library and music clips
Valentino, Inc.
500 Executive Boulevard
P.O. Box 534
Elmsford, NY 10523-0534
914-347-7878
800-223-6278

Software

Your chosen multimedia software may handle all of the media
management duties you need. On the other hand, as your presen-

tations become more complex, you may need additional features for sound production or editing, or for video management. A separate software package—or two or three—can significantly enhance the tools provided as part of your multimedia software.

The best advice for purchasing additional software is to work with the basic multimedia software first. Once you know what you can do and what you want to do, you can start researching the additional software power that's available. The companies in this list can help you.

The Quest authoring package was used to develop the IBM portions of the Ultimedia Tools Series disk included with this book. Allen's product has been around a long time, by multimedia standards. The company began its work in 1981. The basic Quest package runs under DOS, but an add-in product, WINPOST, lets developers work in Windows and deliver a fully interactive product in DOS. The advantage of developing in Windows is the friendly and familiar user interface. The advantage of delivering the presentation in DOS is the speed and control software can maintain without the Windows overhead.

Quest
DOS and Windows authoring tool
Allen Communication
Lakeside Plaza II
5225 Wiley Post Way
Salt Lake City, UT 84116
801-537-7800

MCS Stereo
.WAV file sound editor
Animotion Development Corporation
3720 Fourth Avenue South, Suite 205
Birmingham, AL 35222
205-591-5715

Animator Pro
Animation software
Autodesk, Inc.
2320 Marinship Way
Sausalito, CA 94965
415-332-2344

Playmation
Animation software
Cineplay Interactive
25580 NW Upshur
Portland, OR 97210
503-223-4449

Arts and Letters Scenerio
Pre-fab art for scene design
Computer Support Corporation
15926 Midway Road
Dallas, TX 75244
214-661-8960

Crystal Desktop Animator
3-D modeling, rendering, and animation software
CrystalGraphics
3110 Patrick Henry Drive
Santa Clara, CA 95054
408-496-6175

Sound Impression
.WAV file sound editor
DigiVox Corporation
991 Commercial Street
Palo Alto, CA 94303
415-494-6200

Madison Avenue
DOS-based, user-friendly presentation package
Eclipse Technologies, Inc.
1221 West Campbell Road
Suite 125
Richardson, TX 75080
214-238-9944

The Tempra software package is just one example of the trend toward desktop production in multimedia. Just a few years ago, the only way to record data to CD-ROM was to hire an outside company to handle the master for you, which could cost you thousands of dollars. Today, if you have a CD recorder such as the Philips CDD 521 (about $5000), and software such as the Tempra CD Maker, you can produce your own CD masters right at your desktop PC.

Tempra CD Maker converts DOS files to ISO9660 (CD) format and records it to the CD-ROM media. Once you have the master, you can send it to a duplication house for copying, if desired.

Mathematica also produces a series of graphics and media management software tools, including Tempra Media Author, Tempra Pro, Tempra Turbo Animator, and others.

Tempra CD Maker
CD-ROM mastering software
Mathematica, Inc.
402 S. Kentucky Avenue
Lakeland, FL 33801
813-682-1128

Personal Producer and Matrox Studio
Video editing
Matrox Video Products Group
1055 St. Regis Boulevard
Dorval, Quebec, Canada H9P 2T4
514-685-2630

Photo Factory for Windows
Kodak Photo CD software
The Multimedia Store
5347 Dietrich Road
San Antonio, TX 78219-2997
210-661-8398
800-597-3686

3-D Workshop
Animation software
Presidio Software
2215 Chestnut Street
San Francisco, CA 94123
415-474-6437

D/Vision
Digitized video editing
TouchVision Systems, Inc.
1800 Winnemac Avenue
Chicago, IL 60640
312-989-2160

Wave for Windows
.WAV file sound editor
Turtle Beach Systems
P.O. Box 5074
York, PA 17405
717-843-6916

CameraMan for Windows
PC screen recorder
Vision Software International
524 Second St.
San Francisco, CA 94107
415-541-9333
Fax: 415-541-0555

Publications

An increasing number of multimedia-specific books and periodicals are available to further your learning and help you keep up with the latest industry happenings. Obviously, it would be impossible to list every possible publication here, but these resources will get you started. And, of course, many of these publications list additional resources you may find helpful.

Look for some of these on your local newsstands. Others you'll have to purchase through subscription only. When in doubt, call the company for information.

Presentation Products
Monthly magazine
Full Circle Communications
23410 Civic Center Way
Suite E-10
Malibu, CA 90265
310-456-2283

The Nautilus monthly CD-ROM is indicative of publishing in the future. Each month you receive a CD-ROM disk with several hundred megabytes of software demos, fonts, background music and sounds, digitized photographs and images, as well as software reviews, directories and databases, games, and more

(Figure 8.8). Each disk even includes a "Nautilus Link" facility that offers dial-up support and feedback services with the publisher. Each disk costs about $10.00.

Nautilus
Monthly CD-ROM with music, graphics, and data
Metatec Corporation
7001 Discovery Boulevard
Dublin, OH 43017-3299
614-766-3150
800-637-3472

Figure 8.8
Sample Nautilus
Data Screen

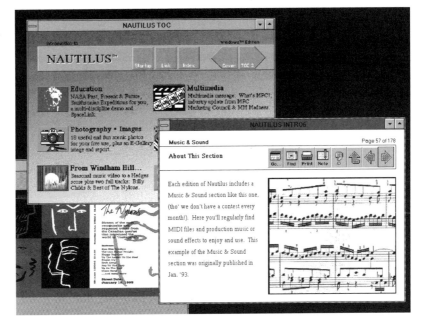

AVideo
Monthly magazine—audio visual topics
Montage Publishing Inc.
701 Westchester Boulevard
White Plains, NY 10604
914-328-9157

Multimedia & Videodisc Monitor
Monthly newsletter
P.O. Box 26
Falls Church, VA 22040-0026
703-241-1799

Multimedia World
Monthly magazine
501 Second Street
San Francisco, CA 94107
415-978-3221

New Media
Monthly magazine
901 Mariner's Island Boulevard
San Mateo, CA 94404
415-573-5170

CD-I World
Monthly magazine—interactive information and entertainment
Parker Taylor & Company, Inc.
49 Bayview Street
Camden, ME 04843
207-236-8524

CD-ROM Professional
Monthly magazine—CD-ROM hardware and software issues
Pemberton Press, Inc.
462 Danbury Road
Wilton, CT 06897-2126
203-761-1466
800-248-8466

Computer Artist
Monthly magazine
PennWell Publishing Company
One Technology Park Drive
P.O. Box 987
Westford, MA 01886
918-831-9423

Computer Graphics World
Monthly magazine
PennWell Publishing Company
One Technology Park Drive
P.O. Box 987
Westford, MA 01886
918-831-9554, Ext. 400

Electronic Imaging Report
Biweekly newsletter
Philips Business Information, Inc.
7811 Montrose Road
Potomac, MD 20854
301-340-2100

Multimedia Week
Weekly newsletter
Philips Business Information, Inc.
7811 Montrose Road
Potomac, MD 20854
301-340-2100

Video Technology News
Biweekly newsletter
Philips Business Information, Inc.
7811 Montrose Road
Potomac, MD 20854
301-340-2100

Videography
Monthly magazine
P.S.N. Publications, Inc.
2 Park Avenue
New York, NY 10016
212-779-1919

Video Magazine
Monthly magazine
Reese Communications, Inc.
460 W. 34th Street
New York, NY 10001
800-365-1008

Roland User's Group
Monthly magazine
Roland Corporation
7200 Dominion Circle
Los Angeles, CA 90040

Desktop Video
Monthly magazine
TechMedia Publishing, Inc.

80 Elm Street
Peterborough, NH 03458
603-924-0100

Videomaker Magazine
Monthly magazine
Videomaker, Inc.
P.O. Box 4591
Chico, CA 95927
616-745-2809

Services

As a presenter of multimedia information, you may never have a need for 600Mb of data on a single, industry-standard disk. On the other hand, once you get into interactive training, multimedia catalogs, and so on, you may want several of your products produced on CD-ROM. The companies in this section provide this service for you, taking your data and converting it to industry-standard CD-ROM format. Once recorded, you have up to 660Mb of information on a single disk. This type of service used to cost thousands of dollars. Today, many companies offer a single-disk conversion for around $250. Production at this price doesn't include much in the way of reformatting or technical time, but if your data is in good form and all the production company has to do is put it on CD, then this is a fantastic deal.

Once you need to distribute your CD data—perhaps thousands of disks at a time—these companies can do that too, for as little as $2.00 per disk after the master is complete. And these companies generally offer additional services, such as design and printing of on-disk color logos or other information, custom cases, mailers, and so on.

CD-ROM mastering
CD ROM, Inc.
1667 Cole Boulevard, Suite 400
Golden, CO 80401
303-231-9373

CD-ROM mastering
CD Services, Inc.
14567 Big Basin Way
Suite 4B
Saratoga, CA 95070
408-867-0514

Comsell offers custom development and consulting services. Comsell develops training courses using multimedia tools for IBM and other nationally known companies.

Comsell, Inc.
500 Tech Parkway
Atlanta, GA 30313
404-872-2500

Multi-Media Solutions is indicative of a rising form of company in this multimedia marketplace. Although tools such as the ones you'll find on the CD shipped with this book make powerful development software available to anyone who needs it, there are many issues that low-cost software can't address. You may need help designing presentations, for example, or simply need help finding the right hardware or software. In addition, as you work on your own presentations, you may need telephone, modem, or on-site technical support. Companies such as Multi-Media Solutions provide this support for independent and in-house developers.

Presentation design, production, and consulting
Multi-Media Solutions
P.O. Box 113
Alcoa, TN 37701
615-681-2573

CD-ROM mastering
Optical Media International
180 Knowles Drive
Los Gatos, CA 95030
408-376-3511
Fax: 408-376-3519

Using Existing Software for Multimedia

An Overview

For really serious multimedia applications, you'll use one of the authoring packages included on the CD-ROM disk with this book, or something similar, and you'll back it up with some third-party applications, such as animation, drawing, or video and sound libraries.

However, if you've been using computers for awhile, you may already have a suite of applications at your fingertips, and some of these already have in them the data you want to present to your multimedia audience.

Can you use what you've already done when it comes time to build that multimedia application?

Certainly!

377

And the process isn't particularly difficult. In this chapter, we'll show you how to use conventional data management products—from spreadsheets to databases—as a source of material for multimedia presentations. We'll show you the most basic steps that apply to the broadest range of packages. However, we should point out that the multimedia arena is gaining interest among all software publishers, who are offering more and more multimedia options with their "conventional" products.

For example, there are spreadsheets and databases that support sound-scanned images and even motion video. You may want to use these utilities to enhance a particular software package's features—a database that includes pictures or video sequences, for example—but you still need a program dedicated to multimedia applications to achieve the kind of presentations we've discussed in this book.

There may be multimedia support in some of the software you're using that's not immediately obvious. If in doubt, contact the software vendor for information on the version you have and to find out what features later versions of the product contain that your version does not.

Also, many Windows-compatible software packages can import objects directly from other Windows applications without any special conversion. These "data links" may work slightly differently among different packages, but in general you select the data you want to link in the source package. Then you load the target application, select Paste or Paste Link (or something similar) from the menu bar, and you've created a live link between these software packages.

Within fairly broad limits, the options available to you for moving information from conventional software into a presentation package are about the same from package to package, only the precise procedure changes.

In general, you have two options:

Import the data directly using the Windows linking feature described above.

Export the data in a format you can import into the presentation software.

In addition, you can use a third product as an intermediary:

1. Copy data from the source application to the Clipboard.
2. Paste the Clipboard data into an intermediate application.
3. Save the data in a file format your presentation package can import.

That said, let's look at some basic ways to use the software you have as a resource for your multimedia package, whatever it is.

Using Spreadsheets

Spreadsheet programs are among the most popular applications for personal computer users, and with good reason. They offer a consistent user interface, automatic data handling, text formatting, creative page design, and graph and chart support.

With a spreadsheet, you can start with basic known data and project future sales, compute profits, figure payments, and plot results. Nearly all businesses with a computer use spreadsheets.

Obviously, if you already have data in a spreadsheet format that would help you in your multimedia presentations, it makes sense to use the information directly where possible, instead of re-entering figures into a presentation package.

Capturing data from a spreadsheet directly reduces the possibility of mistakes when transferring data, and can save you time in the transition from one package to another.

Most spreadsheets offer two types of information you're likely to want to use: numbers and charts.

You want to use raw numbers carefully in a multimedia presentation. Several screens filled with columns of numbers will put an audience to sleep quicker than Uncle George's retirement party slide show. But where comparative numbers make a point, or when you can show progressions or projections with numbers, don't hesitate to use your spreadsheet information.

A graph or chart based on those numbers, on the other hand, is a safer bet. They summarize the data in a way the viewer can interpret quickly, are more interesting, and the information and concepts they contain will be easier to retain.

When you work with numbers and see the trends they present, it's sometimes easy to forget that your audience does not share the same attachment or understanding for the data as you do. Here's a simple, everyday example that may help make this concept more concrete.

Suppose you're late for an appointment and you have several other tasks to complete before you can leave the office. As you work feverishly to catch up, you cast regular—and anxious—glances at the clock. If this is a digital clock, it tells you the time is 3:53. Then you have to process that into "how long is it until 4:00," which is what you really want to know. An analog clock, on the other hand, shows you the minute hand graphically as it approaches the 4:00 mark. You may not internalize the precise time—3:53—but you have a much better idea of how long it is until 4:00.

So it is with graphics information versus columns of numbers. The numbers provide much more precise information about this month's sales, for example, but if you really want the viewer to understand that sales have risen steadily over the past six months, a graph is a much better choice.

With those general ideas out of the way, let's look at some specific spreadsheet programs and show you how to extract data and charts to use in your multimedia presentations.

Using Lotus 1-2-3 for Windows

To use a graph in Lotus 1-2-3, you first have to convert your columns of data into a graphics format.

To convert Lotus data into a graph, do the following:

1. Select the range of data you want to present as a graph.
2. Use Graph New to display the Graph New dialog.
3. Enter a name for the graph in the Graph name: field.
4. Click on OK to plot a line graph (the 1-2-3 default).
5. Use Chart Type to display the Chart Type dialog.
6. Click on the type of chart you want to use, then click on OK to make the change on your display.

Now you have the numeric data presented in a format that will be a lot more meaningful to your multimedia audience. The next step is to get the graph into a form your multimedia package can use.

If you can't establish a direct link (see the discussion of direct links earlier in this chapter), you'll have to save the graph to disk in a format your multimedia package can interpret and load.

Unfortunately, Lotus 1-2-3 for Windows can't directly export a graph into a separate file format that a wide variety of applications can load. Therefore, you have to conduct some interim steps to get the job done.

We'll show you one way here; you probably can think of others, depending on what software applications you have at your disposal:

1. Select a range of cells on the spreadsheet large enough to hold the graph you just created.
2. Use Graph Add to Sheet to display the Graph Add to Sheet dialog.
3. Select the name of the graph you just created. Lotus will place the graph in the marked block of cells you specified earlier.
4. Select this block of cells again and use Edit Copy to place a copy of the graph on the Clipboard.
5. Click on the Down Arrow in the upper-right corner of the 1-2-3 screen to shrink the 1-2-3 application to an icon, giving you access to the Program Manager.

At this point you have a couple of options, depending on what multimedia application you're using. If yours is a Windows-compatible program, simply launch the presentation software, go to the appropriate screen, and use Edit Paste to copy the image from the Clipboard into your presentation software.

If this won't work because you're using a DOS application, or for any other reason, try copying the graph into another Windows-compatible package, saving the file, then importing the file into your presentation.

You can use Windows Paintbrush to capture a graphics file:

1. Open the Windows Program Manager screen, then open the Accessories window, if it's not already open.
2. Double click on the Paintbrush icon (an artist's palette) from among those displayed.
3. Use Edit Paste from the main Paintbrush screen to copy the graph from the Clipboard to the Paintbrush editing window.
4. Now you can enhance the graph, if you wish, using standard Paintbrush editing and drawing tools, before saving it as a separate disk file.
5. To save the file, use File Save As to display the Save As dialog.
6. Choose the appropriate file type from the Save File as Type: field at the bottom of the screen.

The Paintbrush default is 16-color bitmap (.BMP) format. Many presentation applications can import this format. Or, you can choose .PCX format, if your package requires it.

7. Enter a path and filename in the File Name: field of this dialog, then click on OK to save the file in the new format.

Now you have the original 1-2-3 graph stored as a separate file in a graphics format that's compatible with many presentation packages. Load the presentation software and use file import or whatever procedure your package supports to load the image.

If you really must work with rows and columns of numbers (sometimes—but not often—that is the best choice for your multimedia presentations) here's how to get the 1-2-3 data into a format that most presentation packages can use.

You can use the techniques described above for importing a block of a spreadsheet directly into a Windows-compatible application, or you can import it through the Clipboard to Paintbrush, then save it in a graphics format.

Another alternative is to export the range of data into an ASCII file format (.PRN file), then import the text into your presentation:

1. Select the block of cells you want to include in the multimedia presentation.
2. Use File Extract To to display the File Extract To dialog.
3. Select Text in the Save As box at the bottom of this dialog.
4. Enter a path and filename in the File name: field of this dialog.
5. Click on OK to save the file.

Now you have a range of numbers in an ASCII, or text, file that you can import into most any application. The only problem you're likely to encounter with this approach is that as you specify different fonts within your presentation application, the columns of numbers might not line up as they did within the spreadsheet. You can fine tune this alignment by choosing different fonts (non-proportional fonts are easiest to line up) and different font sizes to get the effect you want.

Microsoft Excel

Like other Windows products, Excel supports DDE (Dynamic Data Exchange) links to other products. If your application supports DDE links, this is the best way to share data between Excel and a multimedia software package, If not, then follow one of the procedures noted below.

To create a graph from existing data in Excel:

1. Select the range of cells to include in the graph.
2. Use File New to display the New dialog.

3. Double click on Chart. Excel displays a default bar chart with the data you selected.
4. Use Gallery to display a list of graph types for your selection.

Once the chart is created, copy it to your Clipboard as described in the Lotus 1-2-3 section earlier in this chapter. Although you can save a chart in its own file (unlike 1-2-3 for Windows), you're limited to Excel formats, which won't help you unless your presentation package can import Excel data directly.

If you want to import an entire spreadsheet into your presentation application, you can save a sheet in a specific format that you may be able to use directly.

Here's how:

1. Use File Save As to display the Save As dialog.
2. Specify a path and filename for the chart file.
3. Click on Options to open the Options dialog.
4. Select the file format you want to use from the pulldown list at the top of this dialog.

Which format you choose depends on the application you're using. Excel loads and saves files in the formats shown in Table 9.1, in addition to the normal Excel file format.

Table 9.1 Excel File Format Support	
CSV	Comma Separated Values
DBF 2	dBase II
DBF 3	dBase III
DBF 4	dBase IV
DIF	Document Interchange Format
SYLK	Symbolic Link
Text	ANSI text for Windows
WK1	Lotus 1-2-3 Release 2
WKS	Lotus 1-2-3 Release 1
WK3	Lotus 1-2-3 Release 3, and 1-2-3 for Windows

Of these formats, only CSV, ASCII, or DIF are likely to be much help to you in the multimedia arena. If your presentation package supports one of these formats, use it. Otherwise, you'll have to use the interim software technique described earlier.

If you want to use columns of numbers in your multimedia application, do the following:

1. Select the range of cells you want to use in your multimedia application.
2. Use File Save As to display the Save As dialog.
3. Specify a path and filename.
4. Specify Text format in the box at the bottom of this dialog.

Quattro Pro

Quattro Pro for DOS can generate charts for you to use in your multimedia presentations. However, the process is slightly different from the one you use with a Windows-compatible program, as shown in the following steps:

1. Use Graph Graph Type to specify the type of graph to produce in Quattro Pro.
2. Use Graph Series to specify at least two data ranges: Series 1 and Series 2. the first series becomes the X range and the second series is the Y range in a simple graph.
3. Select View to display the graph.

These steps produce a graph that is separate from the body of the spreadsheet. To return to the spreadsheet READY mode, press any key from the View mode.

Although Quattro Pro is a DOS product, the best way to get a Quattro Pro graph into a presentation-ready format is through Windows.

Here's how:

1. Launch Quattro Pro from a Windows DOS window.
2. Load the file that contains the graph you want to use.

3. With the graph you want to import into a presentation package displayed, hold the **Alt** key and press **Enter** to shrink the Quattro Pro window and display the Program Manager.

Once you've placed a DOS window on a graphics screen, you have access to the Control Panel and you can copy the screen to the Clipboard:

4. Click on the Control Panel icon at the upper-left corner of the screen to display the Control Panel menu, shown in Figure 9.1.

Figure 9.1
Quattro Pro
Control Panel
Menu

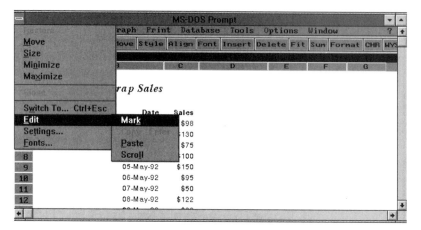

5. Select Edit from the Control Panel menu and choose Mark from the pulldown list.

6. Position the cursor at the upper-left corner of the graph you want to use and hold down the left mouse button.

7. Move the mouse to "paint" or mark all of the Quattro Pro screen you want to use in your application.

8. Press **Enter** to copy the marked area of the Quattro Pro screen to the Clipboard.

Now you can load the copied data into Paintbrush or another application that supports a variety of file formats using the procedure we described earlier. Once you've used Edit Paste to copy the data from the Clipboard into the application you are using to convert from a Clipboard image to a file compatible with your presentation package, you can edit it, and save it in a graphics format your presentation program can use.

Using Databases

You probably won't use database information all that frequently in multimedia presentations. The fact is, database information is (usually) text-oriented. And the large volume of data generally associated with database applications prohibits direct application of database information in your presentations, most of the time.

However, as with spreadsheet information, there may be times when showing lists of information from a database can be useful. And, you may find that you can generate graphic information from inside your particular database program that can be used effectively with your presentations.

The first admonition for using database information with multimedia applications is to reduce the volume of data you'll show on any one screen as much as possible. We can't emphasize this enough. Don't be coerced by the existence of data—however good it may seem—to use it in its original form simply because it's there.

In general, you'll probably produce more useful displays in your presentations by summarizing information from a database in a chart or bulleted list, boiling down the raw data into one or two slides that the user of your application can digest quickly and easily.

There are two basic techniques you can employ to import database information directly:

1. Create a report for the data you want to use and print it to a disk file instead of to a printer.
2. Display the data on the screen and copy it to the Clipboard so you can paste it into the multimedia software or an intermediate software package such as Paintbrush.

If your database is a DOS product, use the technique for copying a screen described in the Quattro Pro section earlier in this chapter.

Using Paradox

Once you've designed the database and extracted the data you want to include in your multimedia presentation, you can design a report to display that information in a variety of formats. Refer to the Paradox documentation if you need help designing a report.

First scan the master data file and produce an Answer file that contains only the records you want to use for the current application. Then design a report for the extracted data.

To send the designed report to a file so you can import it into your presentation, do the following:

1. Press **F10** to display the main Paradox menu.
2. Use Tools ExportImport Export to display the Export menu.
3. Select ASCII, then specify Text ASCII.
4. Type **Answer** at the Table prompt.
5. Enter a filename, including a path, at the File Name: prompt.
6. Press **Enter** to begin the file extraction to the ASCII file.

Now you can use whatever data import features are supported by your presentation package to get the data into a format you can use for multimedia applications.

Using FoxPro

In FoxPro, the procedure for creating an ASCII file is slightly different. Whereas in Paradox you conduct a search and create an Answer file before exporting the data, in FoxPro you extract data from the master file at the same time you send it to the ASCII file.

1. Use File Open to open the file with the data you want to use.
2. Use Database Copy to to display the Copy To: dialog.
3. Click on For to open the selection criteria dialog if you want to print less than the full data file.
4. If you're selecting data from the main file, enter the selection criteria on the data selection dialog.

5. Enter a filename and path in the Save As field of this dialog.
6. Pull down the TYPE: list and select a file type.

> Although FoxPro supports a fairly wide range of data formats, there are relatively few that are likely to be useful in multimedia packages. One of the delimited ASCII formats, DIF., or SDF, is probably your best choice. Consult your multimedia software documentation.

7. Click on OK to start the extraction and copy process.

As with other files, when you've created the transfer file, load the presentation software and use its import features to load the data.

Using Word Processors

As with database applications, word-processing software will be of limited use to you in a multimedia presentation environment. The main reason you might want to import word processor data into a multimedia package is if you have complex tables, mathematics formulas, computer commands, or other material that has been proofed and proven. Frequently this type of information is difficult to verify, and if you attempt to retype the data in a presentation package, you run the risk of introducing errors or you force an extra editing step into the process.

Fortunately, because most word processors are versatile, support many fonts, and offer WYSIWYG (what-you-see-is-what-you-get) or near-WYSIWYG display, it isn't too difficult to use information from these products in your multimedia presentations.

As with the other products discussed in this chapter, you always have the option of using the Windows Clipboard to copy a screen or a block of data from one application to another. Even if yours is a DOS-based word processor, you can use the Clipboard by shrinking the DOS window and using the Control Panel editing features. (See complete instructions for this process in the discussion with Borland's Quattro Pro spreadsheet product.)

Beyond that, each product has some features of its own that you might find useful in building multimedia presentations. We'll discuss some of these for the most popular word-processing packages.

WordPerfect

WordPerfect for Windows has the same options available as other Windows-compatible products. The quickest way to get information from WordPerfect for Windows to your multimedia application is through the Clipboard. All you have to do is select the data, use Edit Copy, then load up your presentation software and use Edit Paste.

The Clipboard retains original document formatting and screen appearance. Usually nothing is lost in the transition.

If you're using WordPerfect for DOS, you can use the technique described earlier of running WordPerfect from a Microsoft Windows DOS window, then shrinking the WordPerfect window to a graphics image. Then you can use the Windows Control Panel to mark the block you want to use and copy it to the Clipboard.

Of course, you can save the WordPerfect data as an ASCII file, which most other applications can import.

To create an ASCII file in WordPerfect for Windows or WordPerfect 6.0 for DOS, do the following:

1. Select the file you want to save, then use File Save As to display the Save As dialog.
2. Select ASCII from the pulldown format list on this dialog.
3. Enter a filename and path in the Filename: field.
4. Click on OK to save the file.

To save an ASCII file in WordPerfect for DOS prior to version 6.0, do the following:

1. Press **Ctrl+F5** to display a file menu.
2. Select DOS Text from the list (number 1 from the menu).
3. Enter a filename, including path, for the ASCII file.

For a few products, you might also be able to use an encapsulated PostScript file (EPS). Not all presentation products can load and use EPS files, and those that do generally cannot display the information from that file on a screen—you can only print it. So this approach isn't a broad-based solution, but it might get you "out of the woods" in some situations.

Here's how to create an EPS file from inside WordPerfect for DOS (including version 6.0):

1. Press **Shift+F7** to display the Print screen.
2. Choose Select Printer, then choose Edit from the Select Printer menu.
3. Choose Port from the Select Printer: Edit screen.
4. Choose Other from the options at the bottom of the screen.
5. Enter the filename, including path, at the Device or Filename: prompt.

Now when you print the file or selection, instead of going to the printer, it goes to the named disk file in the format of the selected printer. So if you select a PostScript printer before printing, the file you create will contain instructions for printing on a PostScript device.

Remember to return the printer output to LPT: when you've completed the current print job. Otherwise, the next time you try to print to the printer, it will appear as if nothing happens. It may take you awhile to figure out why nothing is coming out of your printer.

To create an EPS file from inside WordPerfect for Windows:

1. Use File Print to display the Print dialog.
2. Click on Select to display the Select Printer dialog.
3. Choose PostScript printer from the list. Make sure the WordPerfect printer drivers box is selected.
4. Click on Setup to display the Printer Setup dialog.
5. Select File from the Port: pulldown list.
6. Enter the path and filename in the Filename: field below the Port: button.

7. Press **Enter** or click on OK to accept the setup changes.

8. Click on Select to return to the Print dialog.

9. Press **Enter** or click on Print to start printing the current document to the specified file.

Microsoft Word

Like WordPerfect, Microsoft Word comes in two versions: DOS and Windows. You have the same options with this product as discussed for other Windows and DOS products.

If you want to use ASCII text information to import into your presentation product, export the file from Word for DOS or Word for Windows this way:

1. Use File Save As to display the Save As dialog.

2. Enter a filename in the File Name: field of this dialog.

3. Select the disk drive and subdirectory from the pulldown list under Directories:.

4. Choose Text Only from the Format: list on the right side of this dialog.

5. Click on OK to save the file.

In addition, you can print to an EPS file by following the procedures below.

To create an EPS file in Word for DOS:

1. Use File Print (**Shift+F9**) to display the Print dialog.

2. Click on the File: button in the To window of this dialog.

3. Enter a filename and path in the File: label field.

4. Click on OK to begin printing.

To create an EPS file in Word for Windows:

1. Use File Print (**Ctrl+Shift+F12**) to display the Print dialog.

2. Click on the Print to file button, then click on OK.

3. Enter the filename to print to, including the path.

4. Press **Enter** or click on OK to start printing.

Drawing and Art

Drawing programs are a much better resource for multimedia applications than word processors and database applications. Although most multimedia programs include some drawing and graphics support, some of them are rather limited when you compare the facilities of CorelDraw! or another mainstream graphics package.

Besides, you may already be using a drawing package, and that experience and familiarity makes it easier to get your work done than if you have to learn a new package. In addition, drawing programs frequently support multiple file formats, including "universal" formats such as .TIF (tagged information file) or .WMF (Windows metafile).

Remember, you always have the Clipboard option from inside Windows, whether you're using Windows or DOS programs. For many applications this is an easy and effective way to get information from one application to another.

As we said in the last section, you also can export to an .EPS format, but this is probably not the best choice for inclusion in multimedia applications because you normally can't view an .EPS file on the screen, although you can print it.

In the next section, we'll describe how to use various file formats with CorelDraw!, one of the more popular drawing packages.

CorelDraw!

CorelDraw! has been around for some time and is considered among the premier PC-based drawing applications. Once you've created an image you want to use with another multimedia application, it's easy to export it into a format your presentation package can recognize:

1. Select the drawing or drawing component you want to use with your presentation.
2. Use File Export to display the Export dialog, shown in Figure 9.2.

Figure 9.2
CorelDraw! File
Export Dialog

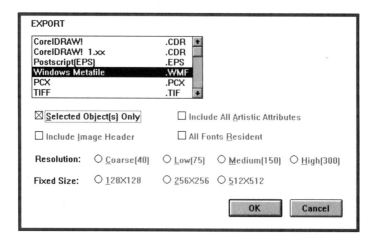

3. Select the file format you want to use from the list in the upper-left corner of this dialog.
4. Click on OK. CorelDraw! displays the Export Path: dialog.
5. Enter a path and filename.
6. Click on Export to begin the export process.

CorelDraw! can support a number of file formats, including those shown in Table 9.2.

Tempra Pro

Tempra Pro is another increasingly popular application, more slanted toward multimedia than other standalone drawing packages. You can use it with Mathematica's Tempra Media Author, or create images for export to other file formats supported by another authoring package.

Tempra Pro is a DOS-based program, but you can run it in a Microsoft Windows DOS window as described previously in this chapter. This lets you mark and copy screens to the Clipboard if you need to. However, Tempra Pro supports a variety of file formats, making it fairly easy to save an image in a format you can use with another application.

Once you have an image you want to use in the Tempra Pro workspace, you can save it in a number of popular graphics formats.

Table 9.2 CorelDraw! Supported File Formats	
Description	**File Extension**
Encapsulated PostScript	.EPS
Windows Metafile	.WMF
PCX	.PCX
TIFF (Tagged Image)	.TIF
Computer Graphics Metafile	.CGM
GEM Draw Metafile	.GEM
WordPerfect Graphic	.WPG
SCODL	.SCD
Video Show	.PIC
HPGL (Outlines Only)	.PLT
AutoCAD (Outlines Only)	.DXF
IBM PIF (GDF)	.PIF
MAC (PICT)	.PCT
Illustrator	.AI

To save Tempra Pro images to a different graphics format, do the following:

1. Click on Disk from the main menu bar to pull down the Disk menu.
2. Click on the Files button to display the Files menu options.
3. Choose the file extension you want to use from the file extension list. Specifying the extension automatically selects the proper file format, as shown in Table 9.3.
4. Specify the filename and path for the file to be saved.
5. Click on Save to store the file.

File formats supported by Tempra Pro are listed in Table 9.3.

Table 9.3 Tempra Pro File Formats	
Description	**File Extension**
TIFF (Tagged Image)	.TIF
TrueVision Targa	.TGA
CompuServe Graphics	.GIF

continued

Table 9.3 Tempra Pro File Formats (Continued)	
Description	**File Extension**
TrueVision Targa	.WIN
Bit Mapped Graphics	.BMP
Encapsulated PostScript	.EPS
PC Paintbrush	.PCX
LinkWay (CGA) Format	.PCC
Pens	.PEN
Masks	.MSK
Palettes	.PAL
Fonts	.BSF

Going on Your Own

The specific examples in this chapter should get you started on the right path for using whatever application you already have with your multimedia presentation software.

The basic guideline is to be imaginative and, when you have data in one format that you'd like to use with another application, to try to come up with ways to make the conversion. If you can't use the copy to Clipboard or export to file technique to derive a file that your presentation package can use, then you may need to try some form of conversion software.

Several popular conversion packages are readily available. One of our favorites is PictureEze from Applications Techniques, Inc. (10 Lomar Park Drive, Pepperell, MA, 01463, 508-433-5201). This Windows-based program can load and convert dozens of file formats and can conduct limited editing on the images. The included CapturEze application lets you capture whole Windows screens, or active windows in a format you can load into PictureEze for conversion or editing.

Another good choice for file conversion is Hijaak (available for DOS or Windows) from Inset Systems, Inc. (12 Mill Plain Road, Danbury, CT, 06811, 203-775-5866, 800-828-8088). Hijaak also includes a screen capture utility as well as data conversion utilities.

Both programs have user-friendly interfaces and help you select the source and destination file format easily.

If you plan to do a lot of conversions, you might want to purchase one of these or another graphics conversion program. If your needs are modest, on the other hand, you can probably find someone in another office to handle the conversion for you.

Also, don't overlook the possibility of having the computer store where you purchased your hardware or software do the conversions for you. Even if you bought your machine from a mail order source, you can probably get good response if you walk into a computer store with your original images and ask someone to run through a quick conversion for you, using one of the software packages they market. This is a good chance for you to see firsthand what works and what doesn't, and it gives the salespeople an opportunity to sway you to their products.

Finally, for modest conversion needs, don't spend too much time trying to reuse an image than it would take you to recreate in the presentation package you're using. Sometimes when you try to save time and money, you lose it instead.

Multimedia Software Reference

The IBM Ultimedia Tools Series CD-ROM software sampler disk included with this book contains over 30 demonstrations of multimedia presentation software, plus 16 working software applications that you can use to create multimedia presentations of your own. While the working models have some features disabled or limited, you can still get a realistic feel for how the packages work and what they do.

Now instead of just reading about what you can do with multimedia software, you can load a package of your choice and view a self-running demonstration, or build your own presentation.

This software covers a wide range of products, including authoring software, animation, graphics, video products, and multimedia utilities. Not only can you do some useful work with the demonstration software, but you can get an excellent, hands-on look at some of the main offerings from a number of companies. This will help you to understand what multimedia software in general is all about, as well as to assist you in making a purchase decision when it comes time to install your own working presentation software.

In this appendix, we'll categorize the software on this disk and offer some definitions of different multimedia software.

Types of Multimedia Software

It's difficult to categorize a given multimedia package into one pigeon hole. The problem is that today's software all does so much! Take IBM's Storyboard Live!, a functional package that nevertheless is considered relatively low end. Not only does it arrange images into a slide show, but you can use its modules to:

- Draw graphics images
- Capture graphics and text screens from other computer applications
- Record and play back digitized sound
- Record and play back full motion video
- Create animated "sprites" that can move through your slides
- Load graphics images from a variety of formats and save them to other formats

So, is Storyboard Live! (for example) a multimedia utility for drawing and editing graphics, or is it an authoring package for building multimedia presentations?

IBM says it's an authoring tool, but it certainly offers more limited features than something like AimTech's IconAuthor, say, or Authorware Professional by Macromedia. However, Storyboard Live! requires relatively fewer computer resources than these packages, and it operates under DOS without requiring Microsoft Windows. It also provides a drawing tool, screen capture utilities, graphics editing features, and more. We'll call it an authoring tool and follow IBM's lead.

So, while many of the packages on the Ultimedia Tools CD-ROM included with this book (and most other multimedia offerings as well) offer a multitude of features and functions, it's still useful to categorize them by their major features.

Authoring Software

Authoring software lets you build complete multimedia applications from simple or complex presentations to interactive training and education and point of sale applications. These full-featured applications include elements from other types of applications, such as drawing, graphics editing, audio support, video, and more. But the main function of authoring packages is that they enable you to take graphics, sound, and animation files and combine them into one clear, well-organized presentation.

Animation Software

Animation is a useful attention-getting device to help focus the viewer's attention. Although many authoring packages include some animation support, some multimedia software take this feature as their strongest point. Animation can range from simple text and whole graphics movement, to complex 3-D movement programs.

Autodesk's Animator Pro, for example, comes with many megabytes of pre-programmed animation clips that you can mix and match for your own projects. You can build animation from scratch by designing your own text or graphics screens, or you can start with a scanned image that the software can animate for you.

Graphics

Drawing and paint programs generally are classified together as graphics applications. Drawing applications, such as Lumena or Professional Draw, and paint software such as Fractal Painter or PC Paintbrush, are useful for creating individual presentation components such as catchy backgrounds, figures for inclusion in presentation slides, or as opening screens. Also in this category are image editing and enhancement products such as ZSoft's PhotoFinish and Gold Disk's Professional Draw.

Video

Multimedia video applications take a variety of forms, from simple small-screen video players to complex desktop video studio products. Increasingly, motion video support is an important part of multimedia capability. Full-featured authoring packages usually support some form of video, but for really top-notch video components for your presentations you'll want something such as Matrox Personal Producer or the Personal Picture Processor from Montage. These packages can catalog, sequence, edit, and record everything from simple video clips to full-blown desktop movies.

Utilities

Multimedia utility packages cover a wide variety of features, from file conversion and screen capture, to clip art or animation libraries, music and sound editors, and image enhancement products. As we said in the beginning of this book, it's doubtful whether you can produce all of the multimedia components you need within a single package. You'll need more than one tool for creating the basic presentation, plus one or more utility packages to support other features you might want to include.

Ultimedia Tools CD-ROM Reference

The Ultimedia Tools Series CD-ROM disk was developed to help potential users get acquainted with multimedia software through hands-on experience. This CD provides an interactive encyclopedia of multimedia software, plus the information the desktop-PC user needs to compare multimedia software products. The CD is designed to let you *see* and *hear* the multimedia software products, and let's you "test drive" them so you can make purchasing decisions at your own pace.

While the Ultimedia Tools Series CD navigation, selector, and tutorial applications are DOS-based programs, many of the self-running and working copy demonstrations require Windows 3.1 or higher. When launched, those demos will find Windows in your system's path statement and load the Windows environment when it's required. If you haven't installed Windows, you'll be told that the tools demo cannot be launched.

To launch the Ultimedia Tools Series main menu, select the CD-ROM drive as the default or current drive, then type **UTSDOS** at the DOS prompt, or UTSOS2 at the OS/2 prompt.

Note the following requirements for running this demonstration software:

- DOS 5.0 or later is required to run this CD-ROM.
- Many of the modules require at least 565K of available conventional memory space for execution. You may have to move some device drivers to high memory to get enough conventional memory with some configurations.
- Up to 10Mb of free space on your hard drive is needed as temporary storage during execution of some of the demonstrations and working models. This space is reclaimed and made available at the end of each session.
- To take full advantage of the sound files that accompany the *Introduction*, *What is Multimedia?*, *Multimedia Tutorial*, and *Animation* modules, you need DOS audio device drivers for your sound card. Refer to your audio card's installation instructions. A SoundBlaster (Creative Labs) sound card or a fully compatible equivalent is required for sound support from these programs. Notice that some cards, including the Pro Audio Spectrum 16 from Media Vision, that claim SoundBlaster compatibility won't work properly with the software on this sampler CD-ROM.
- Most of the Windows-based demonstrations on the CD require Windows with Multimedia Extensions (or Windows 3.1 or later).
- The Tools Series CD may not launch correctly from DOS running inside Windows. You should exit Windows and launch the CD from the DOS prompt.

After you type **UTSDOS** at the DOS prompt, the main Ultimedia Tools Series menu shown in Figure A.1 is displayed.

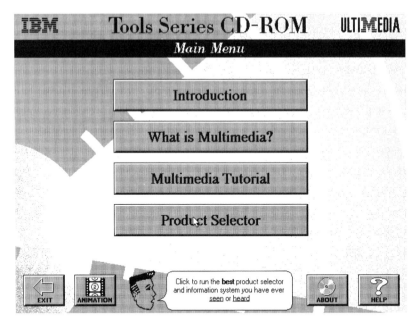

From this main menu, you can get a demonstration with some background on multimedia, plus you can:

- See and hear a quick introduction to the Ultimedia Tools Series
- Learn a little more about using multimedia
- Get a quick hands-on tutorial lesson on the media types
- Select specific tools by category, operating system, and features, then see presentations and test-drive many of the tools in the Tools Series

Some Windows Demonstrations and Working Models require that you manually exit the Windows Program Manager to return to the Product Information screen. A quick way to do this is to press **Alt+F4**. A quick way to exit the CD-ROM is to press the **X** key from the Product Information screen.

Ultimedia Features

The features of this disk are easy to access and are pretty self-explanatory. However, here are a few guidelines.

You can access the software products on this CD by product name simply by using the scroll bar to the right of the Product Selector screen until the product you want to access is displayed. (To display the Product Selector screen, click on Product Selector, the last item in the main menu.)

From the Product Selector screen, click on the product name to display a logo and prompt specific to that product. Figure A.2 shows the Product Selector screen with a product selected.

Figure A.2
Product Selector
Screen with
Product Selected

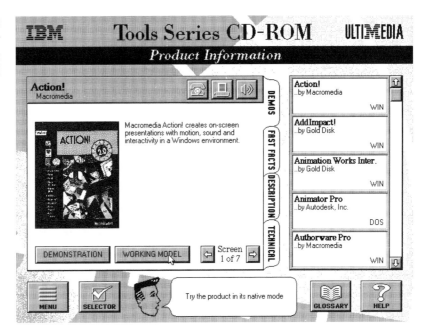

In addition, you can display a list of software by product type, and each tool type is also sub-indexed by tool characteristic or function. Select by Tool Feature/Capability. Click on the Feature button to search for all tools that have a particular capability or function. Figure A.3 shows the results of one such search.

You can also sort the tools by product name or by the name of the company that produces the product. You can limit the search by specifying an operating environment: Windows, DOS, or OS/2. Figure A.4 shows products grouped by company name.

Figure A.3
Products by
Feature Search
in Product
Selector

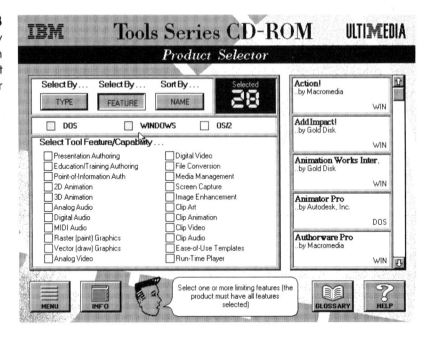

Figure A.4
Products
Grouped by
Company
Name in
Product Selector

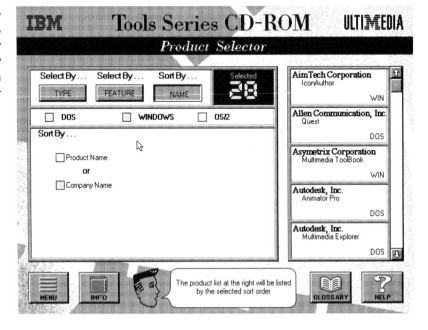

Once you select a specific product from the list, information about the product is presented on the screen in a book format. You select topics, or *chapters*, by clicking on named tabs, including Demos, Fast Facts, Product Descriptions, and Technical Details. The first page displayed when you select a particular product shows a scanned image of the product packaging and a short description. From there you can choose Demo or, if it's available, the working version of the package.

The following sections describe data included in each of these sections of the Product Selector Screen.

Demo Button

What you see behind the demo button varies somewhat by product, but in general you can page through several screens—sometimes with a menu or with additional selection buttons—to view highlights of the selected product and its key features. For most products, you'll also see one or more screen images that represent the tool's user interface. IBM calls these screens of basic information *PIPs*, for product information presentations. PIPs are designed to run on VGA (or better) DOS-based systems, so you can scan the PIP information with a basic system.

In addition, many products include interactive demonstrations. Some of these demonstrations run directly from the CD; others have to be loaded to the hard drive before you can execute them. This is handled automatically for you.

Also, some demonstrations require Windows and some require the multimedia extensions to Windows. If you're using Windows 3.1 or later, these multimedia features are supplied as a default. To view the product demonstration, simply click on the Demonstration button, if it's displayed. If you don't see a Demonstration button, it means the selected product doesn't provide this feature.

At least half of the products supplied on the CD-ROM with this book include a working model so you can use the product interactively. Select the Working Model button when it's displayed to access this feature. These demonstrations are designed to give you detailed information about the specific capabilities of the selected product in its normal operating environment. Therefore, your system must be equipped with the operating system and multimedia extensions required to successfully run the working models. If the product requires Windows or OS/2, the tool launcher will look for those systems in your path and take over from there, or notify you that they cannot be launched. The Working Model button is displayed only if the respective product has a model loaded on the CD.

Fast Facts Tab

Fast Facts give you at-a-glance information about each tool, including its basic functions, the recommended system and software configuration, and a suggested retail price.

When you click on a different tool in the list box, you'll see the Fast Facts for your second choice. This is a great way to compare tools. This Selector feature works in this manner for the Description and Technical Tabs as well.

Description Tab

When you select this button, a scrollable window presents detailed information about a tool's features, functions, and capabilities.

Technical Tab

This section provides technical information about a tool's operation.

Many screens include other buttons that help you get even more information about the Ultimedia Tools in general and about selected products specifically. These include:

Help button: Clicking the Help button causes the "balloon" at the bottom of the screen to present a short description of the function of each selectable area on the current screen. Figure A.5 shows a typical Help display.

Figure A.5
Typical Help
Display with
Full Balloon

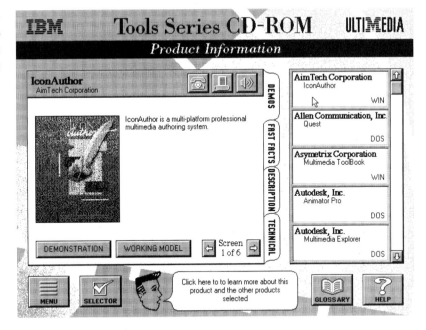

If you paint the screen with the mouse pointer, you'll see short messages in the balloon describing the function of the selected area. The Help feature is a toggle: click it once and the balloon contains continuous help information as you move the mouse pointer around the screen. Click again on the Help button and the balloon stays blank.

You might want to turn off continuous help if you're using a slow CD-ROM drive. Otherwise, leave Help enabled to receive continuous help and feedback on the operations you perform with the Ultimedia Tools disk.

Glossary button: The Glossary button presents a window that allows you to enter a word you would like to find in the Multimedia Glossary. The search starts when you key the first letter and updates following each keystroke. The glossary consists of approximately 300 multimedia-related words or phrases. Figure A.6 shows a glossary selection displayed on the Ultimedia Tools screen.

Figure A.6
Glossary
Display

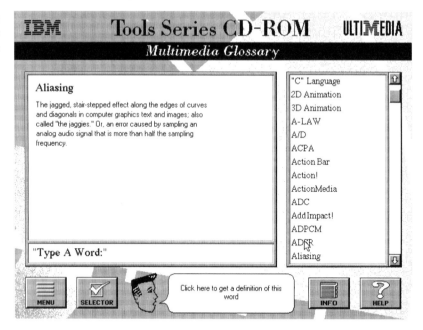

Order (telephone icon) button: When you select the Order button, a single page displays information describing how to get additional information about the Ultimedia Tools Series tools, and how to order via telephone, as shown in Figure A.7. Press the Return button to go back to the previous screen.

Audio (speaker icon) button: This button plays a 30-second narration file associated with each tool. Clicking the button plays an audio narration file through your system's sound card and speaker or through your system's PC speaker via a sound synthesis software driver included on the CD.

Print (printer icon) button: The Print button allows you to print a file describing the textual information catalogued for the selected tool.

Data Compression Technologies

Multimedia data changes the rules from traditional, text-based computer information. As soon as you start storing high resolution graphics, scanned images, photographs, sound, and motion video, storage requirements for even a very brief application skyrocket. The only practical way to handle these storage needs is to compress the data so that only the most essential information is actually stored on disk. When you retrieve the information, associated decompression software reconstructs the original data in real-time as it comes off the disk and is displayed on the screen.

In this appendix, we discuss some of the most common data compression technologies.

DVI

Live video is essential to the future development of PC-based multimedia, but at 30 frames per second, even a short video clip would quickly fill up the average hard disk. (30 seconds of uncompressed, full-motion video requires about 600Mb of storage, for example.) So, if practical motion video were to appear on the digital desktop, some form of aggressive video compression was necessary.

411

DVI products such as the ActionMedia II board and associated software support not only motion video compression, but also JPEG (Joint Photographic Experts Group) still image processing and stereo audio. The quality of these multimedia images and sound is about the same as a standard VCR—perhaps not "broadcast quality," but certainly good enough for presentations and training.

The advantage of DVI video is the large amount of data that can be compressed and decompressed in real-time to present full-motion, full-screen images. Technologies that use less-aggressive compression, or compression that can't be conducted on the fly, can't produce full-screen images, or the playback must be at fewer frames per second.

Not only does highly compressed video let you reduce storage requirements, but such digitized video can be shared over a network or transmitted among different sites at distant locations. To achieve this, however, video must be compressed at least by a factor of 100 to one. DVI accomplishes much of this compression by dropping redundant information. An area of blue screen, for example, uses the same pixel information over and over again. A compression algorithm can reduce storage requirements by storing one blue pixel, then specifying how many times to replicate it during playback.

Additional compression can be achieved by storing only representative pixels, sampling some number of pixels but not storing everything within an area of the screen. During playback, the decompression software re-creates the missing pixels by averaging the known pixel information. This process is called *interpolation*.

And, still further compression is achieved in motion video by dropping redundant information on a frame-by-frame basis. Motion video is made up of a series of sequential frames of information, each one very like the preceding one. A shot of a tiger leaping out of a tree, for example, is composed of a sequence of frames that shows the tiger in various positions, but the tree, the sky, the grass, and so on, change very little, if at all. DVI compression can store only the new information for each frame after the first and reconstruct the actual frames by copying redundant information during decompression.

This three-level compression can achieve video output nearly equal to VHS VCR quality. As a practical matter, IBM's ActionMedia II technology supports two separate levels of video quality: RTV (Real Time Video) and PLV (Production Level Video). RTV quality, nearly but not quite as good as standard VHS video, is produced on your desktop by the ActionMedia II card, while PLV, a higher level of quality equal to VCR video, can be produced by licensed vendors off site.

DVI compression enables producers to store up to 72 minutes of PLV-quality video on a single CD-ROM disk. This level of compression can support practical end-user video editing and production with conventional hard disks or MO removable cartridge drives.

JPEG (Joint Photographic Experts Group)

JPEG is a compression format that's getting a lot of attention in the press and among graphics image users these days, but it's still not considered to be *the* accepted compression standard for still photographic images. One reason is the same problem that plagues so many other so-called "standards" in the computer industry. There is sufficient room in the specifications that many vendors develop their own version of the process, generating multiple compression and file formats and decreasing the universality of the format.

In general, JPEG compresses still-color photographs digitized for computer use. As with motion video images, the real drawback to using digitized photographs is the disk space required to store the images and the large amounts of data that must be transferred when such images are transmitted over network links.

A full-resolution 35mm slide, for example, can require 10Mb of space to store without some form of compression. Depending on the compression used, you can reduce digitized photographs to one-tenth or one-fiftieth its original size. The problem has been, and remains, the acceptance of a broad-based standard for data compression that is workable and accessible by everyone who needs it.

JPEG is working to develop just such a standard for virtually all continuous-tone still-image applications.

Already, software and hardware products are available to support JPEG. Hardware implementations are desirable because they can encode and decode compressed data faster than software-only implementations. Software, on the other hand, can be more responsive to varied data and may, in general, be more flexible.

Digital Audio Reference

Audio—music, sound effects, and narration—is an integral part of successful multimedia presentations. Nearly all presentation software supports audio in one form or another.

The challenge of computer hardware and software that uses sound is to convert natural or analog sound into a format the computer can understand and use, then turn it back into analog sound for playback through an amplifier and speaker.

Although the actual process of making these conversions is complex, it's common enough these days, through hardware and software (*firmware*) devices called ADCs (analog to digital converters) and DACs (digital to analog converters).

Natural sound occurs as a series of continuous, infinitely variable waves. We identify the components of these waves in terms of amplitude, frequency, and wavelength:

Amplitude: The height (and depth) of the wave from the zero baseline.

Frequency: The number of waves per unit of time, or how many waves move past a fixed point in one second. Frequency is measured in cycles per second, commonly expressed as Hertz (Hz) or kilohertz (KHz, 1000 Hertz).

415

Wavelength: The distance between wave peaks or valleys. Wavelength decreases with a rise in frequency; a lower frequency results in a larger wavelength.

Figure C.1 shows the relationship among these sound components.

Figure C.1
Sound Wave
Labeled

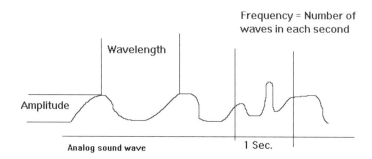

We hear the results of this wave motion through the air. These vibrations are established in some device that produces sound—vocal chords, a falling tree, a car horn, a guitar string—and the vibrations are transmitted to our ear drum. This analog vibration is carried into the inner ear where it eventually is translated into electronic pulses that the brain can understand. We recognize certain frequencies and blends of frequencies as a child's voice, our *own* child's voice, a guitar, a trumpet, and so on. This is because these familiar sounds are stored as electronic memories in our brains.

Notice that while we live in a world of analog sounds, we don't interpret or "use" these sounds in their natural form; we must first translate them into a form the brain can understand.

So it is with the computer. Analog waves are *digitized*, turned into a series of 1's and 0's for storage and manipulation by the computer. In multimedia applications, incoming analog sounds—sent into the computer through a microphone or amplifier port on an internal sound card (see Chapter 1)—typically are sampled 44,100 times every second.

Remember that analog sound is continuous, so to reproduce sound precisely, we would have to sample the wave an infinite number of times per second. Obviously this isn't practical or possible. Luckily, it isn't even necessary. A sampling rate of 44.1KHz produces a reasonable facsimile of the sound, requires a reasonable amount of hardware and software, and can be stored in a reasonable amount of disk space.

Actually, when you're digitizing speech, some sound effects, and possibly even music for some applications, you can live with a lower sampling rate. The result is lower quality sound, but also much less disk space is required to store a smaller sound segment. Most sound recording and playback software lets you choose a sampling rate. The range of samples available depends on the software, but if you can stand the storage requirements, select 44.1KHz or higher.

Why 44.1KHz as the typical sampling rate? Experimentation has shown that a sampling rate of at least twice the highest frequency you want to reproduce results in reasonable sound quality and reproduction. Since the human ear interprets sound roughly in the range of 20Hz to 20KHz, the standard 44.1KHz sampling rate was chosen. However, a minute of 44.1KHz, 16-bit sound (see discussion of resolution, next page) will take about 10Mb of storage. For short sequences, this isn't excessive, but for full-blown multimedia applications with narration, sound effects, and music, storage requirements escalate quickly. See why CD-ROM is becoming such a popular medium for multimedia productions?

Even with a 44.1KHz sampling rate, when you play back a digitized sound, you are hearing only small time slices from the actual wave. Have you every watched time lapse photography, where one frame of movie film or video is taken every few seconds, minutes, or hours? Through time lapse photography of a flower growing, you can watch a seed germinate, sprout, grow a green stalk, bloom, and die in a few seconds of film. You get the picture, you understand the process, but the quality of the motion is not natural.

The same thing happens with sampled and digitized sound. However, at the higher sampling rates it's difficult or impossible to tell that you aren't listening to the complete sound wave.

As sampling rates fall, so does sound quality. You can tell when sound has been digitized at a lower than normal sampling rate because the voice or music is "fuzzy," without depth and clarity. However, some sound—such as voice narration—may do very well at lower rates. Experimentation is the best way to determine the needs of a particular application.

Another factor that determines digitized sound quality is *resolution*, the number of bits used to store information about each sample. Early sound cards were 8-bit devices; now most new offerings are 16-bit cards. An 8-bit digitized sound can use a maximum of 2^8 (256) possible values, whereas a 16-bit sound can be stored with up to 2^{16} (65,536) values. Interestingly, when recording sound for interpretation by the human ear-brain combination, 65,536 values are enough so that the sound is impossible to distinguish from "natural" sound.

Some applications use their own formats to digitize and compress sounds, storing the data in a file with a custom extension. And, most presentation software also supports standard audio formats such as MIDI (Musical Instrument Digital Interface) and WAVE files.

WAVE (wave form) format is used for general sounds and music, and is the format you're most likely to find in multimedia production. WAVE sounds are digitized wave forms, generally compressed at some level, that can be stored to disk and replayed through a sound card with appropriate software.

MIDI sound, on the other hand, is more like a computer program. A MIDI file can be much smaller than a WAVE file of comparable complexity and length because more of MIDI playback is handled by the MIDI hardware (and firmware) attached to your system. MIDI hardware can be an external device (and usually is), or it can be an integral part of your plug-in sound card inside your PC.

Whereas WAVE sounds store digitized samples of sound (see discussion above), MIDI files store information *about* sound: pitch, duration, loudness. A device that can interpret this stored information can play back sound that is very close to the original.

MIDI uses a serial data transmission protocol for exchanging musical information between compatible electronic musical devices. In the multimedia world, MIDI allows a computer to control an internal or external hardware device, and it allows the MIDI hardware to feed sound commands to the computer for storage and playback. MIDI devices include a hardware interface between a computer and a MIDI cable. The MIDI interface is labeled either MIDI-IN, MIDI-OUT, or MIDI_THRU and can be built into the computer or it can be an add-on adapter.

MIDI sound definitions include a channel specification for various devices or types of sounds. The MIDI protocol assigns a channel number from 1 to 16 to each MIDI data type to allow a response from only the desired synthesizer.

For more information about sound hardware for your multimedia PC platform, see Chapter 1.

Video

In this appendix, we'll introduce one of the fastest growing and most fascinating areas of multimedia on PCs—motion video. We'll survey some of the hardware and software you'll need to get started and present the basics of PC-based video editing.

Motion Video Overview

For several years, there has been a movement among semi-professional and professional videographers and editors to move to PC platforms for video editing. The power of the computer coupled with its user-friendly interface and relatively low cost are providing video producers with more features at their fingertips than ever before.

Now, the megabuck editing platforms (cheap by professional video standards but still expensive for average industrial computer users) are getting cheaper and more available. Companies such as Matrox, IBM, and Touch Vision Systems are producing hardware/software packages that let you capture motion video directly to your PC. You can grab pictures from videotape recorders, video cameras, CDs, and other sources, digitize the images, and in some cases add timing codes or other video tracking information. A video editing station based on a desktop PC, as shown in Figure D.1, is now not only technically feasible, but well within the budget limitations of almost any business.

Figure D.1
PC-Based
Video Editing
Station

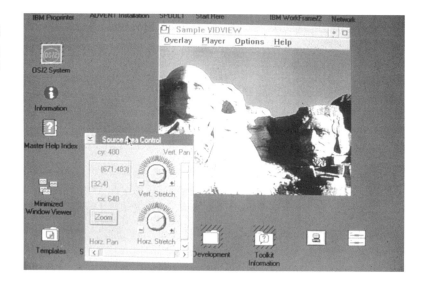

From there you can store the actual images to a hard disk or save information about the source and length of the clip. The software then lets you string these video bites together in whatever order you like, adding titles, computer-generated graphics, and sound, such as narration, sound effects, or music. Then you either dub the digitized images off of your hard disk onto a fresh videotape, or have the software use the resultant Edit Decision List (EDL) to prompt you for the proper tape to place in a source machine to be copied in the proper sequence to the destination recorder.

Either way, the result is a professional-looking video production that would be difficult or impossible to do by simply copying an original tape from one machine to another using a mechanical start/stop/recue/start process. And, the technology is improving as the cost goes down, so look for even more exciting motion video features on your desktop in the near future.

Once you've used the PC and its attendant hardware and software to produce the final edited tape, you have a number of options on how you'll use it. You may simply use it as a standalone tape for presentations, sales, or training. Since you were able to use computer-based graphics images, titling, sound, and so on, you have a finished production that makes use of the multimedia aspects of your computer during production, but which is displayed and distributed on standard VHS videotape or other format.

If the target for this PC-produced tape is a computer-based training, educational, or presentation product, then you'll likely incorporate the finished tape with other material and run it on your PC. Training and instruction are excellent applications for such productions. You can establish a graphics- and menu-based application that lets the user request text or graphics material, perhaps answer questions or take tests, and where more information is needed about a particular subject, the video you just edited can be called up in a window or for full screen display, like the example in Figure D.2.

Figure D.2
Motion Video
Window as
Part of MPC
Presentation

You can experience video in a window with the CD supplied with this book. Use Product Selector from the main menu to find the StoryBoard Live! demonstration, then select Number 1 from the demonstration screen.

With the proper presentation software, you can run the motion video in a window that's part of the presentation display, while text or other information shows up elsewhere on the screen.

Motion video can personalize the presentation (the company president or other known figure provides an introduction, states the goal or purpose of the program, and so on) and help explain difficult material (for example, demonstrate a maintenance or manufacturing process).

However, when you use a lot of video on your computer, you'll need a large and fast hard disk because, even with highly compressed images, motion video requires a lot of storage. D/Vision, from TouchVision Systems, for example, is one of the few editing packages that fully digitizes the video being edited to your hard disk. It uses good compression, but even so, 75 minutes of video require a gigabyte of storage. While 75 minutes may be long enough for a finished film, you may need even more storage to hold all of the various motion clips you wish to use in the finished production.

In this section, we'll show you the basics of incorporating video into your presentations and discuss some of the features of readily available hardware and software that can help you get the job done.

First the basics.

What You Need

To begin using video in your multimedia productions, you'll need a few basic components that go beyond the standard MPC hardware setup. Here's the general list. In the next section, we'll show you some specific products:

- Video input (or input and output) hardware
- One or more video source devices (VCR, video camera, laser disk player)
- Cables for video input/output, plus audio input/output cables
- (Optional) Controller interface for your video sources
- (Optional) Video editing software
- (Optional) Drawing, painting, or titling software
- (Optional) One or more video output devices (VCR, video camera)

The ultimate video-interface setup for multimedia includes both input and output video devices and the software needed to edit video (TouchVision D/Vision, Matrox Personal Producer, or similar software). We'll discuss such a system first, then show you how to incorporate video into your MPC productions with a simpler (and much less expensive) configuration.

PC-Based Video with Editing

You don't have to include video editing capabilities on your multimedia PC to use motion video with your MPC productions. You could elect to input tapes edited elsewhere. However, if you're doing video editing with a simple hardware setup (for example, using two VCRs to dub master tapes to a production tape), then incorporating video editing into your MPC configuration can make the job easier, produce professional results, and give you more flexibility.

If, on the other hand, you either have a professional editing facility at your disposal (or someone else to do the editing), or if you have not yet tried video editing and production yourself, then editing capabilities as part of your MPC configuration probably should take a lower priority.

Matrox Personal Producer

How do you set up your system for video editing? One possible configuration is shown in Figure D.3. This is a dual-VCR configuration that includes a sound card, a hardware controller, and a video I/O card. This particular configuration is used with the Matrox Personal Producer package with the Matrox Illuminator-Series video card.

With this configuration, you can use the Personal Producer software package to view source video, electronically tag segments, arrange clips in the order you want them to appear in the finished video, add audio, and produce computer graphics or titles to overlay the video.

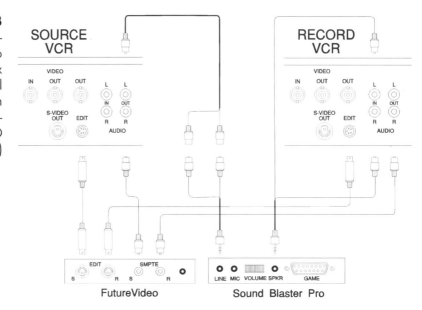

These procedures are conducted from user-friendly screens that show you graphically what operations you're conducting and that help you configure the editing facilities. Figure D.4, for example, shows a Personal Producer video clip editor screen that includes level meters, control knobs, and so on that are

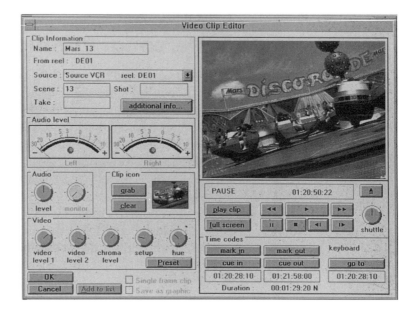

presented on the screen in a format similar to configurations you might use with conventional editing hardware.

It's with a screen similar to this one that you select video clips for inclusion in a finished production with the Personal Producer. The image displayed in the video window of the Clip Editor is a representative image, designed to help you remember what the full clip is. The clip may be a few seconds or a few minutes long.

You can give the clip a name, adjust video levels, and more, before saving information about the clip back to disk. Note that with the Personal Producer, the video information itself remains on a source device (most likely a VCR player), rather than being digitized and stored on the hard disk. The clip selector and editor track information about which master tape the clip is stored on, as well as the frame count for the clip.

When you've identified all of the individual clips you want to include in the finished production, you can assemble them in the order you want them to appear with a storyboard editor. The Matrox Storyboard is shown in Figure D.5.

Figure D.5
Matrox
Storyboard
Editor Slide

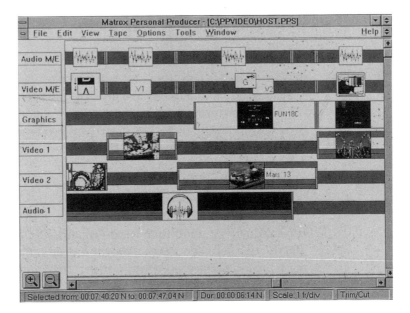

Each line on the storyboard holds a different component of the finished production. One line shows the video clips (which include synched audio) you selected in the Video Clip Editor, one shows any computer-generated art or titling you've added, another holds any music or other mixed audio, and so on. These storyboard lines are displayed on the screen over a calibrated timeline that tracks the timing of the finished piece.

Once you have all of the components in place on the storyboard, you can select a "record to tape" option to build the final production. Because you've named each video clip and other components, and the clip editor keeps track of the source tapes, the software can prompt you to insert the appropriate videotape or other video source when it's needed as the production is assembled.

Although you can use an electromechanical counter to keep track of where you are on the source and destination tapes, you can't edit down to the frame level this way. With the Personal Producer and other professional editing systems, accurate frame count is maintained through an on-tape signal. Depending on the system used, this time code information may be recorded with the video, may reside on a track of its own, or it can be recorded on one of the audio tracks.

If you're using a professional camera or an external dubbing system, chances are this electronic time code is placed on your master editing tape automatically. For most of us using consumer-level equipment, there is no time code recorded as part of the original tape. In this case, you can pre-record a tape with a machine controlled by the Personal Producer.

This process records a solid black video signal accompanied by a time code control track along the entire length of the tape. Whenever you plan to use a tape for an edit master or destination tape, it's a good idea to pre-record a black signal to ensure clean cuts between takes. And, the time code signal obviously can provide more accurate editing than a tape with no time code tape.

Other Software Options

The Matrox Personal Producer is just one of a growing number of software/hardware systems you can use for desktop video editing. There are others, some of which we'll discuss next.

TrueVision's D/Vision

D/Vision from TouchSystem Systems, Inc. uses the Intel/IBM ActionMedia II DVI interface card for video and sound I/O. This software provides features similar to the Personal Producer, but with some differences. For one thing, D/Vision (for "Digital" vision) can capture source video, compress it, and store it on a fast hard drive. D/Vision uses Intel's RTV (Real Time Video) compression algorithm to store the images.

Now you can assemble these video clips in any order you wish—even frame by frame—and play them back on a display attached to the ActionMedia II card. With a fast, high-capacity hard drive (SCSI interface performance level), you can actually view the assembled digitized clips in real-time at a standard 30 frames per second.

The disadvantage to this approach, of course, is the requirement for a gigabyte or more of storage and a SCSI interface. But if you're serious about PC-based video editing, the advantages far outweigh the disadvantages. Once the images are digitized, you can play them, move them, or copy them as much as you want without any degradation of image quality.

When the time comes to record the finished tape, you can print the finished production to a recorder and maintain at least as good a quality as VHS tape, regardless of how many times you've copied, viewed, or moved the clips.

In addition, you can edit digitized images a frame at a time, if required, and it's relatively easy to mix additional sound, graphics, or titling with the original material.

The process of preparing a video with D/Vision is similar to the Personal Producer process, except that instead of capturing only a representative frame of video, you digitize all of the information you'll use in the finished piece.

Once you've captured and compressed the video, you're ready to begin the editing process by placing clips and effects in the proper order.

To begin editing, you display a Source Catalog that shows a still image from each of the captured clips, similar to the one shown in Figure D.6.

Figure D.6
D/Vision Source
Catalog

From this catalog, you can arrange the clips in any order you like by placing the representative still shots on a timeline, like the one in Figure D.7.

Once the images are arranged in the order you want, you can play them back from the previously stored and digitized clips without having to use physical tapes or assemble an edited digital video file. You can play a simulation of an edited file because the clips (TrueVision calls them *events*) are stored on disk with information about disk location, length, and so on.

Figure D.7
D/Vision
Timeline

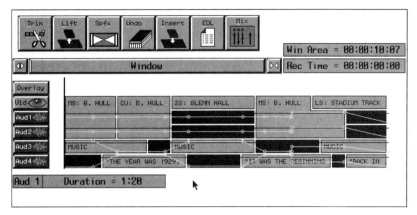

The information about event order is stored in an *edit decision list* (EDL). With the EDL, you can continue the editing process by adding events, merging effects, or removing material at will without having to copy over the previously digitized motion video.

And, the digitized approach lets you arrange video data—even single frames—in any order you like, create special effects such as dissolves and wipes, and edit and mix multiple audio tracks. Once the events, effects, and audio are assembled in the proper order with the EDL, you have three options for completing the finished production.

Your first option is to produce an "online disk" that includes the EDL along with the original time code information. You can take this disk to a professional production facility that will use this information and your original source video to produce a finished, broadcast-quality composite tape. This approach provides the highest quality output, but it also is the most expensive.

Another alternative is D/Vision's "SupeRTV," a TouchVision enhanced RTV process that allows full-screen, 30-frames-per-second video at "industrial video" resolution, equivalent to three-quarter-inch Umatic quality. To do this, you must recapture the events you've chosen from the original pool at the higher resolution. Any special effects and audio you created with the original EDL are reproduced at the enhanced resolution. Then you can play the digitized images back to a master tape, creating a finished production without using outside resources.

Your third option is to assemble a finished master tape with RTV resolution and Intel's DVI (Digital Video Interactive). This process is useful when you want to incorporate your edited, full-motion video into multimedia presentations that support DVI.

Gold Disk VideoDirector

The Gold Disk approach is entirely different from either Matrox or TrueVision. With VideoDirector, you can build an edit decision list and copy information from a source tape to a record tape, but you never actually input any video into the computer.

The VideoDirector package consists of a serial cable for video control and software for specifying the clips you want to use and the order in which you use them. You attach the cable to a serial port on your computer. The other end of the cable has two branches: One is a stereo mini-plug, compatible with the serial port on many camcorders and VCRs (LANC or Control-L Interface); the other branch contains an infrared transmitter that can control a VCR through its infrared remote control interface. A typical hookup for VideoDirector is shown in Figure D.8.

Figure D.8
VideoDirector
Hookup
Diagram

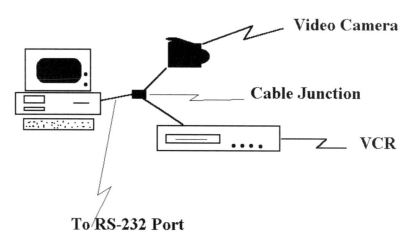

In addition to this supplied interface (one that does not require additional hardware), VideoDirector is compatible with third party video editing interfaces, such as Sony's Vbox and Selectra's VuPort.

With VideoDirector, you view video clips on a source machine, displaying them on a separate video monitor, not your computer's integral display. When you find a clip you want to use in the finished production, you give it a name, identify the start and end point, and specify which tape it's on. You can make individual clips as long or as short as you wish.

Each clip is saved in a tape library. You can display a list of clips in the tape library and use the library images to build an edit decision list (Gold Disk calls it an Event List). Unlike the Matrox and TouchVision products, you don't actually see the video images you're editing on the computer screen. Rather, you build an event list like the one shown in Figure D.9.

Figure D.9
VideoDirector
Sample Event
List

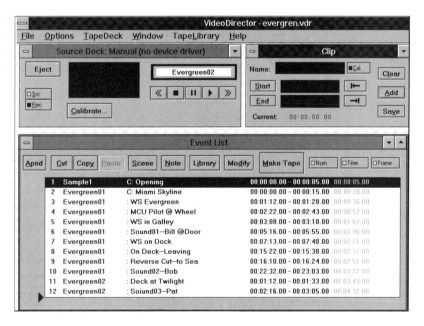

The advantage to this approach is that the software doesn't have to include video capture, compression, and manipulation features. Moreover, the Gold Disk product costs hundreds of dollars less than either Matrox or TouchVision products.

However, from an MPC standpoint, you should consider VideoDirector for relatively simple projects, and ones that don't need to include computer art or text. And, if you intend to incorporate VideoDirector productions into your MPC presentations, you'll still need some form of video capture board. On the other hand, the initial cost of VideoDirector is low, and for many of the clips you might want to incorporate in MPC presentations, it certainly is adequate.

Video Software Solutions

A full description of all of the video manipulation options now available to the desktop-computer user is beyond the scope of this book, but you can see from the discussion of the three main-line offerings in the previous section that the options are varied and useful.

In addition to full video editing software, as discussed earlier, there's a growing body of video software designed for low-end editing or for capturing video for inclusion in databases and multimedia presentations.

Among the most visible products of this type for PC users is Microsoft Video for Windows (VfW). Using one of the available video capture boards, VfW converts external analog video to digital format for display on the computer screen, editing, inclusion in multimedia presentations, and storing on a hard disk. If you're using previously digitized video, you won't need a video capture board; you can run VfW on any reasonably high-end PC.

The basic VfW displays video only in a small on-screen window (160 by 120 pixels) at 15 fps (*frames per second*). Regular, full-motion video plays at 30 fps and on a full screen. Additional compression/decompression hardware will display VfW video in full-screen, 30-fps format. VfW uses Microsoft's AVI (Audio Video Interleaved) storage format, which alternates frames of video with audio information. An application program interface (API) lets either Microsoft's Multimedia Viewer or third-party developed applications display the captured video.

Apple's QuickTime, originally available only for Macintosh computers, is now moving onto the PC desktop through Windows. Although there are a number of application and technical differences between these two products, they provide very similar functionality. For now, it's a good bet the Video for Windows will gain the initial lead in the PC world over QuickTime, simply because of the large base of Windows users, if nothing else. Eventually, however, the two likely will gain almost equal status in the PC world as their capabilities and features merge and as an increasing number of developers work in both applications.

One of the factors that is slowing broad acceptance of any product as "the" video capture and editing tool, is the lack of an industry standard as to which file format and other video issues should be adopted. While that issue won't be solved immediately, the definite movement of such products as VfW and QuickTime will tend to settle things down, somewhat. In addition, groups such as the SMPTE (Society of Motion Picture and Television Engineers) are working on the problem. As this book is being written, the SMPTE task force on Digital Image Architecture has released a report outlining the basic concepts for a digital video architecture that will help different countries, industries, standards, and applications exchange video.

There are really two issues here: broad international standards for using digital video for recording and editing at the professional level, and the standards that will be used across multi-vendor computer systems for video capture, editing, and storage. Both of these issues likely will merge somewhat as the technology—and the standards—evolve.

File Format and Extension Reference

The following two tables will help you to decipher some of the file types and extensions you may encounter as you work with the Ultimedia Tools Series CD. Table E.1 is sorted by application; Table E.2 is sorted by extension.

Some formats, such as .PCX or .BMP, are popular and used by a number of packages. Others are unique to a particular vendor or package and may not be widely used or supported.

While these tables by no means cover every possible file format you're likely to encounter, they should help you with the majority of software you'll be using as you work with this book.

437

Table E.1 File Format Reference—by Name

Application	Extension
Algor	.BTM
Amiga Interchange Format File	.IFF
Application Technology Pizazz Plus	.PZI
AutoCAD	.DXF
Autodesk Animator	.FLI
Autodesk Animator Pro	.FLC
Bit Mapped Graphics	.BMP
Claris Macpaint	.MAC
Computer Graphics Metafile	.CGM
Device Independent Bitmap	.DIB
Digital Research GEM Image	.IMG
Digital Vision Computer Eyes	.CE
Dynamic Link Library	.DLL
Electronic Arts Delux Paint	.BBM
Electronic Arts Delux Paint	.LBM
Encapsulated PostScript	.EPS
Excel Spreadsheet	.XLS
Fonts	.BSF
GEM Draw Metafile	.GEM
Graphics Image File (CompuServe)	.GIF
Harvard Graphics	.CHT
HPGL	.PLT
IBM PIF (GDF)	.PIF
Illustrator	.AI
Image Object Content Architecture (IOCA)	.ICA
LinkWay (CGA Format)	.PCC
LinkWay (EGA Format)	.PCE
LinkWay (MCGA 256 Format)	.PCM
LinkWay (MCGA Format)	.PCH
LinkWay (VGA Format)	.PCV

continued

Table E.1 File Format Reference—by Name (Continued)

Application	Extension
Lotus 1-2-3, Storyboard Live!, Grasp	.PIC
M-Motion Video Files	.VID
MAC (PICT)	.PCT
MacroMind Director (Animation)	.MMM
Masks	.MSK
Media Cybernetics, Dr. Halo	.CUT
Micrografix Designer/Draw	.DRW
Microsoft Paint	.MSP
Musical Instrument Digital Interface (MIDI)	.MID
Palettes	.PAL
PC Paintbrush and others (Bitmap)	.PCX
Pens	.PEN
PostScript	.EPS
Resource Interchange File Format (RIFF DIB)	.RDI
Resource Interchange File Format (RIFF MIDI)	.RMI
Resource Interchange File Format (RIFF WAVE)	.WAV
Rich Text File Format	.RTF
RIX Softworks ColorRIX	.VMG
RIX Softworks WinRIX	.RIX
SCODL	.SCD
SoundBlaster (Creative Labs) Voice Files	.VOC
Space Separated (ASCII)	.TXT
TIFF (Tagged Image)	.TIF
Truevision Targa	.TGA
Truevision Targa	.WIN
Video Show	.PIC
Windows Metafile	.WMF
Windows Palette	.PAL
WordPerfect Graphic	.WPG

Table E.2 File Format Reference—by File Extension

Extension	Application
.AI	Illustrator
.BBM	Electronic Arts Delux Paint
.BMP	Bit Mapped Graphics
.BSF	Fonts
.BTM	Algor
.CE	Digital Vision Computer Eyes
.CGM	Computer Graphics Metafile
.CHT	Harvard Graphics
.CUT	Media Cybernetics, Dr. Halo
.DIB	Device Independent Bitmap
.DLL	Dynamic Link Library
.DRW	Micrografix Designer/Draw
.DXF	AutoCAD
.EPS	Encapsulated PostScript
.EPS	PostScript
.FLC	Autodesk Animator Pro
.FLI	Autodesk Animator
.GEM	GEM Draw Metafile
.GIF	Graphics Image File (CompuServe)
.ICA	Image Object Content Architecture (IOCA)
.IFF	Amiga Interchange Format File
.IMG	Digital Research GEM Image
.LBM	Electronic Arts Delux Paint
.MAC	Claris Macpaint
.MID	Musical Instrument Digital Interface (MIDI)
.MMM	MacroMind Director (Animation)
.MSK	Masks
.MSP	Microsoft Paint
.PAL	Palettes
.PAL	Windows Palette

continued

Table E.2 File Format Reference—by File Extension (Continued)

Extension	Application
.PCC	LinkWay (CGA Format)
.PCE	LinkWay (EGA Format)
.PCH	LinkWay (MCGA Format)
.PCM	LinkWay (MCGA 256 Format)
.PCT	MAC (PICT)
.PCV	LinkWay (VGA Format)
.PCX	PC Paintbrush and others (Bitmap)
.PEN	Pens
.PIC	Lotus 1-2-3, Storyboard Live!, Grasp
.PIC	Video Show
.PIF	IBM PIF (GDF)
.PLT	HPGL
.PZI	Application Technology Pizazz Plus
.RDI	Resource Interchange File Format (RIFF DIB)
.RIX	RIX Softworks WinRIX
.RMI	Resource Interchange File Format (RIFF MIDI)
.RTF	Rich Text File Format
.SCD	SCODL
.TGA	Truevision Targa
.TIF	TIFF (Tagged Image)
.TXT	Space Separated (ASCII)
.VID	M-Motion Video Files
.VMG	RIX Softworks ColorRIX
.VOC	SoundBlaster (Creative Labs) Voice Files
.WAV	Resource Interchange File Format (RIFF WAVE)
.WIN	Truevision Targa
.WMF	Windows Metafile
.WPG	WordPerfect Graphic
.XLS	Excel Spreadsheet

Glossary

MULTIMEDIA PRESENTATIONS

 You can search an interactive glossary provided on the CD-ROM disk included with this book. To view the CD-ROM glossary:

1. Make your CD-ROM drive the default from the DOS prompt. If the CD-ROM is located on drive F:, for example, simply type **F:** and press **Enter** from the DOS prompt.
2. Type **UTSDOS** and press **Enter**.
3. From the main Ultimedia Tools screen, choose Product Selector (the last item on the menu).
4. From the Product Selector screen, click on the Glossary button at the lower right-hand side of the screen to display the interactive glossary.

A/B Roll   The two video sources used to produce a finished video or film. The "A" roll is generally the primary (frequently a synched sound source) source and the "B" roll is generally the secondary (frequently "voice over") source. Cutting between A and B rolls helps add interest to a video or MPC production.

A/B Track   The two audio tracks used to produce a finished "soundtrack" or audio track for a video, film, or MPC presentation. The "A" track is generally the primary track; the "B" track is generally the background sound or supporting audio track.

ADPCM   Adaptive Differential Pulse Code Modulation. A digital audio storage format.

Analog   Numeric values that represent physical data such as current or voltage. A volt meter is an analog device as is a mechanical volume control.

Analog Video   A video signal that contains an infinite number of smooth gradations between video levels. (See also Digital Video)

443

API   Application Programming Interface. A published or documented method for linking software applications or software layers. A way for different applications to share data and other facilities.

Access Time   The total time required to locate desired data and begin transferring it to another storage, memory, or display device. Access time usually consists of seek time plus settling time.

Access   To locate information you wish to retrieve from a hard disk, CD-ROM or other storage device.

Alias   Image distortion characterized by jagged edges on characters or graphics images. (See also Anti-aliasing)

Anti-aliasing   An electronic video technology that reduces the number of rough or jagged edges on character and graphics displays. The result is smoother curves and fewer jagged edges on all text and image displays. Anti-aliasing is achieved by inserting several intensities of color between the foreground and background colors.

Artificial Intelligence (AI)   Computer software that lets the computer use accumulated information and experience to determine future actions. Non-AI software can only perform the functions pre-programmed by the developer.

ASCII ("Ask'-ee")   American Standard Code for Information Interchange. An 8-bit data code used to store and transfer computer information.

Aspect Ratio   The ratio of height to width in a displayed image. Maintaining the same aspect ratio as images are re-sized reduces distortion and keeps the appearance of the image close to the original. The aspect ratio for a video frame or screen is 3:4.

Audio Object   An object (usually represented by an on-screen icon) that holds digitized audio material.

Audio-visual Shows   Presentations developed using audio and video source material.

Authoring   Creating and editing audio-visual shows with a multimedia PC system. The authoring process usually involves writing or designing a program as well as physically producing the finished presentation. All of the authoring steps may or may not be conducted by the same person.

AVA   The Audio-Video Authoring language used in IBM's Audio Visual Connection system during authoring.

AVC   IBM's Audio Visual Connection package.

Background Object   An audio or video object that is not primary. A background object usually is used in conjunction with a foreground object (text, graphics, or sound).

Batch   A series of DOS commands stored in an ASCII file. These commands can be executed by issuing the filename without typing individual commands from the keyboard.

Baud   A commonly-used unit for data transfer speed. One baud is generally equal to one data bit transferred per second.

Baud Rate   A measure of or predicted rate of data transfer. At relatively slow speeds—below 1,200 baud or so—baud rate is equal to bits per second. At higher speed, data transfer techniques can make one baud represent more than one bit.

Bit   The smallest unit of computer memory or data. A single bit stores either a 1 or a zero, signifying an on or off state. Eight, 16, or 32 bits are used together to form computer "words." (See also Byte)

Bit-mapped Graphics   A form of graphics where images can be defined (addressed) bit-by-bit. In bit-mapped graphics every location within the image can be accessed or changed individually.

Block   A contiguous series of objects (text, images) or simply an area of the display screen that can be marked together and acted upon by software commands or functions.

Buffer   Memory or storage used to hold information temporarily during transfer operations. Storage buffers are commonly used to take the place of RAM memory; memory buffers frequently are used to speed up data transfer by freeing up the CPU or the data link by avoiding having to wait on slow mechanical devices. A printer buffer, for example, stores printed pages temporarily in fast RAM memory, feeding it out to the printer as the printer is able to take it. Thus, the main CPU doesn't have to wait on the slow printer or handle the printer interface duties.

Bus   A common circuit or electronic path that carries electronic information in a computer system. Various components within the computer share this data path, each one using it one at a time. Common computer buses are 16- or 32-bits wide.

Button   A graphics screen element that represents a switch or toggle for software operations. An on-screen button is "pushed" by clicking on it with the mouse.

Byte   A string of 8 bits used together to represent one data character or other information. Computers use single or multiple byte words (See also Bit).

CAI   See CBT

Capture   To digitize images or sound using a software application compatible with the display or source.

CBT   Computer Based Training. A program of instruction based on (usually) interactive computer software. Also known as computer-aided (or assisted) instruction. (CAI)

CCITT   Consultative Committee for International Telephone and Telegraphy. A standards organization that establishes international communications protocols.

CD-I   Compact Disk Interactive. A Sony and Philips compact disk format that supports audio, digital data, still graphics, and limited motion video.

CD-ROM   Compact Disk Read-Only Memory. The compact disk platter used to store information in digital format for access by a CD-ROM Player. CD-ROMs use the same physical format as CD music disks common with entertainment systems. Each CD-ROM stores approximately 600 megabytes of data.

CD-ROM Player   The hardware used to retrieve information from a CD-ROM disk. This hardware is essentially the same as used to play CD music disks with the addition of a computer interface. Many CD-ROM players can be used to play standard CD music disks with the addition of appropriate software.

CD-ROM XA   Compact Disk Read-Only Memory Extended Architecture. An extension of CD-ROM technology that supports interleaved ADPCM audio with visual images, which improves performance during data retrieval.

Color Map   Defines the color characteristics of a color palette.

Color Palette   The set of all colors that a specific hardware/software system is capable of displaying or the colors visible in a current image.

Composite Video   An analog system used to transmit and record video information. Composite video contains all image and audio information in one signal. Composite signals usually conform to the NTSC standard in the United States or to PAL or SECAM standards elsewhere.

Computer-aided Instruction   See CBT

Computer-based Training   See CBT

Control Track   A portion of a video or audio tape used to record synchronizing data that is used during editing.

Crop   To mark and remove portions of a displayed object, usually causing the remaining portion of the cropped object to fill the entire screen or window display area.

Current Image   The image object that is currently selected or that is currently being displayed.

Cursor Keys   The arrow keys on a computer keyboard that are used to move the cursor (screen pointer) to a specific screen location.

Cut-and-Paste   A method of removing text or graphics information from one location in a document or file and inserting it at another location in the same document or file or into a different document or file.

DAT   Digital Audio Tape. A consumer-oriented audio recording standard that produces high-quality audio recordings.

Device Driver   Software that enables a software or hardware device to function properly with a host computer. Device drivers most frequently are installed through the DOS CONFIG.SYS file to allow a peripheral—disk, printer, display—to communicate with the computer or with a software application.

Digitize   To convert analog audio and video signals into a digital format for storage or manipulation through computer software.

DVI   Digital Video Interactive. An Intel Corporation technology (originally developed at RCA's Sarnoff Labs in Princeton, NJ) that compresses digital audio and video data. DVI hardware and firmware can be installed in a personal computer for real-time compression and decompression that presents motion video and other data on a computer screen for presentations and training. A CD-ROM using DVI can store up to 72 minutes of full-screen video, about 2.5 hours of half-screen video, or 40,000 medium-resolution (7,000 high-resolution) images.

Electronic Mail   A hardware/software system for transmitting text, graphics, voice, or video information to a remote location for retrieval by another computer system or person.

Environment   A computer system's operating configuration, including hardware type, operating system, and so on.

EPROM   Erasable Programmable Read-Only Memory. A form of PROM that can be erased and re-programmed several times.

Field   One half of a complete video frame. A video field is composed of every other scan line and occupies 1/60th of a second in NTSC (1/50th of a second in PAL and SECAM).

fps   Frames Per Second. Used to describe how motion video is displayed. (See Frame)

Frame   In motion video, one complete image. Motion is created by playing a series of frames in sequence, usually at a rate of 30 frames per second (fps) (25 fps in PAL and SECAM). A field consists of 525 scan lines in NTSC (625 scan lines in PAL and SECAM).

Frame Rate   The rate at which sequential video frames are displayed, measured in frames per second. (See fps)

GUI   Graphical User Interface. A system that allows a computer user to interact with a computer application through a series of on-screen pictures (objects). A GUI reduces training time and can provide consistency among different computer applications.

High Sierra Format   A standard used for recording and retrieving CD-ROM information. The original format was revised and adopted as ISO 9660.

HIS Colors   Colors identified by their Hue, Intensity, and Saturation.

Hot Link   A software application feature that lets you attach an object from one application (the source) into another (the destination) in such a way that when the linked source data changes, the new information also appears in the destination application. This technique is useful in presenting spreadsheet or database information within a word processor document, for example.

Hue   The shades of individual colors, as in a color wheel.

Hypermedia   An extension of hypertext that links text objects with other forms of data such as graphics, motion video, or sound.

Hypertext   A system of linked text objects that allows a user to read through or study a topic via a custom path. Hypertext objects are linked in a cross-reference manner similar to the way information is stored in the human brain. The pathways that link various objects can be traveled in a sequence selected by the user.

Icon   A graphic (pictorial) representation of a computer function, task, application, document, file, or data including video and sound. Icons are typically used as an aid in launching applications or in selecting software features during computer operation.

Image   A picture object displayed on a computer screen or stored in digitized format on disk.

Intensity   In colors, the amount of color displayed. Intensity can range, for example, from dark or dim to full intensity or bright.

Interactive Shows   An Audio-visual show that supports viewer input. The direction of the show and the material covered changes with different input.

Interactive   An application that allows the user to ask questions or otherwise to direct the flow of program execution.

Interactive Video   A computer-based video system in which the user can direct the flow of the presentation by entering commands or asking questions.

Interlace   A method of displaying a video image by "painting" alternate scan lines in two discrete video fields.

ISO   International Standards Organization. An international body that specifies technical standards in a number of disciplines.

Kiosk   A self-contained, usually enclosed, computer platform used to house an interactive application for education or direction of the public. Computer-based information kiosks with interactive multimedia presentations help users find restaurants in a new town, locate merchandise at a shopping mall, describe features of an amusement park, and the like.

LAN   Local Area Network. A system of hardware and software that allows two or more computers to share data and resources such as hard drives and printers.

Library   A collection of objects (images, sound, text, etc.) that serves as a source for authoring presentations.

Live Video   An image coming from a video camera, VCR or other video source. With some MPC systems, this "live" motion video can be captured, stored, edited, and incorporated into presentations.

Master   The original version of a video or produced presentation. The master has not been copied but is the first time the data has been recorded. The master is used to make copies for distribution.

Medium   A surface or material that stores information.

Megabyte   A nominal one million bytes (actually 10^{20} or 1,048,576 bytes).

MIDI   The Musical Instruments Digital Interface. A standard that defines how musical objects will be defined and manipulated.

MPC   Multimedia Personal Computer. A PC equipped with sound card, CD-ROM reader, high-resolution display compatible with the MPC standard.

MPC Standard   An emerging standard that specifies hardware requirements for multimedia personal computers. The standard includes specifications for CPU type, CD-ROM performance and memory requirements.

Multitasking   Running two or more software applications at the same time.

Multimedia Platform   A personal computer equipped to produce and play multimedia presentations.

Multimedia   A combination of audio and visual elements from various sources to produce an educational, entertaining, or training presentation.

NTSC   National Television Systems Committee. This is the body that establishes television standards for the United States. It is administered by the Federal Communications Commission (FCC). NTSC also is used to refer to the standards adopted by this body.

Object   Any audio or video component displayed on screen, stored on disk, or incorporated into an MPC presentation.

Object Oriented Programming (OOP)   A method of generating a series of self-contained, intelligent program elements (objects) that together form an application. Each program object processes the data it receives and forwards the results to associated objects in the system. OOP programming also generally makes use of on-screen objects for much of its interaction with the user.

Overlay   A graphics, text, or data element that is superimposed on another object. Also the process of creating an overlay. For example, a graphics image can be overlaid on a solid background or a text paragraph can serve as an overlay on top of a graphics image.

PAL   Phase Alternation Line. The color television standard used throughout Western Europe, except in France.

Pel   The individual elements of a CRT screen that are used to form characters or graphics images. Pel size changes with the video mode and the size and quality of the display device.

Pixel   The smallest picture element of an image displayed on a video monitor. Sometimes used interchangeably with pel.

Pop Up Window   A small window, menu, or dialog box presented by a program to ask the user for information or a menu choice or to display program output.

Post Production   Editing and assembling a video or film from raw material.

Preproduction   All video and film design tasks that occur before actual production begins. Preproduction tasks include project planning, budgeting, script writing, and story boarding.

Production   The stage during which actual film or video production takes place.

PROM   Programmable Read-Only Memory. A non-volatile memory that can be programmed only once.

Pulldown Menu   A menu or list presented by an application at the user's request. The pulldown menu is an extension of an existing menu or list and can be expanded or shrunk upon user command.

RAM Random Access Memory. Solid-state computer memory that can be accessed (addressed) by specific, individual locations. RAM usually is volatile memory that loses its data when power is removed.

Random Access Retrieving stored information by directly accessing the desired block of data. (See also Sequential Access)

Random Access Memory See RAM

Read-Only Memory See ROM

Resolution A measure of the number of pixels or pels per unit area of display screen. The larger the resolution number, the finer the displayed image detail.

RGB Red, Green, Blue. Used to classify colors according to their relative content of these colors. (See also HIS Colors)

ROM Read-Only Memory. A solid-state storage device that can be read but not written to. ROMs are produced in a manufacturing process as opposed to being created in the field. ROM data typically is used for system boot instructions. (See also PROM and EPROM)

RS-232C A serial interface standard frequently used for exchanging data between computers or between a computer and a peripheral device such as a modem or printer.

Run-time System A software component that can be used to display an MPC presentation but which does not include the editing or authoring components of the application.

Saturation In colors, the amount of whiteness in a displayed color.

Script Written instructions for a video, film, or MPC presentation. Also the process of writing such instructions.

SCSI ("scuzzy") Small Computer Systems Interface. A computer Input/Output interface used for disk drives, tapes, CD-ROMs, printers, and other peripherals.

SECAM Sequential *couleur à mémoire* (sequential color with memory). The color television standard used in France and Eastern Bloc republics.

Seek Time The total time required to determine the proper disk location of the data you wish to retrieve and to move a disk's read/write head to that position.

Sequential Access Retrieving data by reading all of the information that is stored ahead of it on the storage medium. Sequential devices can locate the requested data only by reading the information from the beginning to locate the proper storage location. (See also Random Access)

Settling Time   The time required for a disk hardware mechanism to become ready to access data after the read/write head has been positioned over the proper disk location. Settling is required because mechanical devices must become stable above the closely-packed data on a disk before the electronics can retrieve it successfully.

Shareware   Computer software that is provided to users free or at a very low cost. One marketing method lets users acquire shareware programs free via bulletin boards. A fee is requested from the user if the software is considered useful.

SMPTE   Society of Motion Picture and Television Engineers.

SMPTE Time Code   The time code adopted by the SMPTE.

Still Frame   A single video or film frame displayed as a still image.

Submenu   An additional list of options that is displayed when a menu or list item is selected.

Sync Signal   A video signal used to synchronize video equipment.

Synthesizer   An electronic device that can reproduce a variety of music and other audio sounds that emulate other devices. A synthesizer can be made to sound like an organ, piano, violin, or even a combination of musical instruments playing different parts.

Time Code   A series of electronic signals recorded with a video or audio signal or on a separate control track. The time code signal is used in synchronizing video and audio equipment. A time code can locate individual video frames and sync them with appropriate audio information. In video, the time code marks each frame by hour, minute, second, and frame number.

Touchscreen   A video display device that includes electronic sensors to determine where the screen is touched. A touchscreen allows users to interact with a computer application by touching the screen without using a keyboard or mouse.

Undo   An editing function that restores data to its previous state before the last edit operation.

Window   A separate portion of a computer display screen that holds a dialog, an application, or video and other graphics information.

WYSIWYG   What You See Is What You Get. A term that describes a graphics application screen that displays data as it will appear when output to a printer or other device.

Zoom   A software function that enlarges or reduces a display screen or object. Zoom in generally means to enlarge a portion of an image and zoom out generally means to present a larger view of the selected object.

Index

Italic page numbers refer to terms defined in the glossary.